School Level Leadership in Post-conflict Societies

How do different contexts influence the nature and character of school leadership?

This book is predicated on the simple, yet profound, observation that school leadership can only be understood within the context in which it is exercised. The observation is particularly valid in relation to post-conflict societies, especially when they have eventuated from new wars. Schools in these contexts face highly complex circumstances and a level of environmental turbulence requiring different kinds of leadership from those operating in less complicated and relatively stable situations.

By assembling an impressive array of international experts, this book investigates a much neglected area of research. Each chapter highlights the importance of context for understanding the realities of school leadership, and reveals the challenges and influences that school leaders face as well as the strategies they adopt to deal with the complexities of their work. In particular, valuable insights are provided into how intractable problems faced by schools can affect student, professional and organisational learning agendas. There are also important glimpses of the progression that can be made in schools by:

- enhancing the curriculum;
- energising teaching capacity; and
- optimising leadership capacity.

Depictions of post-new war environments include Angola, Ghana, Sri Lanka, Rwanda, Kenya, Solomon Islands, Lebanon, Kosovo, Timor-Leste and Northern Ireland. The book will be key reading for undergraduate and postgraduate students studying educational leadership, comparative education and education policy.

Simon R. P. Clarke is Professor of Education, Deputy Head of School and the Masters Programs Course Coordinator at the Graduate School of Education, The University of Western Australia.

Thomas A. O'Donoghue is Professor of Education at the Graduate School of Education, The University of Western Australia, and an elected Fellow of the Academy of the Social Sciences in Australia and the Royal Historical Society.

School Level Leadership in Post-conflict Societies

The importance of context

Edited by Simon R. P. Clarke and
Thomas A. O'Donoghue

Routledge
Taylor & Francis Group

LONDON AND NEW YORK

First published 2013
by Routledge
2 Park Square, Milton Park, Abingdon, Oxon OX14 4RN

Simultaneously published in the USA and Canada
by Routledge
711 Third Avenue, New York, NY 10017

Routledge is an imprint of the Taylor & Francis Group, an informa business

British Library Cataloguing in Publication Data
A catalogue record for this book is available from the British Library

Library of Congress Cataloging in Publication Data
School level leadership in post-conflict societies : the importance of context /
edited by Simon R. P. Clarke and Thomas A. O'Donoghue.
pages cm
Includes bibliographical references.
1. School management and organization–Cross-cultural studies. 2.
Educational leadership–Cross-cultural studies. 3. Postwar reconstruction–
Cross-cultural studies. I. Clarke, Simon (Simon R. P.), editor of compilation.
II. O'Donoghue, T. A. (Tom A.), 1953– editor of compilation.
LB2805.S4215 2013
371.2–dc23
2012047451

ISBN: 978-0-415-68709-6 (hbk)
ISBN: 978-0-203-36277-8 (ebk)

Typeset in Galliard
by FiSH Books Ltd, Enfield

MIX
Paper from
responsible sources
FSC
www.fsc.org   FSC® C013056

Printed and bound in Great Britain by
TJ International Ltd, Padstow, Cornwall

Contents

1 The case for studying educational leadership at the individual school level in post-conflict societies

Simon R. P. Clarke and Thomas A. O'Donoghue

The central concern of this book is with educational leadership at the individual school level in post-conflict societies, and particularly in post-new war societies. At the broadest level, it is a work that should provoke thinking on the crucial importance of considering matters of context alongside leadership theories when planning educational change for any particular setting. In other words, the book is predicated on the simple, yet profound, observation that leadership can only be understood within the context in which it is exercised and also that decisions on the type of leadership approach to be adopted in any particular circumstance should be greatly influenced by the context within which the circumstance occurs (Bottery, 2006: 169–84; MacBeath and Dempster, 2009).

A number of academics, including Gronn and Ribbins (1996), have argued for some time that because context constrains leadership and gives it its meaning, it is a vehicle through which the agency of particular leaders can be empirically understood. Nevertheless, empirical research into leadership of organisations has traditionally lacked sensitivity to context. In the realm of education, it is only in recent years that the need has been recognised to investigate how different contexts influence the nature and character of school leadership and to demonstrate how leaders in schools located within different environments shape their leadership accordingly. A growing body of work, for example, has emerged from investigations on the ways leadership is understood and practised in the distinctive environment of the small, remote school. Attention has also been devoted to the challenges of leadership in multi-ethnic schools in constructing and nurturing an inclusive school culture. Another area in which there has been interest is leadership as it is exercised in faith schools. Sullivan (2006), for example, highlights the distinctive expectations that are placed on leaders to develop a school ethos that is conducive to the religious faith, to build connections with the faith community, and to articulate the bearing of the faith perspective on how the curriculum is understood.

More poignant from our perspective is the focus on leadership in schools experiencing 'a multiplicity of economic, emotional and social challenges' (Harris and Thomson, 2006: 1) that, in certain combinations, result in constant crisis. Schools representing one group faced with such challenges are often located in inner city, low socio-economic environments, and have spawned a genre of leadership studies known as 'leadership in challenging circumstances'. Such circumstances are characterised by increasing intensity and complexity that engender a level of environmental turbulence requiring different kinds of leadership from those that apply to organisations operating in less complicated and relatively stable situations. An extreme example of environmental turbulence is represented by those societies involved in a 'new war'. These wars are contrasted with the 'old wars' that were waged from the eighteenth to the middle of the twentieth century. By engaging in 'old wars' the state carried out its job of defending its territory against others through its armed forces in uniform, and the decisive encounter was the battle (Kaldor, 2005). Since 1945, however, there have been very few inter-state wars. 'New wars', on the other hand, which have their origins in the informal wars of the second half of the twentieth century, have moved centre stage in recent decades with the disintegration of authoritarian states.

A substantial corpus of work has been produced by educational historians on old wars, including the contribution of schooling to their emergence (Marsden, 2000; Penn, 1999) and the nature of the process of education while they were waged (Dunstan, 1997; Myers, 2010; Stranack, 2005). Some work on the influences of education upon the emergence of new wars has also been undertaken. For example, Coulby and Jones (2001) have explored, in a general manner, the ways in which European educational systems influence culture, identity, ethnicity and politics, and may reinforce ethnic, or national, cleavages, violence and warfare. Another sophisticated theoretically-grounded work is Davies' (2004) *Conflict and education: conflict and chaos,* which demonstrates how complexity theory can be used to provide an understanding of the linkages between education and conflict. Of equal importance is Blair, Miller and Tieken's (2009) *Education and war,* which examines the complex and varied relations between educational institutions and war. Its particular focus is on revealing how people swept up in wars 'reconsider and reshape education to reflect, or resist, the commitment, ideals, structures, and effects of wartime' and on how constituents 'use educational institutions to disseminate and reproduce dominant ideologies, or to empower and inspire those marginalised' (Blair, Miller and Tieken, 2009: iv). A complementary emerging body of scholarship focuses on the needs of learners and teachers in conflict and post-conflict societies, and the challenges presented for them (Davies and Talbot, 2008; Mundy and Dryden-Peterson, 2011; Paulson, 2011).

Notwithstanding the value of the outstanding works mentioned above, much more research is needed on education during new wars, especially on how those schools that stay open develop survival skills in order to deal with the violence and disruption going on around them. Equally, there is a need for research on the experiences of how states adjacent to zones experiencing a new war deal with refugees from the hostilities, including how they deal with the provision of education for orphaned, or unaccompanied, children. Another area on which much more research is needed is that which is the concern of this book, namely, education in post-new war societies. In these circumstances, education systems need to be revitalised out of conditions that are not conducive to enhancing the vibrancy of schools and the communities they serve. For this reason, it is imperative to examine the ways in which school leadership can contribute to harnessing such vibrancy, especially as this consideration currently represents a research lacuna within the broader area of post-conflict education.

Buckland (2006: 7) has identified some of the main problems that are common to many post-new war societies, which debilitate the capacity of education systems to recover from the devastation that the conflict has caused. These include the lack of domestic revenue available to keep education systems running, the chronic shortage of qualified teachers, the oversupply of unqualified teachers, the number of war-affected youth, poor record keeping, corruption and lack of transparency in education governance, and the vicissitudes of international financial and humanitarian support. Also, with many post-new war societies being located in the developing world, it is instructive to keep in mind Oplatka's (2004) conclusion, that although there is no one portrait of school leadership in such settings, some common features are revealed from a review of the literature. These include limited autonomy, autocratic leadership styles, summative evaluation, low degree of social initiation and lack of instructional leadership functions.

The main focus of this book is on leadership in post-new war societies, specifically at the individual school level. As this is a very new field of research, we considered that the best way to 'open it up', so to speak, would be to invite a number of recognised experts to write on the topic in relation to the particular societies with which they have been most concerned in both their academic and professional work. To assist in the task they were provided with a template aimed at ensuring they would include in their chapter an exposition on the following areas:

- the general context out of which the specific post-new war society in question emerged;
- the particular educational context prevailing in that society (with particular reference to schooling);
- the reality at the individual schools' level, and the nature of the leadership being provided at this level;
- implications for the provision of leadership at the individual school level.

At the same time, they were not given any detailed instructions, apart from being asked to address, in the manner in which they felt most comfortable, the areas outlined in the template. Through such expositions, it was felt, a variety of 'grounded' perspectives would become available that would provide insights on the crucial importance of considering matters of context alongside matters of educational theory when planning for the provision of educational leadership in the promotion of educational development at the individual school level in post-new war societies. At this point it is also useful to foreground that while the nomenclature 'school principal' is used in each chapter for the sake of clarity and consistency, different terms, such as 'director' and head teacher', are used in various countries.

It is often the case in a work of this nature to offer a short exposition on each of the contributors. However, because of the great emphasis placed on the fact that the book is based on 'insider' accounts by recognised authorities, we break with tradition by foregrounding the exposition at this point, while also detailing the focus of each chapter. Chapter 2, which is also written by the editors, considers the broad context to considerations of educational leadership at the individual school level in post-new war societies.

Chapter 3, on Angola, is by Lynn Davies, Emeritus Professor of International Education in the Centre for International Education and Research (CIER) at the School of Education, University of Birmingham. Her major research, teaching and consultancy interests are in global educational governance, particularly concerning democracy, human rights, citizenship and gender. She specifically focuses on conflict and education, in terms of how education contributes to conflict and/or to peace, or civil renewal. The role of education in forestalling violent extremism is part of this work. Her experience relating to all of these areas has been in Angola, Sri Lanka, Kosovo, Bosnia, Palestine, Malawi and the Gambia, as well as with UNESCO in its Associated Schools.

Chapter 4 is on Ghana. This chapter is an exception insofar as the focus is on post-colonial, rather than post new-war, influences on leadership at the individual school level. However, it is a valuable case to consider alongside those in the other chapters since it reveals the extent to which the issues are very much the same across all of the countries considered, and also the extent to which the legacy of war and violence can persist for a very long time, including in the educational sphere. The chapter is written by John MacBeath and Sue Swaffield. John MacBeath is Professor Emeritus at the University of Cambridge, Director of 'Leadership for Learning: the Cambridge Network' and Projects Director for the University of Cambridge's Centre for Commonwealth Education. As well as pursuing his interest and research in leadership he has, for the last decade, worked with schools, education authorities and national governments on school self-evaluation. He has also acted in a consultancy role to the OECD, UNESCO and the ILO. The main thrust of his current research and development work is with Commonwealth countries. This includes leading a major national initiative in Ghana (with the University of Cape Coast, the Ghana Education Service and UNICEF).

Sue Swaffield is a member of the 'Leadership for Learning' academic group in the Faculty of Education, the University of Cambridge and a founder member of 'Leadership for Learning: the Cambridge Network'. She co-directed the Wallenberg-funded 'Leadership for Learning Carpe Vitam

Project', working with schools and universities in seven countries. Sue was also a member of the ESRC/TLRP 'Learning How to Learn' project involving forty schools and five universities in England, and worked on the DfES-funded evaluation of 'Schools Facing Exceptionally Challenging Circumstances' project. She is an executive editor of the international journal *Assessment in Education: Principles, Policy and Practice* and an associate editor of *Professional Development in Education* and is on the Editorial Board of *Reflective Teaching*.

Chapter 5, on Sri Lanka, and Chapter 6 on Rwanda, are written by Jaya Earnest, Associate Professor and Course Coordinator of Higher Degrees by Research at the Centre for International Health, the Faculty of Health Sciences, Curtin University of Technology, Western Australia. She has been involved with education reconstruction, school improvement and reform processes in Kenya, Rwanda and Uganda. She has also worked in Sri Lanka and Timor-Leste. She has written extensively on education reform in education systems in transition. She has also been the recipient (2010) of an Australian Learning and Teaching Council award for internationalisation in education.

Chapter 7 is on Kenya. Strictly speaking, the recent experience of conflict there was not that of a new war. However, it is arguable that it very nearly did become such a war. The chapter is written by Aqeela A. Datoo and David Johnson. Aqeela A. Datoo is a doctoral student in the Department of Education at St Catherine's College, University of Oxford. She specialises in the study of teacher development in countries affected by conflict, with a specific emphasis on dealing with, and overcoming, ethnic tensions. David Johnson is Reader in Comparative and International Education in the School of Education, University of Oxford, where he is also Dean and Fellow of St Anthony's College. He has spent many years studying changes and qualitative improvements in educational systems in the developing world. His research has been important in assisting national governments track improvement in their educational systems and has provided international aid agencies with important insights on the relationship between certain types of educational intervention and educational outcomes.

Chapter 8, on Solomon Islands, is by Jack Maebuta. Jack has served as a school teacher, head teacher and deputy principal for a number of years in Solomon Islands primary and secondary schools. He holds an MA from the University of the South Pacific and has worked as a lecturer in education at the Lautoka Campus of the University, which is located in Fiji. He is currently completing his Ph.D. at the University of New England, Australia, under an Australian Leadership Award Scholarship. His research is focused on the role of education in peace-building in Solomon Islands. In 2010, Jack was awarded the Australian Prime Minister's Pacific-Australia Award in recognition of his potential leadership contribution in the Pacific Islands.

Chapter 9, on Lebanon, is by Nina Maadad. Nina is the Associate Head of Learning and Teaching and a Program Coordinator in the School of

Education at the University of Adelaide. She has spent many years teaching in schools in South Australia and her main research orientation is on education, multiculturalism and languages. She has a strong interest in the Lebanese education system, with a focus on its reform and the impact on schools and students.

Chapter 10, on Kosovo, is by J. Tim Goddard and Osman Buleshkaj. Tim is Professor and Dean of the Faculty of Education and Lead Dean (International) at the University of Prince Edward Island, Canada. He has worked as a teacher, principal, superintendent of schools, university professor and education consultant. He has extensive international experience, including a six year period during which he was the team leader of the leadership component of a CIDA-funded initiative to design and deliver an educational reform programme in the former Republic of Yugoslavia, specifically the jurisdictions of Kosovo, Serbia and Montenegro. His focus was on the design of educational leadership training programmes and their delivery to school principals and to regional education officers in post-conflict Kosovo.

Osman Buleshkaj is originally from Istog, a small village in Kosovo, the former Republic of Yugoslavia, where he was a teacher until the NATO intervention of 1999. Following a period as a refugee, Osman returned to Kosovo and worked on two education projects, first with the Danish Red Cross and then with the Education Development Project (Canada). He was involved with the Ministry of Education, Science and Technology in supporting the policy and curriculum development processes in post-conflict Kosovo. He is currently a doctoral candidate at the University of Calgary, Canada, and his research focuses on the challenges faced by educational leaders to ensure quality education in multi-ethnic post-conflict Kosovo.

Chapter 11, on Timor-Leste, is by Margie Beck and Silvanio Araujo. Margie has been working in Timor-Leste since 2002, when she was seconded to the Catholic Teachers' College, Baucau, from the Australian Catholic University (ACU) in Sydney, Australia. She began by teaching unqualified teachers for a certificate in teaching and learning accredited by ACU, and stayed to assist in the setting up of the Teachers' College itself. Since then more than 400 teachers have qualified for the certificate and 250 qualified teachers with a Bachelor of Teaching from ACU have graduated from the College. She continues to prepare the staff at the College, as well as provide training for the certificate in teaching and learning in various places around the country.

Silvanio Araujo is a recent graduate from the Catholic Teachers' College, Baucau, East Timor, and is currently working as a tutor while he completes his Master of Education degree from ACU. He comes from Vikeke, a rural district about four hours' drive from Dili, the capital of Timor-Leste. Through his support, almost 100 young children attend a preschool that he set up in his village. He trained six young people to run the preschool and provides continuing professional development for them, sharing his learning from his time at the College. He also writes for an online journal, *Centro Journalisto Investigativo, Timor-Leste*.

Chapter 12, on Northern Ireland, is by Sam McGuinness, Lesley Abbott and Frank Cassidy. Sam McGuinness' original research was in chemistry. Following periods as a principal of two large post-primary schools (one all-ability, the other academically selective), he moved to lecturing at the University of Ulster, teaching aspiring school leaders in Northern Ireland and the Republic of Ireland towards a master's degree in educational leadership and management. As well as working for the Northern Ireland Regional Training Unit preparing emerging leaders and newly appointed school heads, he advises committees in the Northern Ireland government on STEM education and other educational matters.

Lesley Abbott is also in the School of Education at The University of Ulster. Her interests lie in the area of inclusive practices, integrated education, differentiation in primary classrooms, the use of technology to promote pupils' cross-national awareness, and the professional needs of newly qualified teachers, as well as those of learning support staff in respect of pupils with complex needs. As a research fellow in the UNESCO Centre, University of Ulster, she examined values in teacher education, and as a recipient of the British Educational Research Association's Brian Simon Research Fellowship, she investigated the potential of Northern Ireland's integrated schools to provide a particular model of inclusion.

Frank Cassidy has recently retired as principal of a large Catholic post-primary school. He is now Regional Officer of the Association of School and College Leaders in Northern Ireland and is also a past president of the Association. The role involves organising management training for school leaders and representing their interests through consultation with local administrators and government committees. He was a founder member of the innovative learning partnership, 'Ballymena Learning Together', which developed close collaboration between schools in a deeply divided community.

Chapter 13, written by the editors, is concerned with outlining lessons for educational leadership in post-new war societies from experiences in the field at the individual school level. It highlights similarities and differences in the ways in which school leadership is understood and practised between and among the post-new war contexts featured in the overall commentary. By examining the combination of contexts, it was hoped that it would be possible to reveal more clearly the issues and influences that school leaders face as they perform their work, the nature of the context within which these issues and influences arise, the strategies school leaders adopt to deal with the complexities of their work and the reasons behind these strategies, and the implications of the specific needs, concerns, challenges and problems faced by school leaders in post new-war contexts for policy and practice.

References

Blair, E. E., Miller, R. B. and Casey Tieken, M. (2009) *Education and War*. Harvard, MA: Harvard Educational Review.

Bottery, M. (2006) Context in the study and practice of leadership in education: A historical perspective. *Journal of Educational Administration and History*, 38(2), 169–84.

Buckland, P. (2006) Post-conflict education: time for a reality check. *Forced Immigration Review*, July, 7–8.

Coulby, D. and Jones, C. (2001) *Education and Warfare in Europe*. Aldershot, UK: Ashgate.

Davies, L. (2004) *Conflict and Education: Complexity and chaos*. London: RoutledgeFalmer.

Davies, L., and Talbot, C. (eds) (2008) Special issue on education in conflict and postconflict societies. *Comparative Education Review*, 52(4), 509–17.

Dunstan, J. (1997) *Soviet schooling in the Second World War*. New York: St. Martin's Press.

Gronn, P. and Ribbins, P. (1996) Leaders in context: Postpositivist approaches to understanding school leadership. *Educational Administration Quarterly*, 32(3), 452–73.

Harris, A. and Thomson, P. (2006) *Leading School in Poor Communities: What do we know and how do we know it?* Paper presented at the International Congress of School Effectiveness and Improvement, Fort Lauderdale, 3–6 January 2006.

Kaldor, M. (2005) Old wars, new wars and the war on terrorism. http://www.lse.ac.uk/Depts/global/Publications/PublicLectures/PL_Old%20 Wars%20Cold%20War%20New%20Wars%20and%20War%20on%20Terror1.pdf (accessed 4 November 2010).

MacBeath, J. and Dempster, N. (eds) (2009) *Connecting Leadership and Learning: Principles for practice*. London: Routledge.

Marsden, W. E. (2000) 'Poisoned history': A comparative history of nationalism, propaganda and the treatment of war and peace in the late nineteenth- and early twentieth-century school curriculum. *History of Education*, 29(1), 29–48.

Mundy, K. and Dryden-Peterson, S. (eds) (2011) *Educating Children in Conflict Zones: Research, policy and practice for systemic change*. New York: Teachers College Press.

Myers, K. (2010) The hidden history of refugee schooling in Britain: The case of the Belgians, 1914–18. *History of Education*, 30(2), 153–62.

Oplatka, I. (2004) The principalship in developing countries: context, characteristics and reality. *Comparative Education*, 40(3), 427–48.

Paulson, J. (ed.) (2011) *Education, Conflict and Development*. Oxford: Symposium Books.

Penn, A. (1999) *Targeting Schools: Drill, militarism and imperialism*. London: Woburn.

Stranack, D. (2005) *Schools at War*. Stroud: The History Press

Sullivan, J. (2006) Faith schools: A culture within a culture in a changing world. In M. de Souza, G. Durka, K. Engebretson and A. McGready (eds) *International Handbook of the Religious, Moral and Spiritual Dimensions in Education*. Heidelberg: Springer, pp. 937–47.

2 Educational leadership at the individual school level in post-conflict societies

The broad context

Thomas A. O'Donoghue and Simon R. P. Clarke

Introduction

This chapter provides the broad context to the next ten chapters, each of which deals with educational leadership at the individual school level in a particular post-conflict society. In keeping with the specific emphasis on post-new war societies, it opens by differentiating between 'old wars' and 'new wars'. The range of issues relating to education in post-new war societies that can be identified in the current literature is then considered. This is followed by a brief exposition on the importance of focusing on the individual school level when planning for the promotion of educational development in such societies, while not losing sight of the equally important task of promoting leadership at the system-wide level. Finally, the question of what kind of leadership is required at the individual school level in post-new war societies is examined. Here, emphasis is placed on the notion that it would be folly to seek answers in the form of sure-fired prescriptive blueprints from the existing range of leadership theories without also considering the variety of contexts within which post-new war societies can be located. This then sets the scene for the exposition in the following chapters on the great variety of contexts which, in fact, do exist around the world.

'Old wars' and 'new wars'

While the notion of 'new wars' is used by a number of political scientists, and in a variety of ways, the meaning attached to it in this book is that provided by Kaldor. She distinguishes between 'old wars' and 'new wars'. 'Old wars' refers to 'an idealised version of war that characterised Europe between the late 18th and the middle of the 20th century' (Kaldor, 2005: n.p.). These wars contributed to the development of modern nation states because of their ability to monopolise organised violence, eliminate private armies and establish professional armies subservient to them. The state carried out its job of defending its territory against others by engaging in wars fought by armed forces in uniform and the decisive encounter was the battle.

'Old wars', according to Kaldor, were, at least in theory, fought according to certain rules, which were codified in the late nineteenth and early twentieth centuries at the Geneva and Hague Conventions. These rules were essential to establish the legitimacy of wars and were related to such matters as minimising civilian casualties and treating prisoners well. At the same time, they did not succeed in curbing the escalation of 'old wars', which reached their pinnacle during World War 2. On the contrary, through the application of science and technology, and through the utilisation of the increased mobilisation capacities of states, 35 million people were killed in World War 1 and 50 million were killed in World War 2. Furthermore, civilians comprised a great proportion of these fatalities.

While the middle of the twentieth century witnessed 'old wars' reaching their apex, what followed was also the high point of state building. The very forces that brought about mass killings led individual nation states to the conclusion that they could not fight wars unilaterally (Kaldor, 2006: 31). The centralised totalitarian state emerged, as did blocs of states and associated ideas of democracy against totalitarianism, and socialism against fascism (Kaldor, 2005; Melander, Oberg and Hall, 2009). Alongside the construction of NATO and the Warsaw Pact as the major post-war alliances, 'a network of military connections was established through loose alliances, the arms trade, the provision of military support and training', creating 'a set of patron-client relationships which also inhibited the capacity to wage war unilaterally' (Kaldor, 2006: 31). The outcome is that since 1945, there have been very few inter-state wars (Bousquet, 2012).

'New wars', on the other hand, have their origins in the informal wars of the second half of the twentieth century, 'starting with the wartime resistance movements and the guerrilla warfare of Mao Tse-tung and his successors' (p. 32). Their character, Kaldor argues (p. 32), was obscured by the dominance of the East-West conflict during the Cold War, when they were perceived as peripheral in the central conflict. In recent decades, however, they have moved centre stage with the disintegration of authoritarian states due to globalisation. At the most obvious level, they have the following characteristics:

> These are wars fought by networks of state and non-state actors, often without uniforms, sometimes they have distinctive signs, like crosses or Ray-Ban sunglasses as in the case of the Croatian militia in Bosnia Herzegovina. They are wars where battles are rare and where most violence is directed against civilians as a consequence of counter-insurgency tactics or ethnic cleansing. They are wars where taxation is falling and war finance consists of loot and pillage, illegal trading and other war-generated revenue. They are wars where the distinctions between combatant and non-combatant, legitimate violence and criminality are all breaking down.
>
> (Kaldor, 2005: 3)

Also, Kaldor (2005: 3) concludes, these are wars that 'exacerbate the disintegration of the state – declines in GDP, loss of tax revenue, loss of legitimacy, etc.'

The 'new wars' have been contrasted with 'old wars' in terms of their goals, the methods of warfare and how they are financed. First, the goals of the new wars 'are about identity politics in contrast to the geo-political, or ideological, goals of earlier war' (Kaldor, 2006: 7). In other words, the claim to power is on the basis of national, clan, religious, or linguistic identity. The labels signifying the particularistic cultural identity are used, but so also are the symbols of a global mass culture. Furthermore, because of the processes of globalisation, diaspora communities can have a great influence owing to ease of travel and enhanced communications (Mukendi, 2012: 15). Second, on the methods of new warfare, the main defining property is the emphasis on controlling the population by getting rid of everyone of a different identity, by instilling terror, and by mobilising 'extremist politics based on fear and hatred' (Kaldor, 2006: 9). Third, while the financing of old wars was 'centralised, totalising and autarchic', new war economies are decentralised, unemployment is extremely high, they are heavily dependent on external resources and participation in the war is low (Kaldor, 2006: 10).

A variety of critiques of Kaldor's position could be considered, including the historical efficacy of her definitions of both old and new wars. Kaldor herself also recognises that new wars have much in common with wars in the pre-modern period in Europe, and also that it is possible to identify some elements of new wars within old wars. The point, however, is that the distinction is not meant to be historically accurate in every detail. Rather, in a manner akin to Weber's notion of an 'ideal type' (Giner, 1972: 36), what Kaldor offers is a model that we can use to engage in structured conversations aimed at helping us to understand the context of what has been happening in very recent times in post-new war societies and to consider what we need to do about it. She also concludes as follows regarding what needs to be done in post new-war zones:

> The key to any long-term solution is the restoration of legitimacy, the reconstitution of the control of organised violence by public authorities, whether local, national or global. This is both a political process – the rebuilding of trust in, and support for, local authorities – and the legal process – the reestablishment of a rule of law within which public authorities operate.
>
> (Kaldor, 2006: 12)

This calls for a strategy aimed at controlling violence that would include political, military and economic components (Kaldor, 2009). Furthermore, the maximisation of the possibility of its successful implementation, she argues, requires not just the involvement of transnational institutions, but also of the establishment of an alliance between these institutions and local defenders of civility.

Here, it is also useful to consider that being in a post-conflict situation is not the same in every setting. In big international wars, as Brown, Langer and Stewart (2007: 4) point out, 'a formal surrender, a negotiated cessation of hostilities, and/or peace talks followed by a peace treaty' mark possible ends to conflicts. It is often not so simple, however, when it comes to many new wars (Macpherson, 2011). Hostilities do not normally end abruptly and complete peace rarely follows (Bengtsson, 2011). Certainly, there may be 'agreed peace', but fighting may often continue at a low level, or sporadically. Also, splinter groups unready, or unwilling, to cease hostilities, may frequently disrupt genuine attempts at reaching peace (Blattman and Miguel, 2010). Thus, Brown, Langet and Stewart conclude, rather than take one, or a number, of conditions to define the beginning and end of post-conflict, it is more productive to think in terms of a process that involves the achievement of the following peace milestones:

- cessation of hostilities and violence;
- signing of political/peace agreements;
- demobilisation, disarmament and reintegration;
- refugee repatriation;
- establishing a functioning state;
- achieving reconciliation and societal integration;
- economic recovery.

Taking a process-oriented approach, they conclude, means that post-conflict zones should be seen as 'lying along a transition continuum (along which they sometimes move backwards), rather than labelled more or less arbitrarily as being "in conflict", or "at peace"' (p. 5).

Education in post-new war settings

While not specifically mentioned by Kaldor, education is proposed by a variety of authorities as a crucial area for action through alliances between transnational institutions and local defenders of civility (Barakat, Connolly, Hardman and Sundram, 2012). Johnson and Van Kalmthout (2006) have noted that international aid donors are becoming increasingly supportive of education in post-conflict societies and that multilateral organisations such as the OECD, UNESCO and the World Bank are engaging in documentation, research and evaluation aimed at informing educational decision-making in such situations. They go on to state that 'UNICEF is now strengthening mechanisms for generating and applying experiential knowledge based on lessons from the field, to inform policy and design intervention strategies, as well as identifying and promoting "recommended practices" that are supported by evidence' (Johnson and Van Kalmthout, 2006: 3).

This emphasis on education in post-new war societies is not difficult to understand (Brock, 2011). It has long been recognised that investment in education is crucial for the promotion of economic progress, particularly in developing countries (Davies and Harber, 2002). After all, no country has reached sustained economic growth without achieving near universal primary school education. Conflict, however, can be a major obstacle. As Toure (2006: 17) points out, such physical, psychological and social consequences of violence and conflict as sexual harassment, lack of sanitation and the spread of HIV/AIDS, can seriously hinder the development of education. The situation is aggravated by unemployment, lack of funding, lack of facilities and infrastructure. Also, since education is a key determinant of income, influence and power, it can, as Johnson and Van Kalmthout (2006: 3) state, 'entrench intolerance, create or perpetuate inequality and intensify social tensions'. These authors are particularly concerned to draw attention to the fact that inequalities in educational access can lead to other inequalities, including in income, employment, nutrition and health, as well as political position. In similar vein, Davies (2005: 357) points out that, far from reducing violence and conflict, education can exacerbate it 'through the reproduction of inequality and exclusion, through perpetuation of ethnic or religious divisions, and through its acceptance of the dominant aggressive masculinities'.

While it is important not to be blind to this situation, education must also be seen as a crucial area of concern in post-new war societies (King, 2011). At the most fundamental level, and echoing the decrees in the 1948 Universal Declaration of Human Rights, the 1959 United Nations Declaration of the Rights of the Child, the 1962 Convention against Discrimination in Education and the 1989 United Nations Convention on the Rights of the Child, the Save the Children Alliance (2006: 11) argues that every child in the world has a right to education, whatever the circumstances. It goes on to detail a number of advantages of providing quality education through schools and other places of learning in post-conflict societies (Save the Children, 2006: 11–15). These advantages, and related ones highlighted by other significant individuals in the field, are that education can:

- help protect children from physical harm, exploitation and violence, since post-conflict settings can still be very dangerous;
- provide psychological support and healing by signalling a return to stability, thus 'helping children to deal with the traumas they have experienced, and in developing their social skills and self-esteem' (Save the Children, 2006: 12);
- assist the affected society more widely by helping to 'restore normalcy, safeguard the most vulnerable, provide psycho-social care, promote tolerance, unify divided communities and begin the process of reconstruction and peace building' (Johnson and Van Kalmthout, 2006: 3);

- offer an entry point for 'triggering longer-term social, economic and political change, especially for the poorest families', being one of the key ingredients of democracy building, as 'universal literacy is essential for creating politically active citizens and strong societies' (Save the Children, 2006: 12);
- yield some of the highest returns of all development investments when it involves investment in girls' education, since such investment can result in 'both private and social benefits for individuals, families and society at large' (Save the Children, 2006: 14).

Dwelling on the latter point, the Save the Children Alliance goes on to argue that education can increase women's labour force participation rates and earnings. Furthermore, it can create intergenerational benefits, since a 'mother's education is a significant variable affecting her children's survival, as well as their educational attainment and opportunities' (Save the Children, 2006: 14).

In the literature on schools in post-conflict settings, emphasis is also placed on the importance of teaching children about conflict, including teaching about difference, about rights and about justice. This raises serious questions for curriculum developers. As Davies states:

> We know in the Balkans, for example, that countries and entities are trying to 'harmonise' curriculum and remove hostile references to previous 'enemies'; but how do they then present this complicated history and set of identities? How do Rwandan teachers teach about the genocide? What are government policies – are teachers, as in India after the riots following the assassination of Indira Ghandi, asked not to mention the conflict and teach 'as normal'.
>
> (2005: 357)

What is especially promoted is 'peace education'. Initiatives in this area by the UN have stressed the idea of a culture of peace, of shared meanings and values, and diversity between different peoples of the world (Bretherton, Weston and Zbar, 2003). Associated peace education programmes tend to be offered in the form of separate subjects, be spread across the curriculum, or be offered through a whole-school approach, promoting the goal of living peacefully together through education and intercultural dialogue. The literature also highlights the need for trained teachers, facilities and resources for peace education, and also the need to connect with the local culture.

Authors in the field provide enlightenment on how to plan, construct and implement peace education. McGlynn, Zembylas, Bekerman and Gallagher (2009), for example, offer theoretical, pedagogical, empirical and contextual perspectives from different projects in such troubled parts of the world as the Middle East, Cyprus, Northern Ireland, Burundi and Macedonia. Similarly, Spence (2009) emphasises the reconciliation aspects of education, including education for truth in Northern Ireland and South Africa, education for justice in Rwanda and Solomon Islands, and education for security in Mozambique and Sudan.

The reality faced by those attempting to promote education, including peace education, in post-conflict societies, however, is a daunting one (Mundy and Dryden-Peterson, 2011). As Bretherton, Weston and Zbar (2003) point out, during a violent conflict the education system is likely to have been seriously affected through the dislocation of children and teachers, damage to schools, and non-payment of teachers because of the breakdown of infrastructure. Indeed, post-conflict education programmes often have to start from a situation where material resources are very scarce, where children are not in school at all and even when they are in attendance there can be a major lack of trust if they are drawn from opposing sides in the conflict. Buckland (2006: 7) details these and other related problems common to many post-conflict states, as follows:

- there is often a chronic shortage of qualified teachers;
- the sheer number of war-affected youth, demobilised soldiers and young people who have not completed basic education can seem overwhelming;
- poor record keeping, corruption and lack of transparency in education governance (e.g. salaries are often paid to 'ghost' teachers) can exacerbate an already daunting situation;
- the 'relief' bubble in international financial support often subsides before a more predictable flow of reconstruction resources can be mobilised;
- skills training for youth is seriously under-resourced, and even when available, vocational training programmes often fail to prepare people for locally available employment opportunities;
- as education involves an interface of humanitarian action and development in complex ways there is often a plethora of coordination mechanisms, which in turn lead to coordination challenges;
- failure to develop successful initiatives to build the skills of young people and prevent their recruitment into military or criminal activity, can lead to youth being seen as a threat to stability;
- few programmes value young people as an important resource for development and reconstruction.

Both Buckland (2006) and Ahlen (2006: 10) also recognise failure to reintegrate refugees into mainstream national education systems as an area of serious neglect, and argue that while there is general consensus that the ideal curriculum in refugee education is, in principle at least, that of the country of origin, realising this ideal is frequently not possible.

While it is important to recognise such problems, it is also necessary to consider possible ways forward. One approach offered by the United Nations (2003) distinguished between the short- and the long-term initiatives that need to be taken in rehabilitating education in any post-conflict society. The short-term initiatives include building schools, providing teaching materials, desks and stationery, providing teachers and making sure they get paid and getting students back into the schools as soon as possible. The long-term strategy involves taking initiatives aimed at raising attendance levels, increasing literacy rates, reducing any gender imbalance in enrolment and attendance at the various levels, reducing drop-out rates, educating enough teachers and providing pedagogical support material to help teachers attain high quality levels of teaching. A key to attaining such aims, according to UNESCO's (2004) International Institute for Educational Planning, is the adoption of a coordinated approach to education. Such an approach, it is claimed (International Institute for Educational Planning/UNESCO, 2004: 881), has been found to have at least five advantages:

1   a coordinated education system becomes a connective tissue linking people from the same country (recognised or *de facto*) together;
2   a coordinated emergency education system promotes the acceptance and utility of humanitarian work because it addresses a fundamental value shared by families, committees and nations engulfed by war. Education is the most practicable, durable and encompassing peace-making enterprise available to humanitarians;
3   available, quality education is valuable because it limits the chances that trauma, abduction, forced labour, or a range of social and economic obligations will consume the lives of war-affected children and youth;
4   promoting education can, because it constitutes a mammoth sector in any nation, involve entire communities and their recognised or *de facto* government in a potentially uplifting endeavour during times of profound stress, uncertainty and tragedy. The work of education can also keep children and their teachers busy on useful activities;
5   coordinating the education sector facilitates the practice of humanitarian work by signifying the humanitarians' response to a widely shared and fundamental value. Coordination is of towering significance to the practice of education during emergencies and early reconstruction because a coordinated education system magnifies the coherence and utility of education for students, teachers and their communities. Displaced people such as IDPs and refugees, within and outside countries, have been cast adrift from their homes and distanced from their peace-time lives.

This brings us back to Kaldor's (2006: 12) position, already outlined, that the maximisation of the possibility of the successful implementation of strategies emanating from coordinated approaches requires not just the involvement of transnational institutions, but also that of local defenders of civility, and the establishment of an alliance between both. Equally, we argue, what is required, and what is greatly neglected in the educational literature in the field, is 'appropriate' leadership. Thus, while the provision of such leadership at the individual school level in post-new war settings is the area of focus in this book, we recognise the importance of locating considerations within a context which also takes cognisance of transnational institutions and of their relationship to local stakeholders.

Leadership at the individual school level in post-new war societies

Our focus on the individual school level in post-new war societies is partly because it provides a useful entry point for considering leadership and education in such societies more broadly. We were more influenced, however, by the fact that this is the 'coal face', the actual place where policy is enacted in a way that is meant to result in real change for students. At the same time, we recognise that appropriate initiatives also need to be taken at the macro level. As the Save the Children Alliance (2006: 17) argues, while government structures and ministries are often operating under increased pressures and, in some cases, limited capacity, in societies affected by conflict, they are the primary duty-bearers in the fulfilment of their citizens' rights. Thus, to ensure that all children enjoy the rights set out in international standards, governments need to put in place policies and plans to achieve education for all. Also, international donors have a vital role to play in supporting governments, especially through providing direct aid to enable basic services such as education to function and through providing the technical support to guide them. This includes making 'financial commitments to support curriculum renewal, modernisation of teacher training and supervision, as well as a significant investment in building technical capacity' (Save the Children, 2006: 30).

Such top-down initiatives are necessary in order to provide the framework within which appropriate leadership can be provided at the individual school level. This leadership, in turn, needs to be provided at the three levels of learning outlined by Knapp *et al.* (2003), namely, the organisational level, the teacher level and the student level. While they can constitute distinct foci, it is important to emphasise that these levels are interdependent in a complex variety of ways; an interdependence that will vary with context, but one that always requires great sensitivity and attention on the part of school leaders.

Regarding leadership at the organisational level, emphasis is placed in the post-conflict literature on the need for capacity building and encouragement of participation and coordination between communities, teachers and their organisations, local authorities and other stakeholders in order to build the appropriate culture (Buckland, 2006: 8). Also, there is emerging consensus that the efforts of local communities and authorities already active in supporting education should not be brought into competition with the efforts of external support agencies. A major safeguard in this regard, it is held, can be provided by establishing a decentralised educational system.

Furthermore, the resultant community participation, Nicolai suggests (2006: 23), should not be confined to mobilising labour to rebuild and repair schools. Rather, space should be given to parents to be involved in school governance (Buckland, 2006: 8). Adopting the same position, Brown (2006: 20) injects a sense of realism, arguing that this is a particularly challenging task in urban areas where a sense of community is often lacking. Furthermore, Greeley and Rose (2006: 14) caution that parental involvement in a decentralised educational system in post-conflict societies should not be seen as a panacea. As they put it, there is need for caution since reliance on communities can 'intensify inequality, particularly where communities are fractured as a result of conflict. School management committees can be captured by local elites, and can themselves give rise to conflict' (p. 14).

Various examples of projects geared towards promoting greater community involvement in post-conflict areas are available, although it is difficult to calibrate the extent to which they have been 'successful'. Spence (2009) has reported on a project in Solomon Islands, where communities were ripped apart as a result of lawlessness related to old grievances over land. One of the main requirements of a large donor peace and restoration fund which ran from 2000 to 2004, and of which education was one component, was that communities had to concentrate on projects that were of mutual rather than individual benefit. Intra- and inter-community cohesion was encouraged through such teamwork activities as leading labour teams and transporting materials, with youths being allowed to experience aspects of leadership in preparation for future roles. The aim also was for the community to become reassured through witnessing youths working productively and constructively.

A second example relates to the formerly violence-strewn Indonesian province of Aceh. Here, the Australia Indonesia Partnership for Reconstruction and Development (AIPRD) focused its relationship-building on a 'Communities and Education Project' (CEPA) which sought to promote reconciliation and village-level democracy through the education sector at the community level. The project aimed to build relationships and good communication across the whole community through school governance structures. Parties to the former conflict gained representation on individual school committees and made mutual decisions about school management procedures, fundraising and resource acquisition (AusAID, 2006). Such community participation, it was held, could lay a foundation for engagement in local democracy processes and promote peace and reconciliation.

A third example comes from Timor-Leste, one of the world's newest nations and born out of violence. Here the '100 Friendly Schools Project' (100 FSP), which was a component of the UNICEF and national government's 'Master Plan of Operations' (MPO), had as its aim to strengthen national educational policy and planning, increase the capacity of primary schools to deliver quality education and increase enrolment and completion rates. The project had four components: teacher training, school based management, the establishment of parent teacher associations and improving early childhood education. It has been claimed (UNICEF, 2005) that parents and community members benefited by gaining a sense of ownership of the school and their children's education, becoming aware of how they could support schooling and obtaining a say in the affairs of the school.

Leadership at the second level, namely, that of teachers working in the individual school, is also necessary. It is particularly needed in order to build teachers' intellectual and professional capacities. The efficacy of this process will depend, in the first instance, on teachers and principals recognising that they are learners themselves. Nearly fifteen years ago, Hargreaves (1997), in relation to the realm of education generally, recognised the increasing complexity of teaching, which he regarded as the crucible for teachers' learning, especially by means of collaboration. Factors such as an expanded knowledge base of teaching, increasingly diverse students in classrooms, and the broadening ambit of teachers' responsibilities, serve to buttress the importance of teachers' continuous learning. This situation applies to teachers in post-conflict societies every bit as much as it does in the case of teachers in schools more broadly.

Nicolai has argued that initiatives aimed at improving the quality of teachers in post-conflict situations cannot be postponed until an education system is fully functioning and the curriculum is known, especially in places where the teaching force is inexperienced (2006: 23). This, as Spink implies, is because teachers need to be able to deal from the outset with a range of contentious issues (2006: 16). He points to developments in Afghanistan to illustrate the sorts of difficulties that can arise. Here, he states, complex tasks of curriculum development were not adequately addressed. As a result,

> curriculum and textbook reform remains fraught with political agendas. There is ongoing debate about religious textbooks, particularly how to present non-Sunni religious practices. Ethnic groups are vying for influence over how history is taught.
>
> (p. 16)

The argument is not that this situation could have been avoided. Rather, what Spink is keen to highlight is the importance of teachers possessing the pedagogical skills and subject knowledge to be able to address the situation in a professional manner. While leadership on its own, of course, cannot guarantee such a scenario, it is sorely needed in order to promote initiatives by which it can be addressed.

The third level at which leadership is required in schools in post-conflict societies is that of the student. Leadership at this level is especially important in order to facilitate recognition of the various disorders which may be evident in young students' behaviours. Teachers should not be surprised to be confronted with many student adjustment problems as well as misbehaviour, aggressiveness, violence and lack of motivation. For example, Darweesh

(1992) was able to identify neurotic symptoms, depression, maladjustment and an enfeeblement of intellectual performance related to academic achievement amongst Kuwaiti children as a result of the first Gulf War.

There is a growing consensus that leadership in education is also required so that children can be involved in providing solutions not only to their own problems, but to those of their society (Buckland, 2006: 8). Hart puts the argument as follows:

> Most research in education and conflict focuses on the school system rather than the children. The general failure of educationalists to engage with the reality of children's lives has some serious implications for the timing, design and evaluation of educational initiatives...Children-focused research implicitly rejects the notion that children's ideas, experiences, needs and aspirations are adequately articulated by adults, however well-intentioned. The role of the researcher should be to enable young people to participate in research as fully as they wish, sharing their views safely and to their own satisfaction...When the situation of children is properly understood, innovative programmes can be developed that provide meaningful learning opportunities.
>
> (2006: 9)

Bird takes up the same point in arguing that children should be considered as 'clients' and as the reason for educational intentions. He goes on:

> Children should be placed within the context of the community they live in and the learning processes they are engaged in through community life. This implies consideration not only of formal schooling but also of the informal educative processes that can often be more significant... understanding how they receive information – from teachers in schools, parents, radio, gossip with their peers or storytelling from their elders. By genuinely listening to children and taking note of their concerns and needs in our programming interventions, the policy and research debate can be better informed from a truly 'grounded' perspective.
>
> (2006: 30)

The Save the Children Alliance has pointed out that some organisations, cognisant of such a position, have established children's clubs in post-conflict settings and that these have proved to be 'a remarkable catalyst for change and development within communities' (2006: 20). Luswata has also documented how UNICEF, in Southern Sudan, promoted children's participation by mobilising girls and boys to act as 'advocates within their communities through "creative facilitation", helping to publicise children's voices in the media, and ensuring children's visibility in "Go To School" launches, marches and other public events' (Luswata, 2006: 2).

What kind of leadership is required at the individual school level in post-new war settings?

While the importance of providing leadership at the individual school level in post-new war societies has been stressed a number of times in this chapter, no attention has been paid to the nature of what that leadership might be. If, for example, one was guided by Weber's (1984) early classical typology of leaders, one would ask whether the most appropriate leaders for such settings should be of the traditional, rational or charismatic type. Traditional leaders, according to Weber, are like monarchs in that they come to their role through social conventions, rational leaders are appointed on the basis of their technical, professional and bureaucratic expertise, and charismatic leaders possess a forceful, or magnetic, personality, or intrinsic spiritual endowment elusively identified as charisma.

The study of leadership developed alongside the study of leaders. This field, particularly in relation to education, has generated an enormous amount of interest among researchers and practitioners, although the search for a singular theory of leadership has proved futile (Harris, 2003). Foster (1989), however, identified two main traditions that have influenced the social scientific definition of leadership, namely, that which comes from the political historical disciplines and that which comes from the world of business management and public administration. The study of leadership through the political historical model highlights the role of significant individuals in shaping the course of history. Leadership in this sense is the story of events, actions and ideas of how individuals transformed their social milieu (Foster, 1989). Leaders are individuals who make history through the use of power and resources. On the other hand, the study of leadership through the bureaucratic–managerial model describes the views of scholars and business personnel on leadership. Here, leaders are persons of superior rank in an organisation, leadership is goal-centred and goals are driven by organisational needs. The reason for exerting leadership is to achieve organisational goals. Top executives control the organisation and make individuals perform tasks at their level of competency.

Given the extent to which the study of leadership has progressed in the last twenty years (O'Donoghue and Clarke, 2010: 54–69), it is appropriate at this point to outline a range of definitions of leadership types. Eight of these types are considered.

Managerial leadership

Bush and Glover's (2003) explanation of managerial leadership focuses on functions, tasks and the behaviours of people. It assumes that the behaviour of the organisational members is largely rational. Also, influence on people is exercised through positions of authority within the organisational hierarchy. Leithwood *et al.* (1999) observe that managerial leadership is similar to other leadership types found in classical management literature. Dressler, however, argues differently (2001: 176). Traditionally, as he sees it, 'the principal's role has been clearly focused on management responsibilities'. Now, however, 'global and societal influence has increased the span of responsibility'. Thus, it has come to include interpersonal relationships, sensitivity and communication skills, contextual factors, including philosophical and cultural values, and policy and political influence.

Instructional leadership

Bush and Glover's (2003) interpretation of instructional leadership focuses on teaching and learning, and on the behaviour of teachers in working with students. Student learning via teachers has become the target of the leader's influence. The emphasis is on the direction and impact of influence rather than on the process of influence. For Leithwood *et al.* (1999) instructional leadership is the behaviour and attention teachers adopt while engaging in activities directly affecting the growth of students. In this regard, Southworth (2002) observes that instructional leadership is strongly concerned with teaching as well as with learning. Gelten and Shelton (1991) agree, stating that effective instructional leadership is characterised by a strategy to deploy all the resources available at school to achieve its instructional mission and goal. In similar vein, Leithwood *et al.* (1999) state that instructional leaders possess the expert knowledge and the formal authority to exert influence on teachers. Furthermore, Hallinger and Murphy (1985) affirm that instructional leaders define the school mission, manage the instructional programme, and promote school climate.

Transactional leadership

Transactional leadership is based on exchange relationships between leader and follower. Much of political leadership is viewed as being transactional. In exchange for the voters' support, the leader adopts a programme designed to help particular groups. Transactional leadership in schools is seen, as US observers put it, as being exercised by the superintendent relationship with unions, teachers and parents. The support of the leaders is worked out through the manipulations of various social forces guiding concessions, negotiations and accommodations of needs (Foster, 1989).

Transformational leadership

Transformational leadership is generally defined as the ability of a leader to envisage a new social condition and to communicate this vision to the followers. The leader inspires and transforms individual followers from higher levels of morality that make the promising of rewards unnecessary. Bush and Glover's (2003) interpretation of transformational leadership describes the influence and the increased commitment of followers to organisational goals. Leaders seek to support teachers for their vision of the school and to enhance their capabilities to contribute to goal achievement. The focus is on the transformation process rather than on particular types of outcomes.

Transformational approaches are often contrasted with transactional leadership. Sergiovanni distinguishes between them as follows:

> In transactional leadership, leaders and followers exchange needs and services in order to accomplish independent objectives . . . This bargaining process can be viewed metaphorically as a form of leadership by bartering. The wants and needs of followers and the wants and needs of the leader are traded and a bargain is struck. Positive reinforcement is given for good work and for increased performance. In transformational leadership, by contrast, leaders and followers are united in pursuit of higher-level goals that are common to both. Both want to become the best, both want to lead the school to a new direction.
>
> (1991: 125–26)

He concludes that when transformative leadership is practised successfully, purposes that might have started out being separated become fused.

Moral leadership

Moral leadership is based on the values and beliefs of leaders and provides the school with a clear sense of purpose (Bush and Glover, 2003). It is similar to the transformational model, but with a stronger value base. Sergiovanni comments on this upholding of the importance of values as follows:

> Excellent schools have central zones composed of values and beliefs that take on sacred or cultural characteristics. The school must move beyond concern for goals and roles to the task of building purposes into the structure and embodying these purposes in everything that it does with the effect of transforming school members from neutral participant to committed followers.
>
> (Sergiovanni, 1991: 322–23)

The embodiment of purpose and the development of followers, he concluded, are inescapably moral. Regarding the education domain, he also argued that the challenge of leadership is to make peace with two competing imperatives: the managerial and the moral. In similar fashion, Grace contended that 'the discourse and undertaking of management must be matched by a discourse and understanding of ethics, morality and spirituality' (2000: 244).

Invitational leadership

Bennis and Nanus (1985) propose a more practical, holistic and dynamic model of leadership – one that encourages leaders to pursue more joyful and more meaningful personal and professional lives, and invites others to do the same. Leaders, Bennis and Nanus argue, 'articulate and define what has previously remained implicit or unsaid. Then they invent images, metaphors and models that provide a focus for new attention' (1985: 39). Thus, they are led to the notion of invitational leadership, which is based on unleashing the intrinsic energy people possess and summoning them cordially to see themselves as capable of tackling challenges, overcoming obstacles and accomplishing great things. It acknowledges the integrity, potential and interdependence of the teachers and their responsibility to work for the common good. This, Bennis and Nanus state, involves a generous and genuine turning toward others in empathy and respect, with the ultimate goal of collaborating with them on projects of mutual benefit.

Interpersonal leadership

Tuohy and Coghlan portray the 'normal' life of teachers as follows:

> Much of the teachers' day is taken up in an intensity of relationships . . . with their students; the changing context of their lives and developing appropriate and effective responses to both their personal and academic needs requires constant reflection and adjustment.
>
> (1997: 67)

Thus, they argue, attention to collaboration and interpersonal relationships is paramount. What is needed, in this view, are interpersonal leaders who focus on relationships with teachers, students and other members of the school community and adopt a collaborative leadership approach based on the moral dimension (Timperley, 2008). Such leaders should have advanced interpersonal skills to enable them to operate effectively with internal and external stakeholders (Bush and Glover, 2003).

The presentation of other types of leadership (Dimmock, 2012; O'Donoghue and Clarke, 2010: 54–69) would result in unnecessary repetition of concepts already discussed above. Also, a major lesson to be drawn from the foregoing account is that leadership diversity continues to evolve in response to new complexities in education. At the same time, the history of educational innovation suggests that the initial response of those familiar with the array of leadership types, and who embrace our commitment to the importance of leadership in planning appropriate initiatives at the individual school level in post-conflict settings, would most likely be to advocate for the adoption of the particular type that appeals to them because of its fundamental underlying principles. To proceed in this manner, however, would be to replicate what time and again has resulted in the death of so much educational innovation, namely, the failure to take cognisance of the importance of context (Harber and Dadey, 1993).

This is not to overlook the importance attached to context by a number of enlightened educationalists. Back in the early 1980s, for example, Fullan argued that in order to effect improvement, that is, to effect an introduced change that has the promise of increasing success and decreasing failure, 'the world of the people most closely involved must be understood' (1982: 149). Dove (1986: 212) emphasised the same point in her work on education in developing countries, while Ball (1987) argued that theoretical writing on school organisation was overwhelmingly influenced by systems theory, but had little to say about the way schools are run on a day-to-day basis in various geographical, political and social settings. Others continued to draw attention to the matter in the 1990s. Hughes (1990) wrote about the danger of assuming that management theories and principles can be applied regardless of national and cultural differences, and without taking qualities and circumstances of different communities into consideration. Hargreaves followed up by contending that many social policies fail and nowhere is this more evident than in education where, he held, innovations frequently fail quite disastrously. The one common reason for this, he argued, is as follows:

> [I]n grafting new ideas on to schools, we do it with so little knowledge about the nature of the everyday world of teachers, pupils and schools that our attempted grafts (and various forms of major and minor surgery) fail to play doctor to an educational patient.
>
> (Hargreaves, 1993: 149–50).

He went on to argue that only when we 'understand the precise nature of the host body can we design our innovatory grafts with any confidence that they will prove to be acceptable' (p. 150).

Gronn and Ribbins (1996) argued along similar lines specifically in the case of leadership, indicating that the approach to educational leadership in any particular circumstance needs to take that circumstance into account. Dimmock and Walker (1997) became particularly influential in highlighting the Eurocentric nature of much research, writing and practices in relation to leadership in schools by illustrating that different cultures have different approaches to leadership and that these have solid cultural foundations. While their examples were drawn primarily from Confucian-based learning settings, others have illustrated this point more recently by providing examples from other parts of the world (Juan, Anderson and Bennett, 2010). Fitzgerald (2003a, 2003b, 2004) has also provided insights by drawing attention to how educational leadership may be practised differently by females, by indigenous leaders and by female indigenous leaders. In the case of educational leadership in post-conflict societies, however, including leadership at the individual school level, very little research, as Jansen (2007: 92) has pointed out, has been undertaken on what the nature of such circumstances might be and what challenges they pose for those who are ascribed leadership roles, or who might want to take them on. It is with providing enlightenment on this matter in the case of a range of post-new war societies that the remaining chapters of this book are concerned.

References

Ahlen, E. (2006) UNHCR's education challenges. *Forced Immigration Review*, July, 10–11.

Al-Jaber, Z. (1996) School management in Kuwait after the Iraqi aggression: Problems for principals. *Educational Management and Administration*, 24(4), 411–24.

Anderson, A. and Mendenhall, M. (2006) Inter-agency network for education in emergencies. *Forced Immigration Review*, July, 29–30.

AusAID (2006) *CEPA program outline*. Canberra:AusAID.

Ball, S. (1987) *The Micro-Politics of the School*. London: Methuen.

Barakat, S., Connolly, D., Hardman, F. and Sundram, V. (2012) The role of basic education in post-conflict recovery. *Comparative Education*, iFirst Article, 1–19.

Bird, L. (2006) Education and conflict: An NGO perspective. *Forced Immigration Review*, July, 30–31.

Bengtson, S. E. L. (2011) Fragile states, fragile concepts. In J. Paulson (ed.) *Education, Conflict and Development*. Oxford: Symposium Books, pp. 33–58.

Bennis, W. and Nanus, B. (1985) *The Strategy for Taking Charge*. New York: Harper and Row.

Blattman, C. and Miguel, E. (2010) Civil war. *Journal of Economic Literature*, 48(1), 3–57.

Bousquet, A. (2012) War. In E. Amenta, K. Nash and A. Scott (eds) *The Wiley-Blackwell Companion to Political Sociology*. London: Blackwell-Wiley, pp. 180–89.

Bretherton, D., Weston, J. and Zbar, V. (2003) Peace education curriculum development in post-conflict contexts: Sierra Leone. *Prospects*, 33(2), 219–30.

Brock, C. (2011) Education and conflict. In J. Paulson (ed.) *Education, Conflict and Development*. Oxford: Symposium Books, pp. 17–32.

Brown, G., Langer, A. and Stewart, F. (2007) *A Typology of Post-conflict Situation: An overview*. New York: United Nations Development Programme.

Brown, T. (2006) South Sudan education emergency. *Forced Immigration Review*, July, 20–21.

Buckland, P. (2006) Post-conflict education: Time for a reality check. *Forced Immigration Review*, July, 7–8.

Bush, T. and Glover, D. (2003) *School Leadership: Concepts of evidence*. Nottingham: National College for School Leadership.

Carnoy, M. and Samoff, J. (1990) *Education and Social Transition in the Third World*. Princeton, NJ: Princeton University Press.

Darweesh, Z. Al-A. (1992) The psychological impacts of the Iraqi aggression on Kuwait youth. *Arab Journal for the Humanities*, 10(29/30), 239–57.

Davies, L. (2005) Schools and war: urgent agendas for comparative and international education. *Compare*, 35(4), 357–71.

Davies, L. (2006) Understanding the education-war interface. *Forced Immigration Review*, July, 13.

Davies, L. and Harber, C. (2002) *School Management and Effectiveness in Developing Countries: The post-bureaucratic school*. London: Continuum Press.

Dimmock, C. (2012) *Leadership, Capacity Building and School Improvement*. London: Routledge.

Dimmock, C. and Walker, A. (1997) Comparative educational administration: Developing a cross-cultural conceptual framework. *Educational Administration Quarterly*, 34(4), 558–95.

Dove, L. A. (1986) *Lifelong Teacher Education and the Community School*. Hamburg: Unesco.

Dressler, B. (2001) Charter school leadership, *Education and Urban Society*, 33(2), 170–85.

Fitzgerald, T. (2003a) Interrogating orthodox voices: Gender, ethnicity and educational leadership. *School Leadership and Management*, 23(4), 431–44.

Fitzgerald, T. (2003b) Changing the deafening silence of indigenous women's voices in educational leadership. *Journal of Educational Administration*, 41(1), 9–23.

Fitzgerald, T. (2004) Powerful voices and powerful stories: Reflections on the challenges and dynamics of intercultural research. *Journal of Intercultural Studies*, 25(3), 233–45.

Foster, W. (1989) Towards a critical practice of leadership. In J. Smyth (ed.) *Critical Perspectives on Educational Leadership*. London: Falmer Press, pp. 39–62.

Fullan, M. (1982) *The Meaning of Educational Change*. New York: Teachers College, Columbia University.

Gelten, B. and Shelton, M. (1991) Expanded notion of strategic instructional leadership: The principal's role with student support personnel. *Journal of School Leadership*, 1, 338–50.

Giner, S. (1972) *Sociology*. Bristol: Martin Robertson.

Goldring, E., Crowson, R., Laid, D. and Berk, R. (2003) Transition in a shifting political environment. *Educational Evaluation and Policy Analysis*, 25, 473–88.

Grace, G. (2000) Research and the challenges of contemporary school leadership. The contribution of critical scholarship. *British Journal of Educational Studies*, 48(3), 231–47.

Greeley, M., and Rose, P. (2006) Learning to deliver education in fragile states. *Forced Immigration Review*, July, 14–15.

Hallinger, P. and Murphy, J. (1985) Assessing the instructional management behavior of principals. *The Elementary School Journal*, 86(2), 217–47.

Harber, C. and Dadey, A. (1993) The job of the headteacher in Africa: research and reality. *International Journal of Educational Development*, 13(2), 147–60.

Hargreaves, A. (1997).The four stages of professionalism and professional learning. *Unicorn*, 23(2), 86–114.

Hargreaves, D. (1993) Whatever happened to symbolic interactionism? In M. Hammersley (ed.) *Controversies in Classroom Research*. Buckingham: Open University Press, pp. 135–52.

Harris, A. (2003) Teacher leadership and school improvement. In A. Harris, C. Day, D. Hopkins, M. Hadfield, A. Hargreaves and C. Chapman (eds) *Effective Leadership for School Improvement*. London: RoutledgeFalmer, pp. 72–83.

Hart, J. (2006) Putting children in the picture. *Forced Immigration Review*, July, 9–10.

International Institute for Educational Planning/UNESCO (2004) *Co-ordinating Education During Emergencies and Reconstruction: Challenges and responsibilities.* Paris: International Institute for Educational Planning/UNESCO).

Hughes, M. G. (1990) Improving education and training for educational administrators and managers: Urgent needs. Paper presented to the UNESCO International Congress, 26–30 March. Planning and Management of Educational Development, Mexico.

Jansen, J. (2007) The leadership of transition: Correction, conciliation and change in South African education. *Journal of Educational Change*, 8, 91–103.

Johnson, D. and Van Kalmthout, E. (2006) Editorial. *Forced Immigration Review*, July, 3.

Juan, J., Anderson, L. and Bennett, N. (2010) Democratic school leadership reforms in Kenya: Cultural and historical challenges. *Journal of Educational Administration and History*, 42(3), 247–74.

Kaldor, M. (2005) Old wars, new wars and the war on terrorism. http://www.lse.ac.uk/Depts/global/Publications/PublicLectures/PL_Old%20 Wars%20Cold%20War%20New%20Wars%20and%20War%20on%20Terror1.pdf (accessed 4 November 2010).

Kaldor, M. (2006) *New and Old Wars.* Cambridge: Polity Press.

Kaldor, M. (2009) Cosmopolitanism and organised violence. http://www.dspace.cigilibrary/jspui/handle/123456789/8454 (accessed 8 June 2013).

King, E. (2011) The multiple relationships between education and conflict: Reflections of Rwandan teachers and students. In K. Mundy and S. Dryden-Peterson (eds) *Educating Children in Conflict Zones: Research, policy and practice for systemic change.* New York: Teachers College Press., pp. 137–51).

Knapp, M. S., Copland, M. and Talbert, J. (2003) *Leading for Learning: Reflective tools for school and district leaders.* Seattle, WA: Centre for the Study of Teaching and Policy, University of Washington.

Leithwood, K., Jantzi, D. and Steinbach, R. (1999) *Changing Leadership for Changing Times.* Buckingham: Open University Press.

Luswata, S. (2006) Getting Southern Sudanese children to school. *Forced Immigration Review*, July, 22.

McGlynn, C., Zembylas, M., Bekerman, Z. and Gallagher, T. (2009) *Peace Education in Conflict and Post-conflict Societies: Comparative perspectives.* London: Palgrave Macmillan.

Macpherson, R. (2011) Educational administration and management in Timor Leste. *International Journal of Educational Management*, 25(2), 186–203.

Melander, E., Oberg, M. and Hall, J. (2009) Are 'new wars' more atrocious? *European Journal of International Relations.* 18(4), 505–36.

Mukendi, B. (2010) *Leadership and Change in Post-conflict States.* New York: United Nations Development Programme.

Munday, K. and Dryden-Peterson, S. (2011) Educating children in zones of conflict: An overview and introduction. In K. Munday and S. Dryden-Peterson (eds) *Educating Children in Conflict Zones: Research, policy and practice for systemic change.* New York: Teachers College Press, pp. 1–12

Nicolai, S. (2006) Rebuilding Timor-Leste's education system, *Forced Immigration Review*, July, 23.

O'Donnell, G., Schmitter, P. and Whitehead, L. (1986) *Transitions from*

Authoritarian Rule: Tentative conclusions about uncertain democracies. Baltimore: Johns Hopkins University Press.

O'Donoghue, T. A. and Clarke, S. (2010) *Leading Learning: Process, themes and issues in international perspective.* London: Routledge.

Oplatka, I. (2004) The principalship in developing countries: Context, characteristics and reality. *Comparative Education,* 40(3), 427–48.

Save the Children (2006) *Rewrite the Future: Education for children in conflict-affected countries.* Cambridge: International Save the Children Alliance.

Sergiovanni, T. J. (1991) *The Principalship: A reflective practice perspective.* Boston: Allyn and Bacon.

Southworth, G. (2002) *Leading and Developing Pedagogies.* Keynote address at the Professional Development Network Conference for School Leaders, Surfers Paradise, Queensland. (August).

Spence, R. (2009) Education in post-conflict environments: Pathways to peace. http://devnet.anu.edu.au (accessed 12 November 2010)

Spink, J. (2006) Education, reconstruction and state building in Afghanistan. *Forced Immigration Review,* July, 15–16

Timperley, H. A. (2008) A distributed perspective on leadership and enhancing valued outcomes for students. *Journal of Curriculum Studies,* 40(6), 821–33.

Tuohy, D. and Coghlan, D. (1997) Development in schools: A systems approach based on organizational levels. *Education Management and Administration,* 25(1), 65–77.

Toure, K. (2006) Impact of conflict in Africa. *Forced Immigration Review,* July, 17.

UNICEF (2005) *100 Friendly Schools project: Evaluation report.* Dili: UNICEF.

United Nations (2003) Office of the Humanitarian Coordinator for Iraq Background Paper: Education in Iraq. www.un.org/dpts/oip. (accessed 12 November 2010).

3 Angola

Fostering teacher professionalism and safe schools

Lynn Davies

Introduction

Presenting an argument about school leadership in Angola involves being aware of seemingly disparate pictures. There is the overall country context both as a conflict affected fragile state (CAFS) and as a politically inequitable, or even corrupt, state. There is the general picture of how the education system has been affected by this context and by political history. There are also the government educational reforms, which have a modernising thrust. And then there are the realities of impoverished schools in remote areas whose participants have their own survival agendas. To offer any exposition on school leadership in Angola means that these four pictures have to be overlaid. Before doing so, however, each has to be considered individually.

Country background

Angola's 27-year civil war ended officially in 2002. It is not, however, an altogether 'post-conflict' country. This was illustrated graphically in 2010 when the Togo national football team was attacked in the province of Cabinda by separatists demonstrating about economic inequalities and wanting autonomy over the resources in that province. Angola has a rentier economy, surviving on the sale of oil concessions and corporate taxes, rather than on more traditional taxation. As a result, the political system is devoid of incentives to provide basic education and health that would allow citizens to add to the country's economic development (DIIS, 2008).

The legitimacy of the state is always in question in terms of people's trust in the government to allocate oil and other revenues fairly (Davies, 2011). On this, the Danish Institute for International Studies warned of the absence of 'bonding ties' between the political elite and the general population (DIIS, 2008). There are some positive developments with a UNDP civic education project and a UNICEF business education project, but it is not yet clear whether citizens will have the incentives to demand real democratic representation.

Sogge (2009) disputes the 'resource curse' thesis of countries such as Angola, but agrees on the 'democratic deficits' that are generated by the hydrocarbon industry in fragile states. In Angola, the political space for associational life (that is, civil society) is severely confined and largely depoliticised. Sogge's work reveals how corruption and clientelism extends through all the system, demonstrating the power of the oil industry – and national elites who depend on it – to corrupt and undermine the legitimacy of whatever political system it touches. It is not surprising that press freedom is among the most restricted in Africa.

Angola operates in complex international spheres of influence, not all of which are benign. In France, Mitterrand and dozens of members of the French establishment were found guilty of an illegal trade in landmines and arms relating to the conflict that killed 500,000 (Cage, 2009). The arms came from stocks offloaded by the Red Army after the collapse of the Soviet bloc. Diamonds were the currency of exchange. Now, the Chinese are making huge investments in Angola. They are building roads, but bring in their own labour, which can cause resentment. The government has agreed that 70 per cent of tendered public works must go to Chinese firms, most of which do not employ Angolans. Angola has taken over from Saudi Arabia as China's largest supplier of oil (Swain 2008). Opaque syndicates controlled by the country's president run the oil trade with China, with oil contracts being regarded as state secrets. *The Economist* has revealed three interlinked problems about these syndicates: first, they are linked to personal gain; second, they have failed to meet the obligation of providing schools, housing and transport which they undertook in order to get mining licences (more than 90 per cent of the residents of Luanda are still without running water); and third, their cash props up certain political leaders, thereby fuelling violent conflicts ('The Queensway Syndicate', *The Economist*, 13 August, 2011).

Although people talk of nearly three decades of war in Angola, it is actually four when one considers the 14-year war of independence against Portugal that preceded the civil war in 1975. Out of a population of 7 million in 1980, some 1.5 million were killed and more than 4 million were forced to flee from their homes. A whole generation missed their education. Also, *The Economist* reported in 2010 that while the pace of development since 2002 has been huge, the country has no manufacturing base to speak of, most items have to be imported, the ports are clogged, the roads are potholed and electricity is patchy ('Rising Angola: Oil, glorious oil', *The Economist*, 30 January, 2010). Extreme bureaucracy pervades all transactions. Officially, GDP per head has more than doubled, so that Angola's IMF ranking is 98th out of 189 countries. The 2010 UNDP Human Development Index, however, put Angola near the bottom in almost every category, including life expectancy, infant mortality and adult illiteracy.

Things are improving slightly, with reasonably fair democratic elections having taken place in 2008, a slight easing of press restrictions, some road building and an unclogging of the ports. There is a plan to replace one million homes for shack dwellers by 2012. Landmines are being removed from farmland, and there is a pledge by President de Santos – for the first time – to reduce corruption. Marques de Morais (2009) speaks of generalised corruption as the 'collective mentality' that is paralysing the nation. His experience is that people feel offended, or can even become hostile, when someone exposes the truth. This is not a fear of repression. Rather, it is a preference to survive by hiding behind the illusion that everyday corruption is an act of benevolence by those in power. Their acts also allow others to plunder, fearing losing the property, or benefits, that are to be gained through dealings based on institutional, party-political or family connections.

In comparing Afghanistan and Angola, Davies (2011) found that while there are highly significant differences, the two countries do share characteristics of conflict-affected fragile states (CAFS) around 'normality'. Corruption is normal. Violent solutions to problems are normal. Lack of transparency and trust are normal. In commerce, non-market-based relations are normal. Above all, resilience, survival and opportunism are the normal default mechanisms for the bulk of the population. This makes capacity development efforts themselves fragile, including capacity development for school principals.

The Government of Angola's human rights record continues to be poor. The 2008 *Human Rights Report* (US Department of State, 2009) reported numerous serious problems. Human rights abuses included the abridgement of citizens' right to elect officials at all levels; unlawful killings by police, military and private security forces; security force torture, beatings and rape; harsh prison conditions; arbitrary arrest and detention; official corruption and impunity; judicial inefficiency and lack of independence; lengthy pre-trial detention; lack of due process; restrictions on freedom of speech, press, assembly and association; forced evictions without compensation; and discrimination, violence and abuse perpetrated against women and children. Violence against women is common and pervasive, particularly in urban areas. Domestic violence is not illegal. Religious leaders in the provinces of Lunda Norte and Uige reported that elderly persons, particularly rural and impoverished women and children, occasionally were vulnerable to accusations of witchcraft and subsequent abuse. Women sometimes were killed, beaten, expelled from their families, or died from mistreatment and malnourishment. All this has implications for how a curriculum area around human rights can be implemented in schools.

The situation of education and children

The conflict left the Angolan education system severely underdeveloped, with millions of children out of school, few functional classrooms and a population with very limited education. In the initial post-war years, many under-qualified teachers were taken on to accommodate the massive influx of students. Teacher educational levels are increasing, but not all have formal teacher-training qualifications. Humanitarian interventions have arguably strengthened the culture of dependency.

Save the Children report that the country still ranks as one of the worst places in the world for children to grow up in. It was revealed that the debt-ridden government spent much of its budget on food and health, leaving little for education (Save the Children, 2008). While there has been rapid economic growth because of oil, the benefits have been slow to reach the education system. In 2009, government spending on education was 7.9 per cent of total government spending, one of the lowest figures in the world (UNDP, 2010). Furthermore, only 16 per cent of the 7.9 per cent was allocated to primary schooling.

Post-conflict reconstruction within education has focussed on physical reconstruction (especially of classrooms), on human resource provision, including that of teachers and their training, and on material resources such as textbooks. Save the Children (2010) report that as the country has made the transition from emergency to development, their own response has become more focussed on development and advocacy work. But while primary enrolments increased by two million between 2002 and 2008, it is estimated that around a million still remain out of school. Repetition and drop-out rates are high and, as a legacy of the conflict as well as of poverty, there is a large number of youths who have missed out on primary education, a sometimes dangerous situation as it can lead to recruitment into violence. Some hope is provided by accelerated learning programmes (ALPs) that are being developed to enable out-of-school youths to catch up, and these are proving successful, particularly for girls.

Save the Children say that some of the most damaging effects of the war on the education system are cultural rather than structural. Whilst demand for good education is high, motivation and belief in the capacity of schools to deliver worthwhile education is low. Teachers have little faith in students' abilities to learn and the authorities have little faith in teachers' ability to perform their roles as professionals. As stated in our *Education Action* report described below (Davies, 2008), the instability and population displacements caused by the conflict have contributed to a culture of non-planning. Students are characterised as being 'low brained'.

The *Human Rights Report* of the United States Department of State (2009) held that the government was committed to the protection of children's rights and welfare, but lacked the human and logistical resources required to provide necessary programmes. The country's National Institute for Children (NAC) has primary responsibility for coordinating government action concerning children's affairs. Activists reported that the condition of many urban and rural children remains undocumented. The government has not permitted undocumented children to gain access to the educational system, and fees for birth certificates and identification cards have remained prohibitive for impoverished families. Although the official registration drive ended in 2004, the government continued to partner with

UNICEF to identify and assist undocumented children, and provide limited subsidies to cover fees for families with proven financial need. It also implemented a plan to provide birth certificates in health clinics and maternity wards.

Education is free and compulsory for documented children until the sixth grade, but students often have significant additional expenses. The government began distributing free schoolbooks during 2008, but the books had not reached schools nationwide by the year's end due to a shortage of supply (Davies, 2008). The Ministry of Education had insufficient resources and during the war most of the educational infrastructure was damaged. The Ministry of Education estimated an 85–90 per cent primary school enrolment rate during the year. An estimated 30 per cent of eligible children were enrolled at the secondary school level, rural areas generally lacked access to secondary schools and the number of available places was often limited, even in provincial capitals. There were also reports of families paying bribes to education officials to ensure their child had a school place. According to UNESCO, enrolment rates favoured boys over girls, especially at the secondary school level. Also, child abuse was widespread, with reports of physical abuse within the family being commonplace and largely tolerated by local officials (US Department of State, 2009).

Gender disparities are part of the post-conflict and historical culture in Angola. Female teachers are scarce and are often less willing than males to take up teaching posts in rural areas. In one rural municipality, local police complained to the school principal that two of the female teachers were having affairs. The case was unfounded, but women who live away from their husbands are under great suspicion of infidelity, a matter not considered a problem for men (Save the Children, 2009). Interestingly, there were no reports of teachers treating boys and girls differently, perhaps, from our experience, because often they did not 'treat' them at all, in the sense of talking to them, knowing their names, praising them or finding out if they understood what they were being taught.

In terms of educational leadership generally, a World Bank report states that female teachers and principals are critical for the expansion and improvement of secondary education systems (Leu *et al.*, 2005). Female teachers are important in encouraging the access and retention of female students. Females in leadership positions within schools provide good role models for female students and encourage female student retention. Yet, the World Bank has also said that there is generally a dearth of information in the literature on secondary school principals and gender issues in sub-Saharan Africa. We found the same difficulty establishing the gender composition in educational administration in developing countries as long ago as 1992 (Davies and Gunawardena, 1992). That research situation does not seem to have improved much in the interim. Specifically in connection with research on Angola, it seems almost impossible to find international texts, or reports, that use Angola as a case study. As in the UNESCO *Education for All* annual reports, while Angola appears in the country statistical lists, it does not appear in the literature reviews. It seems there are favourite countries for in-depth research in sub-Saharan Africa, presumably because major international reports are written in English or French, and writers prefer the familiarity of working in these contexts – although children's organisations such as UNICEF and Save the Children do provide substantive reviews.

Education reform

In the context of the uncertain educational opportunities in Angola as portrayed so far, what does education reform look like? There have been considerable changes in the education system and its legal foundations since independence in 1975, with a major reform having been initiated in 2004, guided by the nation's *Action Plan for Education for All* (Republic of Angola Ministry of Education, 2004). The goal was to improve the education system through three phases: emergency (2003–2005), stabilizing (2005–2010) and development (2010–2015). In its current 'development' phase, the focus is on consolidating the interventions of previous phases, while emphasising quality education (UNESCO/IBE, 2010). This has been seen to reduce school dropout rates and grade repetition. The reform also introduced new disciplines such as music, environment, informatics, design, rights, economy and arts into the curriculum (Republic of Angola, 2010a). There has been increased emphasis on English because of its perceived advantage in improving international trade; concerns have been expressed about the fact that there are twelve national languages, six of which are taught at school, but 'interfere' with the teaching of English (Voice of America, 2008).

There was a phase of experimentation or piloting, followed by a generalisation phase from 2006. In spite of encouraging results from the reform, however, the Government of Angola still admits that continuing financial difficulties are affecting production and distribution of learning resources. A Ministry of Education document in 2011 listed a continuing, although improving, situation of a lack of classrooms, libraries, laboratories and sports facilities, as well as deficiencies in the preparation of teachers and school supervisors. Teachers' salaries and qualification levels had also increased, although there were '*documentos falsos e morosidade burocratica*' (false documents and bureaucratic slowdowns) (Government of Angola, 2011). In August 2011, the Deputy Minister for Technical and Professional Teaching reported that his ministry was implementing a new model of inspection in schools. This aims to change the image of the 'punishing inspector' to that of one who is able to identify and assist in solving methodological and pedagogical problems (Angola Press, 2011a).

The Government is committed to the universalisation of quality primary education for all children. Various initiatives are being devised such as a 'literacy re-launch' strategy and a national strategy for the promotion and development of women, including the advancement of gender equality in primary and secondary school education (Angola Press, 2011b). There is an initiative called *Zonas de Influência Pedagógica* (ZIPs) (Republic of Angola, 2010c) which provides a support zone, or cluster, of schools for the continuing professional development of teachers. All the principals of schools which constitute a ZIP take part in a management 'organ' called the '*Circulo de Directores*'. The ZIPs are based on the local needs of teachers. They involve a greater time commitment, but cost less than conventional in-service training. Teachers reflect on their teaching, discuss issues around learning, and plan their lessons together. The value of such clustering will be returned to later.

A 'National Council for Children' has been established which has a comprehensive plan of action with '11 Commandments' that centre on achieving the Millennium Development Goals and promoting universal respect for human rights at all levels of governance, and in public and family life. The Ministry of Education is spearheading the creation of child-friendly schools across the country. UNICEF successfully advocated for the inclusion of a child-rights perspective in Angola's new constitution. This was adopted in February 2010. As UNICEF admits, however, much more work is needed to develop a full agenda for children's protection, particularly on things like cash transfer schemes for the most vulnerable. Child protection begins with birth registration (only one in three Angolan children gets registered at birth) and UNICEF supports the government in identifying orphans and vulnerable children.

As is clear, the Ministry of Education does not act alone. Rather, it is supported in various ways by different agencies and donors. It is sometimes difficult to know who really takes the lead, or drives the work on an evaluation. The UNESCO International Institute of Educational Planning, for example, is involved with the Ministry of Education in a participatory decentralisation approach to place provinces 'at the heart of the planning system'. The aim is to give education a 'more realistic' dimension, often lacking at national level planning. Provincial education planners are being trained. Sylla (2010) has reported that the associated pilot programmes are showing 'remarkable' mobilisation of the provincial education departments, the positive emulation generated by the interaction within and between them, and the steady development of the participants' capacities. There are positive changes in attitudes of participants who are becoming increasingly 'scientific' in their approach to educational issues, with it being commonplace for them to demand proof, or supporting information, on recommended practices, a sign of the awareness of the need for better data (Sylla, 2010).

Concurrently, the United Nations Development Programme (UNDP), as part of the government's big poverty reduction strategy, is putting funds into technical support; curricula, programmes, teacher guides and support material have been distributed for all teachers. Nine provincial 'technical focal points' have been provided and 80 secondary school teachers have been trained, as have provincial education inspectors and education sub-directors.

There is also a move to increase the provision of technical and vocational education (UNDP, 2011).

UNESCO, in conjunction with the Ministry of Education, launched the *capEFA* programme for Angola in 2009, called 'Mainstreaming of Cross-cutting Issues in the Curriculum of Schools and Teacher Training Institutions in Angola'. Before 2009, the emphasis of UNESCO and the Ministry was on teacher education, literacy, HIV/AIDS, and the educational management and information system. They have now identified six inter-related 'cross-cutting' topics to be incorporated into in the curriculum: 'peace and human rights education', 'HIV and AIDS', 'environmental education', 'gender', 'culture/intercultural understanding' and 'entrepreneurship'. The rationale is that after nearly three decades of civil war, the country is now experiencing exponential economic growth; it has become one of the main oil producing nations in Africa, fuelling its fast-growing economy. The view is that the integration of these cross-disciplinary issues will help learners 'to participate in the new global economy, in which Angola is now becoming a stronger player' (UNESCO/IBE, 2010).

Educational realities

Where does school leadership stand in the midst of these reforms and myriad initiatives? My commentary on this is based on two main sources: my experience with a project on school improvement in a remote area of Angola, and a long-term evaluation of Save the Children's work, which generated a rigorous data set to assess impact on quality, and which has been used for a global comparative evaluation study of four CAFS (Save the Children 2008, 2009, 2010; Davies, 2012). I start with a brief description of work between 2006 and 2008 with Education Action (EA) (a London-based NGO that is no longer operating) in Caimbambo, a remote area of Benguela Province. This sets the scene for the following discussion and explains some of my position on leadership (Davies, 2008; CfBT, 2009). A team from EA and the Centre for International Education and Research in Birmingham was engaged in a project on school improvement with schools in an area that had been neglected by government and had little immediate hope of much attention. The task was to work with the schools to help them identify small improvements they could make that would not cost any money. This was somewhat revolutionary in a culture of waiting for aid, or government support.

Contacts were made with school principals. Even within our small project, we found huge variation in their support, from those eager to see improvement, to those who never came to school at all. One school principal had to be removed from the project sample after repeated visits by the local NGO team never found him to be at work. The lack of any accountability in this regard was due partly to the fact that the commune director was more often than not drunk. To interview him, the best time was just after breakfast, when he might be awake, and might have something coherent to say. Yet he wielded huge power. We found later that he was running a racket whereby he recruited 'teachers' who would then give him a proportion of their salary. In the end, he and two others were reported in the national press when they were sacked '*por Ociosidade*' (for absenteeism) (Angola Press, 2010).

The 30 years of conflict and of communist rule had created a culture in which one kept one's head down and tried not to get involved beyond the immediate requirements of one's work. This was helpful for survival, but the legacy of fear and passivity was still marked in the schools we visited. On attempting to run workshops for principals we found them initially reluctant to enter into any discussion, or to talk honestly about their school. When we set activities involving any writing, we found them asking for more paper so that they could write it again 'in best'. They would cheat and copy from the person next to them, rather than venture their own response. This was not a language issue, but a legacy of authoritarian and punitive government. They assumed, communist style, that everything was a test.

A gifted local NGO team managed to break down barriers with spirited, physical ice-breakers and lots of laughter. We then proceeded to some exercises to identify three small changes in the school that would make things better for learning. The eventual aim was for them to include all those associated with the school in such identification. In the workshops we found ways to ask teachers, students and parents for the changes they wanted, using local cultural methods of 'voting' when appropriate. We produced a manual with the activities (CfBT, 2009) and later went back to see what the three changes were for each school. These were often identified as 'teachers who come on time', 'teachers who explain things', 'teachers planning lessons', or 'parents building a teacher's house'. Various actions were to be identified to achieve the changes, whether by teachers, parents or students, and an 'Action for Change' team was to be set up in the school to monitor and record the results (for a full description see Davies, 2008).

The intertwined leadership challenges identified so far can be summarised as fourfold: lack of initiative; lack of collaboration and of democracy; acceptance of violence or immunity; and shaky teacher professionalism with a less than motivated teaching force. First, in terms of lack of initiative as a leadership challenge, our research found that some principals made little effort to get textbooks or other materials. Parents would have been willing to pay for such materials if the principals had gone to town to get them. Other principals, in contrast, galvanised the community to build classrooms. Yet one should not blame principals. The new curriculum mentioned above had been sent to commune offices, but for a principal to obtain the document, he or she would have had to travel there on foot, or bicycle, and copy it out by hand. Unsurprisingly, few did. In the Save the Children study, where materials were more generally available, lesson observations found the teachers sticking rigidly to the Ministry of Education guide for lesson plans, with the result that the lessons looked uniform across all the teachers (Save the Children, 2009). Having materials does not guarantee initiative.

Second, in terms of lack of collaboration as a leadership challenge, the idea of consultation was alien to many principals. Some did consult with parents, but never with students. Principals would 'call' parents to come, but this would be to ask for funds, or for their labour in a construction project. Yet, they understood their communities. On one occasion, we asked if we could meet a few parents for interviewing. The principal called them all, and they sat outside, patiently waiting. We expressed concern at this, but the principal pointed out that if he had called only a few parents, the rest would be aggrieved and would not come another time. They were happy to be part of some process that was going on and they felt involved. Some small breakthroughs came from a desired change such as 'teachers marking homework'. Parents were given the task of looking at their children's notebooks and checking whether work had been set and marked. Even if they could not read, they could see the indications. Accountability began to creep in little by little. Many teachers had never planned a lesson, but a desired change around this area found them engaging in joint planning and enjoying it.

Third, in terms of violence as a leadership challenge, all seemed to accept corporal punishment. One boy we interviewed said: 'Our teacher is very good. He only hits us if we don't learn.' Students accepted the notion that it was their responsibility to learn, not the responsibility of teachers to teach. All thought that discipline was maintained by fear and violence. Here, it is instructive to recall the observation made by Holland when engaged in human rights' education in Angola:

> The strife and violence were so rampant that most Angolans have witnessed or directly experienced situations of the most basic possible violations of human rights, such as murder, rape and torture...a palpable feeling of fear, powerlessness and scepticism was in the air.
>
> (2003: 121)

In the Save the Children (2009) study, most teachers and principals reported that beatings did not take place in schools. Yet, our observations showed otherwise. Also, while there may not be beating as such, other physical and humiliating punishments were reported by students, such as being made to crawl on sharp gravel for coming late to school, being made to slap the wall hard with the palm of the hands ten times for misconduct, being made to kneel throughout the lesson and being made to pay a fine for speaking in the vernacular at school. Teachers would sometimes instruct a student to slap a peer for misconduct in class. This sometimes led the 'punished' student to take revenge outside the classroom, resulting in an escalation of violence. In spite of the parent committee and the possibility of parental intervention, students would hesitate to seek resolution to a conflict with a teacher or principal, for fear of further punishment.

Fourth, in terms of lack of teacher professionalism as a leadership challenge, absenteeism among teachers was common. Also, teachers would abuse their authority, as this typical observation illustrates:

> One teacher comes to class drunk and leaves very early. He drinks in class, starts laughing and beats the children without any reason. When this sort of thing happens, we can talk to the school director but this can make things worse for us, we can get beaten for telling on the teacher.
>
> (Save the Children, 2009: 19)

Angola is not unique concerning acceptance of violence in school (Harber, 2004; Leach and Mitchell, 2006). Yet, this problem is not mentioned in the review of the experimental implementation of the new curriculum (Republic of Angola, 2010a), although sexual harassment by teachers is identified. It is not clear what action is being, or will be, taken though. In the Save the Children (2009) study, the problem of sexual harassment of girls was seen by some parents and community members to lie with the girls' behaviour rather than with the teachers. Overall, however, the parent committees seemed to be making progress, rooting out instances of students having to pay teachers for good grades, and of teachers seducing children, making them work in their fields, or coming to school drunk. Yet of the 23 'constraints' on implementation mentioned in the official curriculum review, the culture of the school and gender relations were not really elaborated upon. This would, nonetheless, as discussed next, have implications for leadership.

Implications for education and school leadership

Thinking about school leadership in such a 'post-conflict' situation – the actual conflict supposedly ended almost ten years ago – it is difficult to disentangle what is specifically attributable to the conflict itself and its causes, and what represents the current mix of poverty, inequity, corruption and lack of political will for change that characterises a fragile state (Davies, 2011). I would argue that the legacy of conflict in Angola, particularly in remote areas, is less about the need for 'reconciliation', as it might be in Bosnia or Rwanda, and more about shifting a culture of passivity, survival and acceptance of violence. The conflict, while supposedly a civil war, was international in its politics, and not tribal. The pro-Western UNITA was bankrolled by apartheid South Africa and by the USA, the communist MPLA by the USSR and by Cuba. Different ethnic areas were taken over by particular leaders at different stages of the war, but this was not an ethnic war. Hence, the postwar task is not 'learning to live together' in UNESCO-type terms, but learning, in Save the Children terms, to 'rewrite the future'.

As Holland pointed out in 1998, 'Angola had not yet become a democratic culture that looks on human rights...as a prime component of a just society' (2003: 122). Neither had it done so by 2008, as mentioned earlier (US Department of State, 2009). As indicated in the first part of this chapter, the plunder of Angola by Chinese interests and the lack of any trickle down of wealth to poorer areas means that the likelihood of any massive influx of funds to education, or roads, is slim. There is denial at government level of any such acceptance of disparity in wealth and the siphoning off of funds. While the education reform does have newer areas of curriculum such as rights, it does not specifically emphasise political education, or anti-corruption education. As said, the new curriculum may not even have percolated through to many parts of the country, let alone have a supervisory structure that monitors its implementation and has expertise in each learning area.

Against this backdrop, the major tasks for school leadership are threefold:

* providing a safe school, which challenges the normalisation of violence and abuse of human rights;
* trying to get resources, but working with minimal resources if necessary, and mobilising the community;
* enhancing the professionalism as well as motivation of teachers.

These are not discrete areas, but come together in 'whole school development'. Leadership training may, as in Holland's view (2003), have to be based on experience, imagination and growth. However, it also has to tackle fear. The participants in our study certainly had to imagine their schools differently.

This raises the question of how far these three areas fit conventional views about leadership development needs. Glassman and Sullivan (2006), for example, report that for sub-Saharan Africa generally, most principals had received no training before taking up their post, and most did not have degrees in educational leadership. At best, they might have attended some workshops on administration and management on such topics as accountability, resource management and record keeping. Principals recognized they needed further training in IT for financial management, strategic planning and human resource management. That said, while the 'human resource management' area might align with enhancing teachers' professionalism, it may equally be concerned with 'disciplining' teachers.

For sub-Saharan Africa as a whole, the World Bank document does delineate generalised models for improving management, including clearly defined roles, selection and training of staff on the basis of clearly identified competencies, delegation of authority, clear channels for communication and timely and reliable information on which to base decision-making (Glassman and Sullivan, 2006: 33). One cannot disagree with these, yet they do not seem to fit the reality of a context such as Angola. Clearly defined roles do not work when it is uncertain how many, if any, teachers will turn up on any one day. The same observation applies to delegation, or communication. Reliable information would be nice, but for principals it is better to inflate pupil numbers and deflate teacher numbers if there is to be any hope of getting more resources. Also, those teacher numbers that are given imply that teachers are in school for the whole day, when, in reality, they may just look in for a while before going off for 'training'.

What we have seen work is a whole school model based on a vision of a safe, participatory school. Save the Children have used the model of 'child friendly' schools in their work in Angola. Training of teachers has been on participatory teaching methodologies and positive discipline. According to Ministry of Education regulations, all schools should have parent committees (CPEEs – *Comité de Pais e Encarregados de Educação*). Save the Children has supported these CPEEs by providing members with training on children's rights and by distributing the regulations to school communities. It has also provided training to children's groups to help them advocate for protection of children's rights in schools. Interestingly, there is little in their accounts of any direct training for principals; the approach seems often to be a 'bottom up', grassroots one whereby community, parents and students are empowered and, presumably, influence the running of the school.

A study for UNICEF South Asia on education in emergencies proposed a three way model: that schools should be child-seeking, child-friendly and child-enabling (Davies *et al.*, 2009). Child-seeking is important for Angola, in that, as said earlier, only one in three children has registration, and principals need to overcome any strictures about having a birth certificate before a child can enter school. The child-friendly school model is able to tackle both the areas of school safety and the involvement of community and parents. It does this through a framework and sound understanding of rights. In parallel with this, what is needed is leadership specifically in the area of teacher professionalism. This links to schools being child-enabling, guaranteeing the rights of children both to learning generally and to learning of specific skills for future personal and economic survival.

Barriers to promoting leadership for teacher professionalism

Leadership for teacher professionalism has been identified as a critical issue in the provision of quality education in Angola. In a Save the Children (2008) survey, principals were generally very positive about their teachers' conduct, but expressed some concerns about their knowledge of the curriculum. Teachers' use of 'participatory methods' was rarely observed as being at acceptable levels.

Professionalism is about *internalising* professional values and understanding why certain teacher behaviours are desirable. Save the Children (2008) had mixed success with behaviours such as lesson planning, but found joint lesson planning seemingly effective. Yet, supervisors in one region conceded that many teachers only wrote plans when they knew that they were going to be observed. Our Caimbambo study confirmed the benefits of joint planning. It also confirmed that when children and parents start to realise that a lesson is better when it is planned, and that planning is a core responsibility of teachers, then planning starts to become internalised, as opposed to being an imposition from outside. This is where ZIPs showed themselves to be potentially very powerful, bringing educators together, sharing problems and sharing supervision. ZIPS also provide greater access to curriculum and syllabi.

'Participatory methods' are difficult to introduce, partly because there can be little understanding of why they are beneficial. In both the Caimbambo and the Save the Children studies, students copying from the board was a common pattern, even if they appeared to have no idea what they were copying. Teachers did not move around to see if children understood the material. Instead, they sat inactive at their desks, or stood at the front of the classroom. Also, they did not adapt the script and language level of their board work to the level of literacy of their pupils; 'There appeared to be a shared concept of "good teaching" among education professionals that prioritised the presentation of material on the board over the comprehension and learning of the students' (Save the Children, 2009: 14). This is a large area in which teacher professionalism is lacking and which needs to be tackled in Angola at the school principal level. Length of training seemed to make no difference to classroom relationships.

How can this matter of teacher development be addressed? Much depends on how teachers themselves learn. We found from work in the Gambia that telling teachers to teach democratically did not work; they had to experience participatory learning for themselves rather than just to listen to lectures (Schweisfurth, 2008). Nsiangengo and Diasala (2008) reported on a project in Angola to train primary school teachers to work in the rural areas. The philosophy was that teachers should be capable of establishing the link between school and life in general, thus assuming the role of community agents for development and, in turn, helping in the reconstruction of the country. The training used teaching methods aimed at adult learners, combining formal and non-formal approaches. Trainees had the opportunity to learn by themselves and take responsibility for their own training, admittedly with access to computers. As well as engaging in teaching practice, they carried out social surveys and did community work. Extra-curricular options often had leadership dimensions, including 'women's leadership', 'entrepreneurship', 'public health' and 'community leadership'. The evaluation concluded that success would not have been possible without a well-defined project, a shared vision (the fight against poverty) and necessary resources.

Even if training is effective, there is the leadership issue of maintaining motivation and full-time commitment. Teacher professionalism is also restricted in Angola by the fact that many teachers have a second job, or are part time students. Distance from school is a further inhibiting factor. At one school in our study, we found that three of the female teachers walked for one and half hours each way to school, with their babies on their backs. This showed considerable, but rare dedication. Save the Children say that reliable data on teacher attendance and punctuality were rarely available. Schools had 'signing-in' books, but in most cases these seemed to be filled out retrospectively. In one school where the principal had designed his own 'signing-in' book format and kept it under strict control to prevent teachers signing-in retrospectively, the attendance rate for the previous week was around 75 per cent. This seemed to be the lowest rate for all of the schools we studied, but in reality it was probably the highest. The principal in question testified that he had seen an improvement since employing his new method of recording teacher attendance. In some other schools, by contrast, 'from a review of students' exercise books and the lesson attendance book at one of the schools, students appeared to be taught on average around one lesson a day, out of a timetable that had at least five lessons' (Save the Children, 2008: 10).

All this raises delicate questions about the supervisory role of leadership in a fragile context. Given poor pay and difficult conditions, should principals condone teachers having second jobs, taking time off for training courses (sometimes unrelated to teaching) or engaging in 'irregular' relationships? A relevant extract from my research notebook read:

> Today we were to visit a remote school, and the new, young, Commune supervisor asked if he could come too, as he had no other way of ever getting there. When we arrived, there were some children, but no sign of the director or any teachers. Eventually the director came, and a young female teacher began her lesson in the 'classroom' – the usual open air construction of wooden palings, with goats, chickens and younger siblings wandering in and out. She wrote things on the board but clearly many children did not understand it, and merely made marks in their notebooks – if they had them. After a while, she and the supervisor disappeared into the bush, leaving the class unattended. They returned after half an hour or so, he tucking his shirt in, she arranging her hair. The director did not seem concerned. I asked [the local NGO person], 'did you see what I saw?' He shrugged. 'They are friends', he said. This makes one recast what is meant by teacher motivation. In remote areas, one has to take opportunities for a bit of excitement where one can. Who am I to judge?

Amongst the various issues that this extract serves to illustrate is the divide between textbook supervisory practices and the need for a principal to work within local, or regional, cultures, mores and relationships. Principals reported less than transparent methods of promotion, or dismissal, regardless of how one did one's job. In risk-averse cultures, where promotions are not merit-based, it is hard to take the risk of introducing change. All personnel are embedded in cultures of survival as well as denial. In trying to support supervisors, Save the Children provided them with motorbikes, but these were commandeered by senior education office personnel and were not available for supervisors. This reminds me of how, in Malawi, an entire new District Education Office, constructed by donors, was taken over by the local government chief for his own use (Harber and Davies, 2003).

This should not mean, however, giving up on promoting the development of teacher professionalism. Teachers do appreciate having their work recognised, and having supervision by principals, or outside supervisors. The question is whether they change their behaviour as a result of this supervision. Teachers in the Save the Children final evaluation said they appreciated the visits of the supervisors and their advice. However, none gave any examples of teaching techniques suggested by supervisors. Most supervision seemed to focus on the mechanics of delivering lessons, such as preparing structured lesson plans and clear board work, rather than on methods that can promote active learning. Also, visits were *ad hoc* rather than part of a clear programme of professional development; advice was generally about 'correcting faults'.

The key question relating to supervision and observation is, then, whether they really increase teacher understanding. By 2010, teachers and students were still unclear as to what was involved in the concept of 'child friendly' schools. As a result, Save the Children shifted the focus of training. In general, there did not seem to be a shared vision of how the school environment could be improved and how the school community (including parents, students and teachers) could participate in the process. Funding for our project stopped in 2009 and we do not know whether the understandings of how to change things have persisted. We did find, however, that the principle that visions for change should be developed and shared by all participants, and realisation of that change, however small, was possible, were reported in such parental comments as the following: 'In the past, you could never see a child's notebook, because they kept it. Now they show you how work is marked, you can see what they are doing'; 'Our task is to find out if the absence of the pupil is because of the absence of the teacher'; 'If there is nothing there, have you been to school?' The parents were showing 'new courage' in examining and reporting issues.

Conclusion

This chapter has focussed on the demands of, and challenges for, school leadership in Angola, taking into consideration its political, economic and cultural contexts. While introducing new curriculum areas is important, this has to be viewed against the background of a more significant need for whole school development and the creation of a culture that would enable any changes in learning content to take place. The latter includes the following: the provision of a safe and non-violent school, founded on rights; working with parents and community, not just in providing material resources for the school, but in raising their awareness of what good teaching is about; and extending teacher professionalism, including improvement in basic attendance and punctuality, but also promoting real understandings of 'positive discipline' and of new teaching approaches. Initiatives such as the organisation of schools into clusters of 3–4 schools (ZIPS), did seem to work well

(Republic of Angola, 2010c). This can also force principals to meet together, thus helping them in their own professional development, problem-solving and thinking about pedagogical issues.

In connection with sub-Saharan Africa more broadly, a 2005 World Bank document on school administration (Leu *et al.*, 2005) commented that many secondary school administrators were ill-prepared to meet the demands posed by the changing nature of their jobs. For principals, it recommended organised and systematic training in educational leadership, and effective and transparent management that goes beyond the occasional workshop currently offered in most systems. Principals' critical new roles as instructional leaders within schools, builders of learning communities among teachers, and developers of strong community participation, were widely recognised, although few principals had any preparation for this array of new responsibilities. Largely, I would agree with these recommendations, particularly on the dubious use of one-off workshops. I asked one principal who had just come back from a management training workshop in Luanda how it was. 'Very good', he said, 'I learned a lot'. 'What are you going to change as a result?' I asked. He could not think of anything. It was enough to have been 'workshopped'. The solution, however, is not the World Bank's proposal for a national, or regional, institution that specialises in advanced degrees or certification in educational leadership. Taking principals out of schools for advanced degrees is not the way forward, although it would be popular. The key to what works is principals who are stable members of the community, working with energy and compassion alongside their school communities to solve real problems, and participating in networks of schools that can join forces in this problem-solving and the development of teachers.

References

Angola Press (2010a) Afastados directors escolares de ensina primáro. http://allafrica.com/stories/201010181168.html (accessed 3 May 2011).

Angola Press (2010b) Education Ministry invests in expansion of professional technical education. http://allafrica.com/stories/201010181168.html (accessed 3 May 2011).

Angola Press (2011a) Education ministry changes inspectors' image. Agéncia *Angola Press*, http://allafrica.com/stories/201010181168.html (accessed 3 May 2011).

Angola Press (2011b) Government committed to universalisation of quality education. Agéncia *Angola Press*. http://allafrica.com/stories/201010181168.html (accessed 3 May 2011).

Cage, A. (2009) The President's son, the Minister and the £450m illegal deals for civil war weapons. *The Times*, 28 October, pp. 41–42.

CfBT (2009) *School Change to Improve Effectiveness: A practical guide for head-teachers.* Reading: CfBT.

Davies, L. (2008) *Base-line Primary Education Research in Angola.* London: CfBT and Education Action.

Davies, L. (2011) Learning for state-building: Capacity development, education and fragility. *Comparative Education*, 47(2), 157–80.

Davies, L. (2012) *Breaking the Cycle of Crisis: Learning from Save The Children's delivery of education in conflict-affected fragile states*. London: Save The Children.

Davies, L. and Gunawardena, C. (1992) *Women and Men in Educational Management: An international inquiry*. Paris: International Institute of Educational Planning.

Davies, L., Harber, C., Schweisfurth, M., Williams, C. and Yamashita, H. (2009) *Educating in Emergencies in South Asia: Reducing the risks facing vulnerable children*. New York: Centre for International Education and Research/UNICEF.

DIIS (2008) *Policy Brief: Fragility and natural resources*. Danish Institute for International Studies.

Glassman, D. and Sullivan, P. (2006) *Governance, Management and Accountability in Secondary Education in Sub-Saharan Africa*. World Bank Africa Region Human Development Working Papers SEIA Thematic Study No 3. Washington: World Bank.

Government of Angola (2011) *Balanço de Implementação da 2 Reforma Educativa em Angola*. Angola: Angola Ministério de Educaçáo.

Harber, C. (2004) *Schooling as Violence*. London: Routledge.

Harber, C. and Davies, L. (2003) Educational decentralisation in Malawi: A study of process. *Compare*, 33(1), 139–54.

Holland, T. (2003) Teaching and learning about human rights in postconflict Angola. In E. Uwazie (ed.) *Conflict Resolution and Peace Education in Africa*. Oxford: Lexington Books, pp. 119–32.

Leach, F. and Mitchell, C. (2006) *Combating Violence in and Around Schools*. Stoke-on-Trent: Trentham.

Leu, E., Mulkeen, A., Chapman, D. and DeJaeghere, G. (2005) *Recruiting, Retaining, and Retraining Secondary School Teachers and Principals in Sub-Saharan Africa*. World Bank Africa Region Human Development Working Papers: Thematic Study #4: Secondary Teachers and School Principals. Washington: World Bank.

Marques de Morais, J. (2009) Angola: Presidential promiscuity has corrupted society. *Pambazuka News*, allAfrica.com. http://allafrica.com/stories/printable/200912040792.html (accessed 1 December 2009).

Nsiangengo, P. and Diasala, A. (2008) Teacher training colleges in the rural areas of Angola. *Prospects*, 38, 247–61.

Republic of Angola, Ministry of Education (2004) *Education for All. Final document*. Luanda: Republic of Angola, Ministry of Education.

Republic of Angola (2010a, September) *Relatorio da Fase Experimentação do Ensino Primário e do 1 Ciclo do Ensina Secundári*. Angola Ministério de Educaçáo CAARE.

Republic of Angola (2010b) *Resumo Sobre o Projecto de Supervisão de Professors*. Luanda: Ministry of Education, Institito Nacional de Formaçáo de Quadros.

Republic of Angola (2010c) *Resume sobre as zonas de influência pedagógica – ZIPs*. Luanda: Angola Ministério de Educaçáo.

Save the Children (2008) *Learning from Those Who Live In It: An evaluation of children's education in conflict-affected fragile states*. London: Save the Children.

Save the Children (2009) *Rewrite the Future Global Evaluation: Angola midterm country report*. London: Save the Children.

Save the Children (2010) *Rewrite the Future Global Evaluation: Angola country report*. London: Save the Children.

Schweisfurth, M. (2008) Education and democracy in The Gambia: Reflections on the position of development projects in a small African state. In D. Johnson (ed.) *The Changing Landscape of Education in Africa: Quality, equality and democracy*. Oxford: Symposium Books, pp. 63–76.

Sogge, D. (2009) *Angola: 'Failed' yet 'successful'* (Working Paper 81). Madrid: Fundación para las Relaciones Internacionales y el Diálogo Exterior FRIDE.

Swain, J. (2008) Africa: China's new frontier. *The Sunday Times*, 10 February, pp. 33–43.

Sylla, K. (2010) Angola: Planning at the provincial level. *IIEP Newsletter*, 28(2), 6–7.

UNDP (2010) Human development report. http://hdr.undp.org/en/reports/global/hdr2010/chapters/ (accessed 1 January 2011).

UNDP (2011) Angola: Poverty reduction. http://www.ao.undp.org/Poverty%20Reduction.htm (accessed 10 January 2012).

UNESCO/IBE (2010, August) CapEFA Programme: Mainstreaming of cross-cutting issues in the curriculum of schools and teacher training institutions in Angola. Workshop to develop national guidelines. http://www.ibe.unesco.org/fileadmin/user_upload/News/2010/AngolaCapEFA_2010_ConceptNote_Agenda_EN.pdf (accessed 12 February 2011).

US Department of State (2009) *The 2008 Human Rights Report*. Washington, DC: US Department of State.

Voice of America (2008) In Angola, Education Ministry aims to expand teaching of English. http://www.voanews.com/learningenglish/home/a-23-2008-04-29-voa2-83138577.html (accessed 29 September 2011).

4 Ghana

Resolving the tensions between colonial values and contemporary policies

John MacBeath and Sue Swaffield

Introduction

The colonial legacy provides a powerful backdrop to the development of schools in Ghana, shaping their relationship with their communities and requiring a quality of leadership that displays a confidence to challenge much of established thinking and practice. This chapter begins with a review of the successive regimes in the country that have attempted to deal with the aftermath of wars on its people, exploitation of its human and natural resources, mismanagement and corruption and its impact on communities, families and children. It goes on to consider current support, partnerships, intervention and subvention issues. This is followed by an examination of current leadership challenges in schools.

After the conflict

Following conquest by the British in 1896 until independence in March 1957, much of the territory of modern Ghana was known as the Gold Coast. The local Ashanti people resisted British occupation and even defeated them in battle a number of times. They suffered a final defeat, however, in the Ashanti–British War of 1900. Nevertheless, resistance in various forms continued over the next four decades. In 1947, when moves toward decolonisation intensified after World War 2, the newly formed United Gold Coast Convention (UGCC), called for self-government as soon as possible. Rioting, involving rural and working class people who supported the nationalist movement, broke out in 1948. The imprisonment of some of the leaders of the movement led to boycotts, strikes and other forms of civil disobedience. Eventually, on 6 March 1957, Ghana became an independent nation.

All societies are shaped by the wars and conflicts through which they live. Sometimes they come out the other side, renewed and reinvented, from dictatorship to republic, from socialism to capitalism, from fascism to democracy, or in a transition from one form of social and political constellation to another. Unlike countries in which the end of a war marked a fundamental realignment of values and principles, the transition from colonialism to independence and self-government in Ghana has not brought with it a sudden release from a colonial mind set. Nowhere is this more apparent than in education, where the post-colonial school, in many essential respects, continues to bear the imprint of its colonial legacy.

Since the gaining of independence from British colonial rule, education has been a high priority on the government's agenda. It has also been subject to a series of changes, with the government constantly in search of the model which would fit the needs of the country and the expectations of its citizens, but unable to shake off the historical legacy of what schools are for, what they do and how they do it. However persuasive the rhetoric of learning and teaching for a new social order, the disconnection between life lived in the school and life lived in home and community has continued to open, rather than close, the distance between children and their families, and between school education and education in the community.

Reform: a continuing process

The overthrow of Nkrumah in 1966, in a military coup, was followed by decades of political instability, marked by corruption, general macroeconomic turmoil and mismanagement of many of the public services (Mfum-Mensah, 2004). The dramatic increase in the number of elementary and secondary schools during the Nkrumah presidency and the momentum for free, universal and compulsory education, established by the 1961 Education Act, faltered. Eventually, as Kingsley (2007) claims, by the 1980s, Ghana's education system had become dysfunctional.

Five decades of political changes followed the 1961 Act, as successive administrations tried to cope with the conflicting demands of a globalisation agenda and Ghana's own national cultural traditions in an attempt to resolve the tensions between economic and social goals. Much of the activity was driven by conditions set down by donor agencies. It was not until the end of the 1980s that many of the dysfunctions began to be seriously addressed, with the 1987 Education Act establishing a national literacy campaign for school drop-outs and adult learners. The extended period of school attendance, it was recognised, was penalising poorer rural children as parents could not afford to have their children in school for that length of time, given their vital contribution to the family economy. In addition, preparation for success in the nation's Common Entrance Examination required extra tuition in order to gain entry to secondary school, something that only the rich could afford (Sefa Dei and Opini, 2008).

The Whole School Development Programme (WSD) launched in 1987 sought to promote:

- child-centred primary practice in literacy, numeracy and problem-solving with the view to improve the quality of teaching and learning in basic school classrooms;

- community participation in education delivery;
- competencies of teaching and learning through school-based in-service training;
- participatory planning and resource management at school and district levels;
- improved efficiency in resource management.

Osei's 2006 study concluded that these laudable aims could not be realised without a quality of leadership that offered teachers the support needed to implement the kind of radical and widespread change implied. Reform, he concluded, requires that teachers 'thoroughly understand the rationale for reforms and are able to engage critically and productively with the key educational objectives of new policies through a solid understanding of contemporary educational theory and practice' (Osei, 2006: 49). This is unattainable, he stated, 'without a formal system of incentives and financial recompense' (p. 49).

The establishment of school management committees (SMCs) in 2001 by the Ministry of Education/Ghana Education Service, was a further step taken to support and oversee provision most appropriate to local needs and priorities. However, it was not until 2005 that primary school education became free as well as compulsory. In 2007, reforms which had been in preparation since 2002, were launched by President Kufuor, introducing new gender-free pathways that were intended to enhance the nation's human resources in the form of a skilled, technologically-advanced and disciplined workforce to service the growing economy. Other elements of the reform included establishing a National Teachers' Council to regulate the profession and a distance education programme to upgrade serving teachers' knowledge and skills, and expanding residential accommodation, lecture halls, laboratories and libraries in the nation's fifteen universities and ten polytechnics.

Living with the colonial legacy

When the British officially colonised Ghana (then the Gold Coast), they used schools to educate intermediaries for colonisation (Segura, 2009). This was essential to their policy of indirect rule so as to impose superiority of knowledge, language and culture, and cut pupils off from their families in order to create new indigenous elites who would align themselves with the culture, values and world view of the coloniser (Antwi, 1992; McWilliam and Kwamena-Poh, 1975). Ghanaian governments from Nkrumha onwards sought to rework the colonial legacy. They had a dream of a new independent nation forging its own identity. They did not, however, succeed in decolonisation of the mind' (Arnot, 2008 p. 27). The inferior status of girls and women was endemic within African communities and was 'buttressed by the colonialist whose Victorian values about girls further reinforced the subordination of women. Colonial schools in Africa taught skills that were exclusive of women' (Sefa Dei and Opini, 2008: 475). This situation continues today. Also, the structure of schools and the nature of the school day continue to mimic the 'Western' layout of classrooms, with rows of seats, blackboards, textbooks and subject timetables, and with inflexible starting times, so that if school starts at 7.45 in the morning, pupils who arrive late tend to be punished by excluding them from lessons and making them tidy the compound.

Up until the last quarter of the nineteenth century, education was an informal process through which Ghanaian communities prepared the next generation. The collectivist nature of education in traditional communities, writes Antwi (1992), encompassed the total way of life of the society. Education as a shared responsibility ensured that the learning of all children was the responsibility of the community. The notion of the African woman as dependent housekeeper, wife and mother confined to the home and economically dependent on the husband, the breadwinner, was introduced into African culture by Westerners (Odaga and Heneveld, 1995: 8). This view ignored the traditional value of African women in public and economic spheres, and the role of women as chiefs in Akan society (the ethnic group that is predominant in Ghana) (Obeng, 2002).

While there is a danger of romanticising traditional practices, there is substantial evidence that the introduction of formal schooling in the Western mould did little to counter the disenfranchisement of girls and, in many respects, created new barriers to educational opportunity. Language is also cited as a factor in marginalisation and colonisation. A study by Quist (2001) in Ghana and Cote d'Ivoire found that all students interviewed preferred to be taught in English, or French, and only 35 per cent could speak their native language. In Ghana also, English has 'cultural capital', with many Ghanaians seeing it as the neutral language that should be used as the medium of instruction (Sefa Dei and Opini, 2008). Sefa Dei and Opini view this privileging of a 'foreign language' as reinforcing cultural imperialism and neo-colonialism, and robbing students of their cultural heritage (p. 479).

In more recent times, 'whole school development' (WSD), the model of school improvement widely adopted in developed countries, has been influential in Ghana, as well as in other African countries. Following a 'Western' decentralised model, principals and leadership teams are expected to carry the responsibility, and be accountable for, improvement in their schools, measured primarily by 'outcomes' in the form of pupils' scores on exams. However, schools sit within a nesting of agencies and authorities that support, direct or constrain their initiative. District assemblies, local councils and school management committees may either facilitate, or constrain, decision-making at the school and classroom level.

'How useful is the Anglo-Saxon model or Eurocentric model of decentralisation for other communities in developing parts of the world?' asks Mfum-Mensah (2004: 153). He problematises the nature of this complex devolution, designed for 'empowerment' of local community voice and agency. He identifies three levels of participation by communities in the organisation and conduct of schooling. These range from local community members playing a supportive role, through to a stronger advisory function, inviting 'voice' and taking account of local concerns, to more fully blown decision-making by community members extending to full community control. However, his in-depth studies of communities in the northern region of Ghana found that, rather than being a tool for empowering them, the shift in locus of control had produced 'conflicts, gossip and tensions among community members' (p. 153). The power struggles and rivalry that emerged were, he argues, a consequence of policy makers placing responsibility on individuals with little or no experience of school management and no grounded understanding of what it means to create the conditions for learning and teaching. Hence, he concluded, 'school governance may draw on conventional attitudes more than empirical fact about what promotes learning' (p. 153).

The economic and cultural challenge

Education in Ghana at the basic level now reaches most young people and has expanded at a rate far exceeding the country's economic growth. It also enables employers to select from a wide pool of educated labour and to demand high credentials from prospective employees. This 'qualification inflation' has produced an 'inflationary' cycle in which people chase higher qualifications. A tendency to shun vocational routes in favour of the academic persists because opportunity and better salaries continue to be found in clerical occupations, especially in the government sector (Boateng and Ofori-Sarpong, 2002; Rolleston and Oketch, 2008).

To make this observation is not to overlook UNICEF's (2006) estimate of 11.6 of the population as 'unemployed'. The Ministry of Manpower Youth and Employment (2002) found that 32 per cent of school leavers had no skills relevant to the world of work. Also, Ghana, like many other African countries, is witnessing the deforestation and de-agrarianisation of rural land, and an acceleration in the migration of young people to cities. These young people often enter the informal economy, where they become vulnerable to criminal activity. Girls and young women, homeless and isolated in the city, are subject to exploitation by night guards, by security personnel and by a whole range of urban predators buying, or requiring, sexual favours. Ghana is also one of the world's major transit areas for the trafficking of cocaine and other narcotic drugs to Europe.

Children and young people are caught between two cultures, differing expectations and the push–pull of life in the community and life on the streets. Having less and less in common with their parents and the older generation, and with increasing access to television, mobile phones and the internet, they look to Western mores in preference to the traditional values of their communities. An economy that depends on a mobile, flexible and skilled workforce does not sit comfortably with traditions of collective responsibility (Arnot, 2008: 2).

Focusing specifically on rural areas, one of the major constraints that militates against girls' access and achievement is the low presence of female teachers (Casely-Hayford, 2007). On this issue, Casely-Hayford states that Ghana's Education Service is reluctant to post women to areas where they would be 'handicapped or fall victim to local chiefs or rich farmers who wanted to take them as their second wife' (p. 5). Hedges has summarised the policy of the Ghana Education Service on this as follows:

> Women teachers, who make up over 30 per cent of training college graduates are not to be posted to rural areas, despite the positive impact this might have on girls' enrolment. It is a practice that recognises two Ghanaian realities: parents' fear that their daughters may lose their 'marriage market' or be put in the vulnerable position, and middle class husbands' reluctance for their wives to work in rural areas.
>
> (Hedges, 2002: 357)

Thus, male teachers predominate in poor, rural areas, reinforcing the view that teaching is 'man's work' and depriving girls of role models and of educated women with whom they can speak about female issues (Sefa Dei and Opini, 2008: 477). The situation is exacerbated by male teachers discouraging female students from studying certain school subjects that could open up certain male-dominated career paths for them (Palmer, 2007: 136).

Launching a new programme in May 2010, directed at marginalised groups, Ghana's then Vice President, John Dramani Mahama, noted that 'whilst enrolment and gender parity rates have steadily improved at the lower primary level, this has not translated into increased retention of children, particularly girls and children with disabilities, in the upper primary and junior high schools' (www.vso.org.uk/news/press-release/27152/). Domestic violence was recorded in almost half the communities visited by Crawford (2010), with reproductive rights being breached because of the relative powerlessness of women to negotiate with their husbands as to sexual activity and family size. Witchcraft allegations and banishment were reported in four communities, despite often being referred to as a thing of the past. Violations of girls' rights occurred in three main ways: abuse of fostering arrangements, forced marriage through betrothal to older men, and the migration of adolescent girls to cities in order to undertake 'head-portering' work, often due to a lack of livelihood opportunities at home.

Fostering is a consequence of extreme poverty. Parents accept the payment of a lump sum of money, or a cow, in exchange for their child's labour. These children are often mistreated. In the case of boys, many 'are forced to continue diving (to tie up or release fishing nets) for several hours a day and are often beaten. One senior official revealed that every month a child dies in the lake because of overwork, or exhaustion' (Fentiman, Hall and Bundy, 1999: 437). There is also a tradition of 'pawning', or debt foster-age, using children as collateral for loans. They work for the creditor until the debt is repaid, giving the creditor rights over the labour of the child for the period of his, or her, indenture. The related practice of last resort of hiring out young females as mothers and carers of younger children limits women's access to, and participation in, education.

Support, partnerships, intervention and subvention

Transformation of the education system is a task beyond the resources of the Ministry of Education alone. It relies on the support of numerous donor agencies, the G8 countries, the World Bank, UNESCO, UNICEF, the Commonwealth Fund, USAID and many other organisations, most with limited life and therefore not able to follow through on, and sustain, change. The system also benefits from voluntary service. For example, Comic Relief and Voluntary Service Overseas jointly provide support for intervention strategies in the most disadvantaged areas of the country and for the most marginalised groups. When its programme was launched in 2003, 54 volunteer teachers took part. By 2006/7, this had grown to 8,000 and in the 2007/8 school year, 13,000 volunteers were posted to all ten regions of Ghana.

Because education is extensively funded by aid (Segura, 2009), the donor agencies are able to set many conditions regarding how it is spent. This, according to Segura, undermines the leadership role of the national government. What it means, he concludes, is that 'colonial powers and donors have set up structures of schooling that carry political meaning and values, and they continue to limit and create possibilities of what school is in Ghana' (Segura, 2009: 13). This situation is related to the economic status of the country. By the mid 1990s Ghana was heavily indebted, and by the end of the decade it was subject to inflation and economic problems. In 2000, Ghana joined HIPC (Highly Indebted Poor Countries) to receive debt relief. This involved accepting more conditions and strictures set by the World Bank and the IMF, including a commitment to education as a 'human right' (UNESCO, 2007). While the latter may be both laudable and uncontentious, the fact that it is viewed as being synonymous with compulsory attendance at school cast in a Western mould is, as Segura argues, to miss the point; 'It is important for the donors to understand that this is a contextual and structural problem and not a managerial problem with technocratic fixes' (Segura, 2009: 7).

The low level of pupil achievement is also a matter of concern. Ghana ranked 47th (out of 47) in 2010 on the international benchmark in mathematics and 47th (out of 48) in science, and is last among the four African countries that participated in the exercise. Testing revealed that as many as 87 per cent of Ghanaian students did not reach the low international benchmark in science and that 91 per cent did not reach it in mathematics. With regard to the intermediate international benchmarks, as many as 98 per cent of the Ghanaian students did not reach this level in science and mathematics (http://news.peacefmonline.com/social/200910).

Clearly there is a need for more and better qualified teachers. However, with pupil numbers growing rapidly, the Ministry of Education has calculated that the total number of teachers needed to keep pace has been doubling every 18 years. It was estimated in 2006 that about 10 per cent of the total number of teachers (around 24,000), most of them serving in rural areas, were untrained (Osei, 2006). Engagement in upgrading of formal qualifications is, however, not attractive because the low salary levels mean that teachers often need to take on part-time jobs out of school hours in order to earn extra money.

Conditions for learning

'Which is better, a child who doesn't go to school or one who has the chance to be taught under a tree?' asked Bannerman Mensah in 2006, in his role as Deputy Director General of the Ghana Education Service. Four years on from that speech it was claimed that while churches and community centres were used to house the growing number of children wishing to attend school, 3,947 schools were still conducted under trees (Editorial, 16 April, 2010, www.afrika.no). What goes on in the 'classroom' is also often uninspiring. Dull puts it succinctly as follows:

> Maintaining student discipline through teacher-dominated methodologies and teacher discipline [is] by following standardised procedures, maintaining orderly classrooms and pleasing supervisors.
>
> (Dull, 2004: 312)

She cites examples of the tutors' and supervisors' view that good practice in lesson presentation is where one never deviates from the textbook, apart from engaging in blackboard work. Art projects and other more student-centred activities are discouraged because of a belief that they may lead to indiscipline, while group work involving discussion is discouraged as it could lead to students playing or chatting. Instead, learning by rote is promoted, partly because it facilitates conformity and order in the classroom, and partly because children have to commit much to memory in order to pass exams.

Matters are not helped by the lack of a home environment conducive to promoting study habits. Obeng's title for her 2002 book, *Home was Uncomfortable, School was Hell*, captures through case studies the difficulties faced by children and young people in trying to balance the demands of the domestic economy with homework and home study. Very few homes have electricity for lighting. Most have kerosene lamps, which come with their own associated accidents and tragedies. Also, in describing her experience as a child she recalled that her grandmother 'saw no need to give us girls her kerosene lamp to study'. Preference had to be given to the boys 'whose duty it was to study well, do well in life and then look after us girls' (Obeng, 2002: 28).

Conditions for teaching

Teachers who live in cities such as the capital, Accra, find it difficult when posted to rural communities to live there without having access to the internet, electricity, drinking water and basic amenities. It is estimated that 10,000 teachers leave the teaching service each year, in large part due to the unpropitious conditions in which they have to work, the resultant lack of job satisfaction that accrues, and the relatively low status that they enjoy. Described by the *Daily Graphic* (a state-owned daily newspaper) as 'the unsavoury ritual', the late payment of salaries reinforces the idea, in the eyes of teachers and the communities in which they work, that they are of low status and that their work is of little use (Hedges, 2002: 359). As qualified teachers leave the profession the gaps are filled by unqualified staff.

In many parts of the country, teachers have to deal not only with the expectations of the District Office, but also with those of the local community (Roberts, 2009). While the District Office has its own professional criteria, exercised to some extent at a bureaucratic distance, the eyes and ears of the local community are ever alert to potential, or real, indiscretions. Villagers know how frequently teachers are absent from the classroom. They are acutely aware of any indiscretion, excessive drinking or sexual impropriety. Underlying this, there is often resentment about accepting a professional in the community, one who possesses an alien authority over their children and who has associated privileges, such as not being required to undertake communal village tasks, and enjoys a lifestyle that creates unfair competition with village men over access to girls and young women.

Most teachers are young men, and most are unmarried, or do not have their wives living with them (Roberts, 2009). As wage earners, they have more money at their disposal for gifts than, for example, unemployed school leavers, or young men dependent upon their relatives. Teachers usually have more privacy in their rented or free rooms, 'while the school building itself is notoriously a place of assignation' (Roberts, 2009: 275).

'Seduction charges' may be brought against teachers, not necessarily because they are responsible for pregnancies, but because they are the only persons who could be expected to pay the large sums involved. Teachers may also be threatened by witchcraft-associated objects being placed on their desks and may experience action taken against themselves, or their property. They may find it difficult to buy food in the village and may, exceptionally, be thrown out of their accommodation. When conflict reaches the point at which village political authority intervenes, the first step is usually to withdraw the privilege that the village considers it extends to teachers as professionals, namely, the waiving of the obligation to perform communal labour.

The leadership challenge

Zame, Hope and Respress (2008: 11) state that education reform in Ghana has ignored the importance of leadership development for principals. While this statement may be rebutted by evidence of programmes in various places in the country, the vast majority of principals do accede to, and tend to remain in, their positions without the benefit of professional development. The Zame *et al.* survey (2008) of 224 principals in the greater Accra region reported 29 per cent of them as having some form of training, with the predominating emphasis being on what might be described as maintenance tasks. Fifty per cent of principals ranked 'managing and organising the school day-to-day functions' as the primary proficiency required of a principal. Assessing pupil performance was allocated to last place out of ten competencies practised by principals in primary schools, with only 1.8 per cent citing it as current practice. While questionnaire items such as those used in arriving at this conclusion are open to differing interpretation there is, nonetheless, consistent evidence as to the primarily office-bound administrative role of the Ghanaian school principal.

Oduro (2009) reported that 76 per cent of principals interviewed had little or no training and that leadership strategies tended to be largely based on trial and error. He said that many principals did not regard themselves as leaders, but as custodians of school properties and implementers of government policies. This echoes an earlier study by Oduro (2003) in which he described principals as performing a range of duties such as supervising the cleaning and tidying of the school campus, monitoring the hygiene of vendors who come on to the school compound, inspecting building projects, and attending to risks, injuries and illness among staff as well as pupils.

In the three districts he examined, Oduro found a high level of school principal absenteeism, which was higher than that of teachers. He also found that 82 per cent of teacher absenteeism could be accounted for by ill health and attending funerals, with another 40 per cent being attributable to attendance at in-service distance lectures. There was, Oduro concluded, an urgent need for intervention strategies that would equip school leaders with strategic approaches to professional development and classroom pedagogy.

Akyeampong (2004) describes whole school development workshops targeted at principals as offering training in how to develop a whole school action plan, including target setting and appraisal, and designing and preparing school budgets. These take the form of cluster in-service workshops in which principals from five to eight schools form a single school-based in-service unit working in close collaboration with a District Teacher Support Team (DTST). The purpose is to identify common unsolved problems relating to teaching and learning with DTSTs and principals acting as resource personnel. Where solutions to problems are beyond the expertise of school principals and the DTSTs, other cluster centres are to be approached for assistance.

With funding and support from the Commonwealth Education Trust, a University of Cambridge team has been working in Ghana since 2009, in partnership with the University of Cape Coast on a 'leadership for learning' programme. The point of entry was with principals, since they have direct responsibility, and accountability, for the quality of learning and teaching in their schools. The reputation of Geroge Oduro, Centre Director at the University of Cape Coast, and the involvement of the Commonwealth Education Trust, UNICEF and the University of Cambridge, were all influential in persuading the Ministry of Education to support the programme.

A vital centrepiece of the programme has been the cadre of 15 'professional development leaders' carefully selected from regional offices and from the University of Cape Coast. Their energy, insight and commitment, sustained over the three-year period, gained the respect of the Ministry and the Ghana Education Service, convincing policy makers to invest in the continuing development of the programme and to extend it country wide.

Professional development for a leading-edge first cohort of 125 principals was the key to building capacity at the system level. Its impact was in:

- providing a model of leadership development;
- embedding a set of principles for learning-inspired leadership;
- creating a collegial network of principals;
- identifying the need for similar development work for those who support principals and monitor school improvement.

The hugely positive evaluation of the impact on this first cohort was convincing evidence of the need to extend the programme with appointees running courses based on 'leadership for learning's' five essential principles (www.leadershipforlearning.org.uk/index.php/lfl-principles). They are as follows:

- maintaining a focus on learning as an activity;
- creating conditions favourable to learning as an activity;
- creating a dialogue about the connections between leadership and learning;
- sharing leadership;
- fostering a shared sense of accountability.

These five 'leadership for learning' essential principles now take pride of place in the *Headteachers' Handbook*, produced by Ghana Education Sevices in 2010 – the 'bible' for school leaders nationwide.

Using the language of reframing, a female principal referred to the recognition of how little learning was occurring in the classroom prior to her direct interest and intervention in the teaching and learning process:

> In the old frame teachers sat the children down and lectured, lectured, lectured, and then asked the children 'Do you understand?' And they answered 'Yes sir'. And yet, there were some who couldn't pick up anything from what was taught.

Another female principal, reflecting on her practice before being involved in the programme, identified embedded systemic issues, stating:

> Formerly we were heads who were not concentrating on the leadership for learning; we were heads who, up and down, didn't involve ourselves deeply into the learning process.

Because the first line of accountability for principals is their circuit supervisors, it was deemed that this significant cadre of people should also benefit from the professional development that principals had experienced. While enjoying a less intensive programme than the principals, it has proved to be a crucial step in also engaging them with the 'leadership for learning' five essential principles and in providing a common reference point in the ongoing dialogue between a group of school principals locally and their circuit supervisor.

The obvious implication in this upward spiral of development was for the Regional and District Directors also to be involved, to be apprised of what their circuit supervisors and principals had experienced, and to be participants themselves in an interactive programme underpinned by the five 'leadership for learning' essential principles. Following a one day workshop with a small group of Regional Directors, 60 District Directors then participated in a two day professional development event. The active support during these two days of the overall Director responsible for basic schools was a testament to how much there had been 'buy-in' to the process of the professional development of school leaders by the Ghana Education Service and the Ministry.

Conclusion

Ghana is a country characterised by a diverse and inequitable distribution of resources and wealth, a consequence of population migrations, religious influence and colonial economic policy. While internal conflicts and north–south division existed prior to colonialism, the ruthless exploitation of its people exacerbated old rivalries and created new ones, further disenfranchising rural areas, particularly in the north. The impact of decentralisation policies has had a destabilising effect on communities, whose leaders, parents and community members lack experience and requisite expertise in the running of schools. There are tensions between the horizontal (collegial and capacity building) purposes of the education system and its vertical (distancing and individualistic) functions. Inflexibility in school routines, protocols and starting times creates problems for households, where children, particularly girls, are required to share in family tasks. Post-colonial practices and the reliance on external donor agencies are reflected in what is widely acknowledged as a cumbersome and inappropriate curriculum. A consequence of this is a lack of engagement by pupils, low levels of achievement and, on the parents' part, a weighing of opportunity costs to the domestic economy. When a school is located a long distance away from the community, girls are less likely than their brothers to attend. Other issues are the pull of cities and migration from north to south. These expose young people to exploitation, abuse and criminalisation, often by the very individuals employed to protect them.

Such issues are deeply rooted in history and culture, and in continuing struggles to resolve the tensions between pre- and post-colonial values and forms of government. While the associated tensions will not be addressed by reforming schools alone, school education can continue to play a significant role in social and economic life as long as there is a quality of leadership whose focus is on learning at the individual pupil level, the teacher professional level, the senior management level and the inter-school level. In this regard, the Centre for Commonwealth Education's 'leadership for learning' initiative has been able to make a significant contribution to recasting the reach and impact of leadership, where the starting point is with a focus on learning, an environment which supports the learning of a whole community, the continuing dialogue around learning, the sharing of leadership, and a shared accountability which refers to those key enduring principles.

References

Akyeampong, K. (2004) Aid for self-help effort? A sustainable alternative route to basic education in northern Ghana. *Journal of International Cooperation in Education*, 7(1), 41–52.

Antwi, M. (1992) *Education, Society and Development in Ghana*. Accra: Unimax Publishers Limited.

Arnot, M. (2008) Educating young citizens: social discrimination, gender equality and global democratic issues. Paper presented to the State Council for Educational Research Conference on 'Democratic and secular education: Kerala in the international context'. Kerala, 4–6 December.

Boateng, K. and Ofori-Sarpong, E. (2002) *An Analytic Study of the Market for Tertiary Graduates in Ghana*. Accra: World Bank.

Casely-Hayford, L. (2007) *Gendered Experiences of Teaching in Poor Rural Areas of Ghana* (RECOUP Working Paper 8). Department for International Development and University of Cambridge.

Crawford, G. (2010) Decentralisation and struggles for basic rights in Ghana: opportunities and constraints. *The International Journal of Human Rights*, 14(1), 92–125.

Dull, L. J. (2004) Democracy and discipline in Ghanaian education. *International Journal of Educational Development*, 24(3), 303–14.

Farrell, J. P. (2001) Transforming the forms of primary education in the developing world: The emergence of a radically alternative model of schooling. Toronto: Ontario Institute for Studies in Education, University of Toronto.

Farrell, J. P. and Mfum-Mensah, O. (2002) *A Preliminary Analytical Framework for Comparative Analysis of Alternative Primary Education Programs in Developing Nations.* Toronto: Ontario Institute for Studies in Education, University of Toronto.

Fentiman, A., Hall, A. and Bundy D. (1999) School enrolment patterns in rural Ghana: A comparative study of the impact of location, gender, age and health on children's access to basic schooling. *Comparative Education,* 35(3), 331–49.

Hedges, J. (2002) The importance of posting and interaction with the education bureaucracy in becoming a teacher in Ghana. *International Journal of Educational Development,* 22(3), 353–66.

Kingsley, E. J. (2007) Ghana@50. www.ghanaweb.com/GhanaHomePage/features/artikel.php?ID=120210 (accessed 9 June 2010).

McWilliam, H. O. A. and Kwamena-Poh, M. A. (1975) *The Development of Education in Ghana.* London: Longman.

Mfum-Mensah, O. (2004) Empowerment or impairment? Involving traditional communities in school management. *International Review of Education,* 50(2), 141–55.

Ministry of Manpower Youth and Employment (2002) *The National Employment Policy* (first draft version). Republic of Ghana.

Obeng, C. S. (2002) *Home was Uncomfortable, School was Hell: A confessionalist-ethnographic account of belief systems and socio-educational crises in the schooling of Ghanaian rural girls.* New York: Nova Science Publishers.

Odaga, A. and Heneveld, W. (1995) *Girls and Schools in Sub-Saharan Africa: From analysis to action* (Technical Report, No. 298). New York: World Bank.

Oduro, G. (2009) The missing ingredient: Headteacher leadership development in sub-Saharan Africa. Paper delivered at the Conference for Commonwealth Educational Cooperation: Looking Ahead at 50. Oxford, 31 March.

Osei, G. (2006) Teachers in Ghana: Issues of training, remuneration and effectiveness. *International Journal of Educational Development,* 26(1), 38–51.

Palmer, R. (2007) *Knowledge gaps and research questions: Informal apprenticeship in Ghana.* Geneva: International Labour Organization.

Quist, H. O. (2001) Cultural issues in secondary education development in West Africa: Away from colonial survivals, towards neo-colonial influences. *Comparative Education,* 37(3), 297–314.

Roberts, P. A. (2009) Whose school? Conflicts over school management in Sefwi Iwaso, Ghana. *Anthropology and Education Quarterly,* 13(3), 268–78.

Rolleston, C. and Oketch, O. (2008) Educational expansion in Ghana: Economic assumptions and expectations. *International Journal of Educational Development* 28(3), 320–39.

Sefa Dei, G. and Opini, B. M. (2008) Schooling in the context of difference: the challenge of post-colonial education in Ghana. In D. Thiessen and A. Cook-Sather (eds), *International Handbook of Student Experience in Elementary and Secondary School.* Rotterdam: Springer, pp. 463–91.

Segura, C. C. (2009) *Lost in Translation: Why the structures of formal schooling are not translating in rural Ghana.* Toronto: International Development Studies, University of Toronto.

UNESCO (2007) *A Human Rights-based Approach to Education: A framework for the realization of children's right to education and rights within education.* New York: United Nations Children's Fund.

UNICEF (2006) *Government of Ghana–UNICEF Country Programme Action Plan.* Accra: UNICEF.

Zame, M. Y., Hope, W. C. and Respress, T. (2008) Educational reform in Ghana: the leadership challenge. *International Journal of Educational Management*, 22(2), 115–28.

5   Sri Lanka

School leadership in the conflict-affected north and east

Jaya Earnest

Introduction

The 30-year ethnic civil war between the Government of Sri Lanka (GoSL) and the Liberation Tigers of Tamil Eelam (LTTE) ended in mid 2009. This conflict seriously undermined the country's enormous development potential. Approximately 800,000 people, a third of whom were children, were displaced. Nearly a million children, amongst them an estimated two thousand child soldiers, lived in the north and the east of the country, the areas most affected by the ethnic conflict. The impact of the tsunami of December 2004 exacerbated the situation here. Furthermore, the peace efforts of international mediators, notably Norway, were thwarted by uprisings in 2006 and 2008. However, by May 2009, the Sri Lankan military finally defeated the Tamil Tigers, marking the end of the civil war.

This chapter examines school leadership in the districts of north and east Sri Lanka, drawing on fieldwork undertaken in 2006 (Earnest and Finger, 2006) and subsequent field narratives obtained in 2010 and 2011. It comprises three main sections. First, the background to the civil war and the impact of the tsunami in 2004 are considered. Second, an overview is presented of the structure and administration of the current Sri Lankan education system. Third, the realities of school leaders' work are examined in order to identify some of the challenges they face.

Background

The island nation of Sri Lanka is a democratic socialist republic situated in the Indian Ocean, off the south-eastern tip of the sub-continent of India. A 22-mile stretch of water known as the Palk Straits separates Sri Lanka from India. Sri Lanka is a small, multi-racial, multi-ethnic and multi-religious country. Nearly 75 per cent of its population of 20 million are Sinhalese who speak Sinhalese and are mainly Buddhist. Sri Lankan Tamils account for 18 per cent of the population. The majority of Tamils are Hindu and live predominantly in the north and east of the country. About 4 per cent of the Sri Lankan population is Muslim and is concentrated in the eastern provinces and Colombo. There are also small groups of Burghers (Eurasians of mixed descent) and Malays, as well as a Christian minority (Human Rights Watch, 2006).

Sri Lanka is a former Portuguese, Dutch and British colony, and gained its independence in 1948. From the 1950s, tension between the Tamils and Sinhalese escalated, especially after Sinhalese was made the only official language in 1956. During colonial times, a Tamil nationalist discourse that advocated for a 'traditional homeland' – 'Tamil Eelam' – for the Tamils in the north-east of Sri Lanka emerged. This discourse gathered strength in the post-independence era (Sitrampalam, 2005).

Following continuing tensions, the Tamil United Liberation Front, established in 1976, openly advocated separatism and made a demand for a separate Tamil state (Goodhand, Klem and Sørbø, 2011). After defeating rival Tamil groups in the 1980s, the Liberation Tigers of Tamil Eelam (LTTE) emerged as the self-proclaimed 'sole representative' of the Tamil cause in Sri Lanka. The LTTE developed from a small, amateurish guerrilla movement into a much larger force that pioneered suicide bombing. It also created its own navy (the 'Sea Tigers'), a small air force, rudimentary government structures and symbols, administrative institutions, tax collection, banks, a flag and a national day (Fuglerud, 2009; Korf, 2006). By the 1990s, the LTTE, led by Vellupillai Prabhakaran, controlled significant territory in north and east Sri Lanka. The movement came to act like a state and its conflict was understood as a process of state-making.

It has been estimated that 60,000 people died in the conflict prior to the peace agreement in 2002 (Goodhand, Klem and Sørbø, 2011). In mid 2006, an outbreak of renewed violence threatened the fragile ceasefire, which ultimately collapsed. Sri Lanka's conflict mutated and expanded over time. Over three decades, the war created new 'ground realities', added new layers of tensions, complex political dialogue and rhetoric, and changed the dynamics of conflict resolution and peace negotiations. The evolution of the conflict unleashed political and social processes that continue to shape the state and society (Goodhand, Klem and Sørbø, 2011).

War in Sri Lanka has reconfigured politics and educational institutions, especially in the north and east of the country. Although major population centres such as Jaffna, Trincomalee and Batticaloa ended up under government and army control, the LTTE retained a major influence. In the so-called 'un-cleared areas' (LTTE controlled), state institutions continued to function, in spite of an economic blockade imposed by the government. Government administrators and basic services like food aid and poverty relief were co-opted by the LTTE in what was an unusual form of hybrid governance (Korf, Engeler and Hagmann, 2010). However, in 2009, after the complete breakdown of the ceasefire, the GoSL launched a major military offensive, resulting in the destruction of a number of arms-smuggling vessels that belonged to the LTTE. This was followed by an international crackdown on funding for the Tamil Tigers, enabling the GoSL to take control of the entire area previously controlled by them. This area included the Tamil Tigers' de-facto capital, Kilinochchi, their main military base in Mullaitivu, and the entire A9 highway leading to Jaffna. The LTTE admitted defeat on 17 May 2009 (Goodhand, Klem and Sørbø, 2011).

The impact of the Tsunami in 2004

On 26 December 2004, an earthquake occurred off the western coast of Sumatra, generating tsunamis that washed over the eastern and southern coasts of Sri Lanka. The tsunami created an 'emergency within an emergency' as it hit Sri Lanka's coastal areas that had already been affected by 20 years of conflict (Save the Children, 2006). The tsunami killed 35,322 people and displaced over one million Sri Lankans. In addition, there was a devastating impact on housing, businesses, livelihoods and infrastructure, as well as on education and healthcare facilities. The north-eastern region of Sri Lanka was particularly hard hit (World Health Organization, 2005). Thousands of children lost their lives and many more were separated from parents, or orphaned. Almost 1,000 children lost both parents and almost 4,000 lost one (Save the Children, 2006). Children who were already living in poverty and in regions affected by the 20-year civil war, were among the most vulnerable victims of the tsunami and its aftermath.

In December 2005, UNICEF Sri Lanka undertook a survey of 323 transitional shelter sites for the internally displaced in the southern, eastern and northern provinces (TNS Lanka, 2006). Nearly 100,000 people affected by the tsunami resided in these shelters. Many vulnerable families there saw that they had few other alternatives other than to send their children to work, or to live with better-off relatives. The tsunami also broke down existing social structures of protection and increased the vulnerability of internally displaced persons (IDPs) to violence and harassment. The majority of transitional sites (63 per cent) did not have adequate health facilities and there was also a problem with food security. Most families (75 per cent) relied on government food rations and 13 per cent of families had fewer than three meals a day (TNS Lanka, 2006). Donor response to the rehabilitation of the north and east of Sri Lanka after 2009 has been determined by the pace of the resettlement process in these regions, with a focus on providing access to quality basic education, health and nutrition, safe drinking water, appropriate sanitation and hygiene, all aimed at building a stronger protective environment for children (UNICEF, 2011).

To summarise this section of the chapter overall, it is against this background of protracted conflict that the country seeks a qualified and skilled workforce that is adaptable to change in a constantly evolving environment. At the same time, educational reformers continue to grapple with issues related to disparities in income distribution and regional development, especially in the north and east of the country. In the complex circumstances that apply in these regions, the provision of education, training and educational leadership plays a critical role (Ministry of Education, Sri Lanka, 2006).

The education system

The modern system of education in Sri Lanka developed in the nineteenth and early twentieth centuries under British colonisation. Traditionally, the education system was highly centralised, academically intense and examination oriented. It was based on class and language differentiation that created, alongside access to knowledge, wide socio-economic and regional disparities. These disparities have continued into the post-colonial decades (Goodhand, Klem and Sørbø, 2011).

Since independence in 1948, the government of Sri Lanka has made education one of its highest priorities. The educational reform of 1988 was based on the aims set out by the constitution of Sri Lanka in 1948, recognising the right of all children to universal and equal access to education. They included several key objectives: an understanding of cultural and religious heritage, an appreciation of contributions made by different ethnic groups, an appreciation of the environment, the acquisition of learning skills relevant to societal needs, a recognition of the arts, literature and science, and the development of a national philosophy of understanding cultural diversity. Other aims included the spiritual and physical development of children and the creation of a technically skilled workforce to meet the needs of the country's economy. Finally, the 1988 education reform also sought to promote lifelong education (UNESCO, 2011).

Sri Lanka's current structure of education consists of the Ministry of Education and Higher Education, the National Institute of Education, the Provincial Department of Education (part of the elected provincial government) and district level, zonal and divisional education offices. The Ministry of Education (MOE) (previously the Ministry of Human Resources Development, Education and Cultural Affairs – MHRDECA) is responsible for general education and teacher education nationwide (UNESCO, 2011). Schools in Sri Lanka are divided into non-government and government schools. Non-government schools consist of estate schools located in plantation areas and *pirivenas,* which are educational institutes attached to Buddhist temples. These latter schools cater for Buddhist monks and also conduct general education classes for male students who do not attend formal schools, or special, certified, and international schools (Gunawardhane, 2011).

The National Education Policy on Early Childhood Care and Development (ECCD) was implemented in 2004, aiming to ensure the best start in life for every Sri Lankan child. This was to be achieved by providing access to adequate health and nutrition services, along with opportunities for responsive psychosocial stimulation. Hence, there has been an attempt to introduce an integrated approach to policy in the early childhood area that brings together health, nutrition, psychosocial stimulation, safe water, hygiene, sanitation and education. Standards and guidelines have been developed that regulate the development and implementation of ECCD programs and that clarify the role and responsibilities of central, divisional, local government and non-governmental agencies in the provision of the ECCD services (UNESCO, 2011).

The five-year primary education program commences for children at the age of five. Primary education is divided into three key stages: grades 1 and 2, grades 3 and 4, and grade 5. Upon completion of primary education, most students sit the Grade 5 Scholarship and Placement Examination. The Grade 5 Scholarship is an important grant made available to students of low income and vulnerable families. Sinhala and Tamil are official languages and English is the link language taught from Grade 3 onwards (Aturupane, 2008). In 2010, a new primary school curriculum was designed by the MOE, focusing on communication, the environment, ethics and religion, play and leisure, and learning to learn. Class-based assessment and frameworks have also been developed as part of the new curriculum (Gunawardhane, 2011).

Leadership in Sri Lankan schools

Change in education is a necessary component of a much broader social, political, legal and economic programme of reform. It is also well documented that educational leadership in many developing countries promotes nation-building by fostering mutual understanding and tolerance, and respect for cultural diversity (DFID, 2000). For this reason, the planning and development of education becomes a vital consideration for ensuring social cohesion and stability (National Education Commission, 2003).

Principals in Sri Lanka belong either to the Sri Lanka Education Administrative Service (SLEAS), or to the Sri Lanka Principals' Service (SLPS). The Sri Lanka Principals' Service is responsible for the selection of principals. The Diploma in Principalship is exclusively for principals, whereas the Diploma in School Management is designed for principals and deputies. Principals in Sri Lanka have administrative roles that include attending to school admissions, maintaining attendance and leave registers and personnel files, and managing student and teacher performance (Gunawardhane, 2011).

Every province in Sri Lanka has at least one teacher preparation centre catering for the in-service preparation of school principals and teachers. These centres provide residential facilities, lecture rooms and staff who conduct management courses for principals that concentrate on the following:

- managerial behaviour that includes effective communication, conducting meetings, interpersonal relations, managing as a leader, the characteristics of an effective manager, and motivating teachers for better performance;

- management processes and functions that involve planning, physical resource management, infrastructure development, financial management and the use of information technology;
- managing the curriculum to ensure effective implementation of the curricula, the contextualisation of the curriculum in different regions, undertaking school improvement strategies and staff appraisal;
- the implementation of education reforms and understanding recent trends in school development.

(Gunawardhane, 2011)

In the last two decades the gradual move towards school-based management for enhancing principals' autonomy has demanded that school leaders have multiple and often non-traditional skills. The way principals lead and manage their schools is not only influenced by their individual skills and capacities, but also by recruitment criteria, posting procedures, evaluation practices, and the provision of an attractive career progression ladder. This observation implies that in order to bolster the role of principals in Sri Lankan schools it is not only necessary to strengthen the way they lead and manage their organisations, but also to support the national education authorities' attempts to develop and enhance the education profession (Kandasamy and Blaton, 2004). For this purpose, the National Institute of Education (NIE), Sri Lanka, was established in 1986, to build the capacity of educational managers, teacher educators and teachers, and to develop school curricula and conduct policy research on education (National Institute of Education, n.d.). The NIE was also mandated to advise the Minister on matters related to education, to initiate and promote innovative practices in the education system, including the adaptation of technology for educational purposes, to provide for improvement of professional competency of all educational personnel and to make available to the government specialist services in education (National Institute of Education, n.d.).

In addition, an in-service advisors' (ISA) mentoring scheme was established by an all-island teacher improvement initiative. ISAs were selected from 'currently employed efficient teachers', with the majority being professionally qualified graduates. It was expected that an advisor should have a specialised knowledge in a relevant subject and pedagogy, and should be able to maintain a healthy relationship with teachers (Gunawardhane, 2011). There have, however, been several shortcomings associated with this initiative. For example, zonal education directors and school principals felt that it was not realistically possible for an ISA appointed for one subject to cover all of the schools in his, or her, jurisdiction. Some ISAs were appointed without adhering to proper recruitment procedures and more than one third of appointees were trained teachers without degrees. Moreover, many ISAs lacked sufficient subject knowledge as well as teaching experience. In spite of these perceived weaknesses, however, in-service training has contributed immensely to the introduction of curriculum revisions and teaching innovations (Gunawardhane, 2011).

The realities faced by schools: glimpses from the field

This section of the chapter draws on a study undertaken in six of the eight districts of north and east Sri Lanka in 2006 (Earnest and Finger, 2006). These areas, which encompass the districts of Jaffna, Killinochchi, Mannar, Mullaitivu and Vavuniya in the Northern Province, and Trincomalee, Batticaloa and Ampara in the Eastern Province, were, as previously outlined, severely affected by the war. The study investigated principals' perspectives on the challenges they faced in performing their work and the strategies adopted in order to deal with its complexities. Personal communication based on the observations of a fieldworker assigned to one of the international aid organisations in this region provided additional insights into the situation covering the period from the end of the civil war to the end of 2011.

Discussions with school principals in the field centred on the impact of the conflict and displacement, as well as the problems resulting from the tsunami. It was clear that several UN and international aid organisations had provided much needed assistance with the supply of latrines, water, sanitation and books. They had also supported the rehabilitation of schools. Nevertheless, there were still considerable challenges being faced by both the education and health sectors. In particular, the number of children dropping out of school was increasing after the tsunami because of their displacement and loss of family.

These circumstances necessitated supervision of younger children while their parents were at work as daily wage earners. There also continued to be a lack of qualified teachers, limited availability of resources and a dearth of contractors to rehabilitate schools in the conflict- and tsunami-affected regions. The restricted access to health and education facilities in the more rural and remote areas was highlighted repeatedly, as was an acute shortage of transport facilities that limited opportunities for the relocation of teachers and for student attendance at schools.

Furthermore, there continued to be a severe shortage of teachers and a need for their ongoing professional development. Particular attention was drawn to the scarcity of qualified language, science and mathematics teachers. Although the MOE had recruited young graduates as teachers for secondary schools, most of these graduates did not have teaching qualifications. Concerns were also expressed about the poor quality of the textbooks translated into Tamil. The books were often translated by those who lacked proficiency in both the subject matter and the language, and many books failed to be delivered on time. These circumstances threatened to place Tamil students located in the north and east of the country at a disadvantage.

The sector-wide approach (SWAp) to education in Sri Lanka, discussed initially in 2004, was formulated and developed as the Education Sector Development Framework Programme (ESDFP) at the end of 2005, and was implemented island-wide from 2006 (Jayaweera and Gunawardena, 2007). This approach postulated the integration of programmes and expenditure on education in a holistic framework and was evaluated in 2007, with recommendations for the decentralisation of the Sri Lankan education system and the creation of the Education Sector Development Project through SWAp. The evaluation also proposed that school leadership in various districts should be administered under newly-created school development committees (Jayaweera and Gunawardena, 2007).

Since the end of the conflict in 2009, UNICEF and Save the Children have contributed over three million US dollars to education in Sri Lanka, specifically to the conflict-affected areas of the north and east. They have also co-led an expansion of educational access and quality for all children, especially in the conflict-affected areas (UNICEF, 2011). As a result of this expansion, which included the rehabilitation of at least 30 permanent schools damaged by the conflict, formal education was re-established for returnee children who had been internally displaced. In all, approximately 6,000 children benefited. Temporary learning spaces were established in areas of return and in host communities while schools were being repaired and rehabilitated. Learning and teaching kits and other educational supplies were provided in these temporary learning spaces and in schools that had been repaired. School principals were supported in the delivery of formal education in these circumstances.

An intensive teacher-preparation programme was delivered to approximately 500 inexperienced primary school teachers in the Northern Province in basic classroom pedagogy and effective classroom management (UNICEF, 2011). School principals, especially primary school principals, were trained in the 'child friendly schools' concept and in the implementation of an accelerated learning program (ALP). The ALP was overseen by school principals, with the support of the Ministry of Education, to reintegrate and retain up to 100,000 children who had fallen behind in their education as a consequence of conflict and displacement. Teachers were also prepared in how to deliver the ALP to their students. To depict some of the more specific challenges faced by school leaders, and the ways in which they are handled, four 'snapshots' are now presented.

Snapshot one: schools in Ampara and catch-up education

In the Kalmunai zone of Ampara district, fifteen primary and secondary schools had been totally destroyed, and two were partially destroyed, by the tsunami. School visits to rehabilitated and temporary schools, and meetings with school principals conducted during Earnest and Finger's (2006) field study, indicated the extreme difficulties the principals had to face post-tsunami. There was a severe shortage of teachers of English, Tamil, science and mathematics as they had been displaced, or had lost their lives, and all of the teachers who were available required in-service professional development.

'Catch-up education (CUE)', with the assistance of UNICEF, was introduced by school principals for students living in IDP camps who had missed school owing to displacement, and for children who had been child soldiers who had been returned to their families. CUE was successfully implemented with these children by school principals in many of the conflict- and tsunami-affected areas, with more than 1000 students receiving assistance. This was particularly important after the tsunami as many additional children had been displaced and were residing in camps. Private teachers were also used to provide children with CUE and the programme operated before and after school for a year.

School principals revealed that the majority of underage recruits (child soldiers) had not been forced to join the LTTE. Girls and boys recruited by the LTTE often came from poverty-stricken families, or from families that had one parent missing. Many of the under-age recruits joined up if their friends and older siblings were already recruited into the LTTE cadres. In other instances, families and villagers felt that they had to give a child to the Tamil cause. Eighty-six per cent of the IDP children who were attending school were enrolled in a school outside of their camp and walked an average of one to two kilometres to get there. The influx of displaced children into school also placed immense pressure on principals and teachers who had to cope with school environments that were still being rehabilitated and were under resourced (Earnest and Finger, 2006).

Snapshot two: high school youth in Batticoloa

Principals in high schools in Batticoloa expressed their concerns about adolescent students. Most high school students had encountered a variety of traumatic experiences during the conflict. Some of them had been separated from their parents. A few had seen their fathers arrested and had to deal with their subsequent disappearance. Sometimes unidentified armed groups stormed houses at night trying to abduct children. If there was resistance, it was quite likely that a family member would be killed. On occasions, fathers were injured and families ended up living in fear.

Principals also revealed uncertainties associated with daily school operations. Schools could not be opened if strikes were called by the LTTE, if road blocks were set up, or if a violent incident had occurred. A large number of young students had lost friends and members of the family to claymore land-mines. Other students had lost limbs. Many families were displaced by the conflict and had no permanent homes. However, in spite of these insecurities, school principals commented that the students still wanted to pursue higher education and become teachers, doctors or lawyers so they could help solve the nation's problems and bring about justice. They were unsure, however, if they would ever be able to realise their ambition for further education. School principals also observed that younger children yearned for peace and security, displaying an extraordinary resilience and capacity to achieve, in spite of the difficult circumstances presented by on-going tensions and the constant threat of renewed conflict (Earnest and Finger, 2006).

Snapshot three: towards child-friendly schools – small steps at a time: reflections from Mannar in 2010

One visionary school principal at a primary school in Mannar, with 120 students and seven teachers (including the principal), initiated the child-friendly schools concept in her school. At the time, the school was experiencing many problems. These included serving a vulnerable rural population affected by war, displacement and hunger, poor student attendance, and children lacking uniforms, shoes and school books. The principal, who had been trained by UNICEF in the child-friendly school approach, initiated a number of innovative methods and strategies in her school. For example, she built fencing around the school premises with the support of a rural development society. With the assistance of the parents, she also ensured that a nutrition programme providing an afternoon meal for the children was established in the school.

Effective communication by the principal with parents and other stake-holders has been the key to bringing about the desired changes in the school. In 2004, UNICEF provided further support by building additional class-rooms and setting up a play area with equipment and attractive wall paintings. The playground added much needed stimulation and was a source of enjoyment for the children. In 2009, the process of preparing the school development plan was also supported by UNICEF and incorporated into the ESDFP.

The teachers, with support and guidance from the principal, have worked continuously to assist students affected by war and displacement to catch up with their learning. There is also a systematic method of identifying students with special needs and providing them with remedial lessons for half an hour every day. Thus, the combined efforts of a hardworking and visionary principal, community members from the villages, and parents and teachers from the school have been instrumental in providing a better quality of education for vulnerable children from the three conflict-affected villages in the catchment area of the school.

Snapshot four: the situation of conflict-affected schools in Jaffna in 2011

In some areas, schools are but a bare patch of land and children often have to walk two-to-three kilometres to attend other schools while their own is being reconstructed. Nevertheless, in July 2011, information disclosed by field staff from international organisations after visiting several child-friendly schools experiencing such circumstances in Jaffna, indicated that the child-friendly process had helped principals in pursuing a supportive school development initiative. This, in turn, made it possible for principals in these conflict-affected areas to focus more on leadership and the quality of education in their schools.

The Special Professional Development fund has provided much needed aid required by the schools. UNICEF, Save the Children, and World Vision continue to supply such resources as libraries, playground material, sanitation facilities and materials for principal and teacher professional learning. Basic scholastic material such as exercise books, pens and pencils, chalk, school bags and drink bottles are also provided, as are teacher kits, recreation activities and some preparation for teachers. To support each other, principals of schools that are better resourced are visited by colleagues in the region. At these meetings, they compile a checklist to identify teaching needs, resource gaps and improvements to be pursued in their respective schools. This is seen as a constructive way to improve leadership capacity, provide peer support and obtain resources for school children (UNICEF, 2011).

Challenges for school leaders

According to government figures in 2011, there were 42,000 female-headed households in north and east Sri Lanka. This situation causes significant economic stress on affected households and has a detrimental impact on the quality of care for children. In order to ease the economic burden on households, children are seeking jobs and dropping out of school, and a large number of adolescent girls are getting married. Many children are behind in their learning, having missed significant periods of the school year. Some children have missed out on education altogether, or require additional support, and school principals and teachers work hard to cater for the needs of those children who are affected.

Children who remain in IDP centres in part of the north require safe play environments and temporary learning spaces while their schools and homes are being rehabilitated. They also require specific assistance to continue their education (UNICEF, 2011). Thus, on occasions, children in north-east Sri Lanka have been excluded from schools and health care facilities, and from participating fully in their communities because of the protracted civil war.

War-affected families often do not have the funds to pay for such requirements as school materials and shoes. This is a constant scenario that confronts school principals. Survival pressures force parents to withdraw their children from school to engage in income-earning activities, or to exclude one child from school to look after the household, or younger children, so that they themselves can go to work (TNS Lanka, 2006). The war has also had an impact on the education system in unexpected ways. Aside from the depletion of resources and psychological effects arising from decades of conflict, school principals face a new set of challenges stemming from a dramatically altered socio-economic makeup. Many of the prosperous and well-educated Tamils have left the island and the student population at school is now disproportionally from poor, rural families (Goodhand, Klem and Sørbø, 2011). Despite these difficulties, the nation is committed to its children, as was evidenced by the National Plan of Action for the Children of Sri Lanka, implemented from 2004–8, with the help of UNICEF, especially in the conflict areas of north and east Sri Lanka, as well as by the declaration of the year 2006 as the 'Year of the Child' by President Rajapakse.

The vital role of sustainable school leadership in north and east Sri Lanka cannot be over emphasised in this context. Indeed, among the foundations on which education is anchored, school leadership is of cardinal importance. School effectiveness research reveals that leadership is a very strong predictor of school performance and has a significant effect not only on student learning, but also on school conditions (Leithwood, 2007). Taking cognisance of this position and the discussion so far, the following challenges to school leaders in Sri Lanka stand out.

- In north and east Sri Lanka, it is important to find a balance between support for school principals in order to improve the quality of school leadership and making resources available within the school. Principals in these areas are in particular need of assistance that is sustainable, regular and consistent.
- The NIE, with a group of principals, deputy principals and officials, has prepared a handbook for principals based on the concept of school-based management. A training manual has also been produced that addresses planning, school development, curriculum delivery, managing resources and setting and achieving standards. Effective use of the handbook and training manual by school principals, however, needs to be initiated.
- The main objective of school-based management is to improve school performance based on the assumption that schools with strong leadership offer a clear vision for the future and can raise educational standards by empowering staff (Kandasamy and Blaton, 2004). The impact of the programme aimed at achieving this objective has been positive but modest. It could be enhanced if used in conjunction with strategies to build the capacities of school principals motivated by a clear focus on quality improvement (De Grauwe, 2005).
- If leadership is expected to have a pronounced effect on education, it must be visionary, transformational and shared. Leadership in schools located in north and east Sri Lanka needs to be developed such that a principal will be not only responsible for tasks in the school, but also be able to secure the collaboration and commitment of teachers, students and the community in achieving effective performance;
- School principals and teachers in the areas of protracted conflict need ongoing professional development, but their backgrounds should be

taken into account when conceptualising, planning and implementing relevant programmes. Also, it would be desirable for the provision of in-service professional development to be differentiated and diversified in order to accommodate the differences in preparedness of teachers.

Conclusion

This chapter has highlighted the impact of protracted conflict on leadership at the school level, particularly as it relates to students in north and east Sri Lanka. In the micro-level setting, a number of constraints to the successful implementation of effective education have been identified. They are the uncertainty of the context, the lack of basic infrastructure in schools, quality of teachers, content and relevance of the curriculum, shortage of human resources, and the acute lack of material resources and finances required to rehabilitate, reconstruct and rebuild infrastructure. Longer-term sustainable funding initiatives are required to strengthen, support and promote school leadership. At the macro-level of the national political context, the challenge for the government is to be able to respond to these constraints.

Currently, Sri Lanka is going through a critical phase, that of building the trust of its Tamil population and integrating them into civil society governance. The nation's situation underscores the centrality of human rights and humanitarian issues entwined with the need to reconstruct schools, reform education and enhance school leadership. Is there the political will to stay the course, to engage in dialogue and work through the immense task of dismantling the IDP centres in the north and east, reintegrate people into their communities, rehabilitate infrastructure (especially schools), and address the needs of vulnerable children? If the answer is to be in the affirmative, it will require educational leaders in north and east Sri Lanka who are empowered to work in transformative and participative ways in order to ensure the effective provision of quality education for the benefit of future generations.

Acknowledgement

I would like to acknowledge the invaluable contributions of a friend and colleague with first-hand knowledge of issues that have made an impact on education in the conflict affected areas of Sri Lanka.

References

Aturupane, H. (2008) *Celebrating 60 Years of Progress and Challenges in Education in Sri Lanka*. Human Development Unit, South Asia Region: The World Bank.
De Grauwe, A. (2005) Improving the quality of education through school-based management: learning from international experiences. *Review of Education*, 51, 269–87.

Department of National Planning (2005) *National Plan of Action for the Children of Sri Lanka*. Colombo, Sri Lanka: Department of National Planning.

DFID (2000) *Towards Social Harmony in Education – Sri Lanka* (unpublished report commissioned by UK Department for International Development in Sri Lanka).

Earnest, J. and Finger, R. (2006) *Resource and Vulnerability Mapping of Children Affected by War in North East, Sri Lanka*. Sri Lanka: UNICEF.

Fuglerud, O. (2009) Fractured sovereignty: The LTTE's state-building in an interconnected world. In C. Brun and T. Jazeel (eds) *Spatialising Politics: Culture and geography in post-colonial Sri Lanka*. London: Sage, pp. 194–215.

Goodhand, J., Klem, B. and Sørbø, G. (2011) *Pawns of Peace: Evaluation of Norwegian peace efforts in Sri Lanka, 1997–2009*. Copenhagen: Norad Evaluation Department.

Gunawardhane, R. (2011) A study on the effectiveness of short-term in-service teacher training in the teaching learning process (unpublished research study). Sri Lanka: National Education Commission (NEC) of Sri Lanka.

Human Rights Watch (2006) Living in fear: child soldiers and the Tamil tigers in Sri Lanka (unpublished report). New York: Human Rights Watch.

Jayaweera, S. and Gunawardena C. (2007) *Social Inclusion: Gender and equity in education swaps in South Asia*. Kathmandu: UNICEF, Regional Office for South Asia.

Kandasamy, M. and Blaton, L. (2004) *School Principals: Core actors in educational improvement, an analysis of seven Asian countries*. Paris: Asian Network of Training and Research Institutions/UNESCO – IIEP.

Korf, B. (2006) Dining with devils? Ethnographic enquiries into the conflict-development nexus in Sri Lanka. *Oxford Development Studies*, 34(1), 47–64.

Korf, B., Engeler, M. and Hagmann, T. (2010) The geography of warscape. *Third World Quarterly*, 31(3), 385–99.

Ministry of Education (2006) *Education Sector Development Framework Programme. Sri Lanka*. Colombo, Sri Lanka: Ministry of Education.

National Education Commission (2003) *Proposal for a National Policy Framework on General Education in Sri Lanka*. Colombo, Sri Lanka: National Education Commission.

National Institute of Education (n.d.) *The Formation and Objectives of the National Institute for Education, Sri Lanka*. http://www.nie.lk (accessed 4 November 2010).

Save the Children (2006) *1-Year Progress Report: Rebuilding lives after the Tsunami through the eyes of children*. London: Save the Children.

Sitrampalam, S. K. (2005) The Tamils of Sri Lanka: The historic roots of Tamil identity. In G. Frerks and B. Klem (eds) *Dealing with Diversity: Sri Lankan discourses on peace and conflict*. The Hague: Clingendael, pp. 231–74.

TNS Lanka. (2006) Report on the assessment of the water supply, sanitation and hygiene status, education needs and social protection services in transitional shelters, camps and settlements: Tsunami affected areas in Sri Lanka. Sri Lanka: UNICEF.

UNESCO (2011) *World Data on Education*, 7th edn. Paris: UNESCO.

UNICEF (2011) *Sri Lanka: UNICEF humanitarian action for children*. www.unicef.org/hac2011 (accessed 1 June 2010).

World Health Organization (2005) *North-East Emergency Reconstruction Project (NEERP): Recovery of the health system in the North-East of Sri Lanka final report (2003–2004)* Colombo, Sri Lanka: World Health Organisation.

6 Rwanda

Challenges for school leadership in a transitional, post-conflict nation

Jaya Earnest

Introduction

Rwanda is a small central African nation that has been more than adversely affected by major political, economic and ethnic upheaval. In particular, the country has faced the challenge of ensuring recovery, rehabilitation, reconstruction and reconciliation after the horrific genocide of 1994 that resulted in the loss of nearly a million lives and the displacement of over two million people. In 2000, the government of Rwanda proposed Vision 2020 (Ministry of Finance and Economic Planning, 2000), a dynamic policy document, resulting in the adoption of the following goals:

- the eradication of illiteracy;
- national capacity building in science and technology;
- and improving quality in education.

This chapter draws on research undertaken in Rwanda between 1997 and 2011. The research utilised qualitative methods to examine the nature of school leadership in this post-conflict transitional society, supplemented by relevant published literature. The findings of the research identified a series of constraints faced by school principals in Rwanda and highlighted challenges that need to be confronted in the implementation of the education reform process. In particular, the following major challenges were identified: running schools effectively with limited infrastructure and resources; progressing professionally with limited opportunity for further learning; seeking to support the professional development of teachers; meeting Ministry of Education goals of quality education when the emphasis is on set examinations; enabling school principals to contribute to the design of a contextually relevant Rwandan curriculum; and improving the status of the teaching profession and working conditions of teachers.

This chapter is in three parts. First, a brief historical background is presented. Second, there is an overview of the country's education system and third, attention is focused on each of the major challenges described above.

The landlocked transitional nation of Rwanda

Rwanda, a small, landlocked country in east central Africa, is known as the 'Land of a Thousand Hills'. It is bound on the west by the Democratic Republic of Congo, on the south by Burundi, on the east by Tanzania, and on the north by Uganda. Germany colonised Rwanda between 1899 and 1916. After the First World War, Rwanda was assigned as a trusteeship to Belgium. The Belgians followed a policy of indirect rule, resulting in a political and administrative monopoly being placed in the hands of one of the major groups in the country, the Tutsis (Eriksson, 1996). The colonial power encountered heightened tensions in the nation due to this Tutsi favouritism and its introduction in 1931 of identity cards that classified Rwandans as either Tutsi, Hutu or Twa. This raises the question as to why the colonial administration strongly supported one group at the expense of the others. Destexhe's (1995) explanation is that it was to weaken the possibility of any national coalition being established to oppose its presence in the country.

At the end of the 1950s, there was a sudden policy shift, with the Belgian trusteeship authorities deciding to support the other major group who were in the ascendency, the Hutus. The monarchy was abolished and replaced by a presidential system. Eventually, independence was gained in 1962. In the lead up to independence and in the period that followed, there was heightened ethnic tension between the Hutus and Tutsis, causing the first flight of Tutsi refugees from Rwanda to Uganda, Burundi, Tanzania and the Democratic Republic of Congo between 1959 and 1962 (Earnest, 2003; Mbabazi, 2012).

A three-year civil war, which began in 1990, left 6,500 Rwandans dead and more than a million displaced. Following the assassination in April 1994 of the Hutu president, Juvénal Habyarimana, the country dissolved into a state of anarchy and terror. Extremist Hutu militia groups slaughtered Tutsis and moderate Hutus. Nearly a million people were killed in 100 days. Tutsis fled in fear of their lives and Hutus fled in fear of retaliation. This was one of the greatest mass flights of people in modern times. Within a few days, two million Hutus fled across the border into Burundi, Tanzania and Zaire. The vast majority of those who fled were innocent of any wrongdoing (Earnest, 2003).

On 4 July 1994, the Rwandan Patriotic Force (RPF) gained power in Rwanda. The RPF put an end to the 1994 genocide and formed the Government of National Unity (GNU) and the Transitional National Assembly (TNA), in coalition with other political parties. They set out to define a new future for Rwanda through the establishment of democratic institutions (Ministry of Economics and Finance, 2000).

Today, 18 years after the genocide, the majority of villages in Rwanda have very basic conditions. Many have no electricity and food is still prepared on wood-burning, or charcoal, stoves. The only light in the evening is usually that supplied by paraffin lanterns. Also, while the nation has made significant progress from its devastated condition following the 1994 genocide, it continues to have an agrarian economy, with over 60 per cent of the population living below the poverty line.

The 2010 World Bank report on Rwanda and the Department of Health Services 2010 survey highlight that the population is 10.62 million, making it one of the most densely populated countries in Africa. Life expectancy according to the Department of Health Services 2010 survey was only 55 years, the fertility rate stood at 5 children per woman of reproductive age, the HIV prevalence in the country was 3 per cent, and only 55 per cent of the population had access to sanitation (Department of Health Services, 2010). Furthermore, the country continues to receive nearly a billion dollars in overseas developmental assistance (World Bank, 2010). However, there is also hope, with rebuilding, reconstructing and reconciling of communities taking place, and with the government committed to the progress of Rwanda's knowledge economy (Ministry of Finance and Economic Planning, 2007).

Overview of the education system

Rwanda's formal education system did not emerge until it was colonised. The first schools in the country were established by Catholic missionaries in 1900. The German and Belgian colonial governments did eventually become involved by providing funding and helping to develop curricula, but 'the operation of the schools remained almost entirely the responsibility of the church' (Bridgelenad, Wulson and McNaught, 2009: 5). An agreement signed in 1965, between the Catholic Church and the government, resulted in many of the Church schools being nationalised and 'led to a system where schools were classified as public, private, or assisted' (Ibid.: 5)

This section of the chapter now provides an overview of the education policies that have been implemented in Rwanda since the late 1960s. The passing of the first education act, implemented in 1966, resulted in a continuation of the pre-independence curricula, with limited national content, especially history, being included. The first education project, implemented in 1977, dealt with general education, while efforts to provide universal access to primary schooling were completed in 1983. It was during this reform period that ethnic and regional quotas were formalised and reinforced, the curriculum was vocationalised, and the national language, Kinyarwanda, and local cultural content were introduced (Obura, 2003). The second project was approved in 1982, and focused its attention on secondary school education. The third project commenced in 1986, and included assistance for enhancing the quality of education and improving the management capacity of each education sector, with a focus on school management and leadership (World Bank, 2000). In 1991 and 1992, further minor education reforms were introduced, but the ethnic quotas were not eliminated (Obura, 2003).

The immediate educational aim in the aftermath of the genocide was to rehabilitate and re-open schools, and to allow students to return to school as soon as possible in order to provide some sense of normality in the communities. The transitional Government of National Unity formed in July 1994, had reopened all schools by September 1994 to facilitate reconciliation and the healing of communities. During the genocide the education system and the teaching workforce had been devastated, 65 per cent of the schools were damaged and 25 per cent of schools in the country housed returning refugees. Of the teachers who survived, only 45 per cent of primary and 33 per cent of secondary school teachers were qualified. Furthermore, the majority of qualified teachers were located in the capital, Kigali (Obura, 2003). Since then, the main educational objective of the government has been to expand access to, and improve the quality of, education, which is regarded as a national project for human development. In view of this, the Rwandan government adopted several national education goals in 1998, focused on the eradication of illiteracy, the introduction of universal primary education, the provision of teacher training and the improvement of national capacity building in science, mathematics and technology (Ministry of Education, 1998; Obura, 2003).

A commission led by curriculum design specialists from Canada, appointed by the Rwandan Ministry of Education in early 1996, produced a new curriculum for primary and secondary schools. The new curriculum documents were published in French and English, and were presented to schools in September 1998. The curriculum was designed to help bring about universal primary education and improve science and technology in an environment severely constrained by limited financial, human and material resources (Ministry of Education, 1998). The National Curriculum Development Centre (NCDC) was also established and since 2000 has been involved with the development of holistic curricular perspectives.

In 2002, the then Minister for Education, Romain Murenzi stated:

> It is generally felt that the education and specifically the school curriculum failed the nation in 1994. The curriculum was silent where it should have been eloquent and vocal where it should have been silent. There was much about human difference and very little about human similarities, too much about collective duty and little about individual responsibility and too much about the past and too little about the future.
>
> (cited in Obura, 2003: 86)

A restructured Rwandan education system began to emerge as a result of the educational initiatives that commenced post-genocide. Rwanda, like many developing countries, also found itself signing up to global commitments to achieve international millennium development targets, notably universal primary education (UPE) and education for all (EFA), and to develop quality teaching, quality management of education and a quality education experience for students (Ministry of Education, Science, Technology and Research, 2003).

Vision 2020: transformation of Rwanda to a knowledge-based economy

Vision 2020 (Ministry of Finance and Economic Planning, 2007), which was developed at the start of the new millennium, espoused a new vision for Rwanda. One of its main pillars was the concept of comprehensive human resource development, encompassing the education, health and ICT skills of the population. It recognised that at the core of Rwanda's on-going development are its people, who are its principal asset. However, the level of human-resource development in the country is low. For example, there is a severe shortage of professional personnel. There is also significant illiteracy among the population, with only 65 per cent of Rwandans being able to read and write. The situation is exacerbated by poor health and the prevalence of malaria, HIV/AIDS, and malnutrition (Ministry of Finance and Economic Planning, 2000).

The government, through Vision 2020, realised that there was clearly a need to educate and train people at all levels – primary, secondary and tertiary – with special attention being paid to the quality of education. There was also acknowledgement that the quality of education had been declining because of the low calibre of teaching staff and poor leadership. Hence, plans were put in place to organise intensive teacher preparation programmes (Ministry of Finance and Economic Planning, 2000).

In identifying priority areas for public action, the 2002 Poverty Reduction Strategy Paper (PRSR), provided by the government of Rwanda made the following commitment in relation to education:

> The government will continue to support quality in education, improving teacher training, distance learning for teachers, and reform of teaching methodology. The curriculum will be evaluated and reviewed in an effort to reduce the drop-out rates so that Universal Primary Education is achieved by 2010, leading to Education for All by 2015.
> (Government of Rwanda, 2002: 48)

Currently, it is the Education Sector Strategic Plan (ESSP) of 2010–15, that is informing the reform of education. Although the government has tried to improve access to, and the quality of, education, this has proved to be a difficult task for several reasons. In particular, while the current primary school (years 1 to 6) enrolment rate stands at between 92 per cent and 95 per cent, the lower secondary (years 7 to 9) rate is less than 40 per cent, and the upper secondary (years 10 to 12) rate is only about 18 per cent. Furthermore, the higher education and tertiary education enrolments are extremely low at 3.2 per cent. Also, class sizes in primary schools are currently at a ratio of fifty four students to one teacher. Concurrently, since 2009, the Ministry of Education has implemented the fast-track Nine-Year Basic Education (NYBE) programme, mainstreamed the child-friendly schools programme, ensured improvement of educational quality through closer integration of curriculum development, improved textbook distribution, sought to improve teaching and learning, and introduced English as the medium of instruction (Ministry of Education, 2010). In pursuit of these initiatives, the government has acknowledged that the leadership and management of schools need to be enhanced.

Teacher preparation in Rwanda

In 2007, the government recognised (Ministry of Education, 2007b) that teachers are the main instrument for bringing about improvement in learning, and that adequate teacher management structures, policies and strategies are key factors that determine teacher performance. Before 1998, there were no institutions preparing secondary school teachers. In that year the Kigali Institute of Education was established. New teacher-training colleges were set up by the Ministry of Education to prepare primary school teachers, while the previous *Ecole Normale Primaire* (primary teacher-training institutes) were phased out. Across the country, eleven teacher training colleges have been established to train primary school teachers. There are two colleges of education for lower and higher secondary schools teachers, and the Kigali Institute of Education was created in 1998 to train teachers for degree programmes, especially in science, mathematics and technology education (Ministry of Education, 2007a).

In 2007, out of 1556 teachers teaching at the higher secondary school level, only 221 had a bachelor's degree with an education qualification, while 440 teachers had a degree without education, or had a teaching diploma. Many teachers in high schools had dropped out of university after two years. Of the small number of qualified teachers who were available, some had moved out of the profession because of extremely low salaries, lack of accommodation in places where they were posted (especially in rural areas) and a dearth of incentives to pursue a teaching career (Ministry of Education, 2007b).

The absence of a policy for teacher management and development until 2007, compounded the problem of acute teacher shortages and the quality of teacher preparation. The Ministry of Education is now committed to overhauling teacher preparation, development and management in order to establish a cost effective pre-service teacher education system equipped to meet increased demand; developing a national teacher qualifications framework; designing a human resource strategy to support increased recruitment and efficient deployment of teachers; providing incentives to support the retention of teachers, such as competitive salaries, housing, bonuses for performance, and credit facilities; introducing teacher preparation mechanisms at pre-service and in-service levels using a range of methods, (participatory, learner-centred and gender sensitive approaches); defining the roles of teachers and enhancing their management capacities; and implementing a quality system of evaluation and management with well-defined responsibilities (Ministry of Education, 2007b). One of the priorities of the Education Sector Policy (2010–15) is to create a skilled and motivated teaching workforce through the advancement of a comprehensive teacher development and management system (Ministry of Education, 2010).

Exploring challenges in educational leadership

Educational reform is a complex process that affects the working lives of school principals, teachers and administrators. For educational change (internally, or externally, initiated) to succeed, the reform process has to deal with the past and its history, changing pre-established practices, values, attitudes and structures within an educational structure (Hargreaves, 2007). To put it another way, school principals across many different contexts are faced with a wide range of challenges because of the nature of the school environments in which they work (Walker and Dimmock, 1999). At the same time, such challenges, like those identified in the rest of this chapter, are in accord with what Fullan (2008) suggests are also opportunities through which school principals involved in education reform and leadership can learn about, and reflect on, their practices.

The challenges for school principals in Rwanda that are now presented have been distilled from interviews with practitioners identified as key informants because of their experiences of the nation's education system after the genocide and because they were accessible to the author. The author also visited 24 schools in diverse rural and semi-urban areas, interviewing principals both formally and informally. This assisted in attempting to sample for diversity rather than representativeness. Furthermore, when visiting Rwanda in 2007 and 2011, the author spoke with personnel at the Ministry of Education and at the Kigali Institute of Education, and with a cross-section of educators. Among the latter were two principals who, while themselves survivors, had lost family members during the genocide. Another had worked as a refugee principal in neighbouring Uganda and had returned after the genocide to assist in the rebuilding of his country. A fourth principal was a Catholic nun in a Catholic girls' secondary school. Another was a young principal of a boarding primary school in which the majority of students were genocide orphans.

Most of the principals interviewed were fluent in English, French and Kinyarwanda. All worked in extremely difficult circumstances characterised by a shortage of financial and material resources, poor water and sanitation, a lack of power supply, limited availability of text books and little access to professional development opportunities for themselves or the teachers in their schools. Most had also been thrust into leadership positions with little preparation and training. Despite these limitations, they tended to be visionary and were looking for ways in which their schools could enhance the vitality of the surrounding communities. Furthermore, while they had endured extreme hardship, grief, pain and trauma, they remained resilient. Overall, they demonstrated a tenacity to survive against great odds and rebuild the education system that had been so devastated during the genocide. In adopting such a disposition they were faced, as has already been pointed out, with five major challenges as school leaders, each of which will now be considered in turn.

Challenge one: running schools effectively with limited infrastructure and resources

Most schools, especially those that are in the government sector and located in rural areas, lack basic infrastructure and basic furniture, equipment and books, while many also have poor sanitation facilities. These circumstances are of great concern to principals. To make this observation is not to overlook the fact that UN agencies, international governments and non-governmental organisations fund economic, health and educational projects. It is important in the context of transitional societies that these organisations view long-term sustainable goals in education as a determinant for funding. In addition to external sources of funding, the Ministry is assisted in its work by such internal sources of funding as school fees, communal budgets, assistance from religious institutions and contributions from parental associations (Ministry of Education, 2010). The harsh reality, however, is that most schools function on minimal resources. Indeed, some schools in the poorer districts have no roofs, desks or chairs, and the majority of schools have little or no access to electricity or water.

The principal of a Catholic boarding school in Gitarama traced the origin of this situation back to the genocide, describing its impact on schools as follows:

> During the genocide there was massive destruction of schools, many teachers were killed and many went to live in exile. Many books were burnt and school furniture was also burnt or used as firewood. Although the government has repaired schools, all schools need further improvement and development of their infrastructure.

In similar vein, a rural school principal commented:

> The new government will have to support us for several years as no schools have sufficient material. There is still a lack of schools in many rural areas, especially secondary schools, and the government will have to build schools according to the school mapping exercise it undertook.

Trends, however, are in a different direction, with the Ministry of Education seeking to devolve financial responsibilities to schools and to parent–teacher associations.

The financial burden of school maintenance, provision of textbooks and, in some instances, even teachers' salaries, is carried by schools and their communities. One principal, struggling to look after his school and its boarding facility, made the following revelation:

> Most of the children in my school are unable to afford the fee-paying schools, as they are orphans. Sometimes I feel that as the children in my school are poor they have no hopes, except to become farmers, look after cattle or become drivers.

It is true that many private schools were established after the genocide. This, however, only succeeded in increasing social divisions based on wealth, connections and class. There is some concern, therefore, that 'quality' education is only available to members of the financial and political elite who can pay for it and that this is resulting in severe disparities in educational provision and quality between urban and rural areas. Over the nine years of basic education (NYBE), students do not have to pay fees, but they have to pay for uniforms, shoes and books. Also, with the introduction of the fee-free NYBE, teachers have experienced an increased workload, with an expansion in class sizes needing double-shifts that require them to teach both in the morning and in the afternoons.

Since 2007, primary schools have received from the Ministry of Finance, 2,500 Rwandan francs (US$ 4.30) per child in a monthly capitation grant to meet their operational costs, and an additional 1,800 Rwandan francs (US$ 3.10) per child to pay for contract teachers and teachers' allowances. The challenge across the sector now is to ensure that the Education Sector Strategic Plan (2010–15) is fully funded, so that the school component of the capitation grant will increase to a target of 6,000 Rwandan francs (US$ 10.50). Yet, even that amount will not be enough to meet the school needs of students and teachers. Concurrently, principals of local schools have to seek funds to run their schools, or to buy food and grain if boarders are in attendance. In other words, a major challenge for most principals is to run their schools effectively, while at the same time devoting considerable energy into exploring avenues to obtain financial assistance, support and resources for them.

Challenge two: advancing professionally without the opportunity for further learning, while also supporting the professional development of the teaching staff

Although professional development activities for school principals and teachers exist in Rwanda, they tend not to take into account the realities of school life. In-service training usually consists of 'one-shot' retraining courses, arranged in centres and run by educators who often have little understanding of the context, history or complexity of teaching and learning in a transitional environment. Also, very few schools in Rwanda have their own professional development plan. In this connection, a principal from a well-known rural, government school stated:

> There are no facilities for professional development at our school. Most teachers work individually. Many are not motivated and feel demoralised. Sometimes government salaries are not regular and we survive on contributions from the parent-teacher association (PTA). In this situation, can you expect us to upgrade our qualifications or improve our classroom teaching practices?

Indeed, it is not going too far to say that, in general, a principal of a Rwandan school is more of an administrator than a mentor, or initiator, of professional development activities. As one deputy principal commented: 'Teacher professional development does not exist in the school and teachers do not meet to exchange views or discuss pedagogical issues.'

This situation is compounded by the difficulties associated with the Ministry of Education's immense task of upgrading the skills and qualifications of more than 50 per cent of Rwandan teachers. While 97 per cent of primary school teachers are deemed to be qualified, the challenge is particularly daunting in the secondary school sector, where just 48 per cent of teachers (lower and upper secondary) are deemed qualified at the appropriate level. The Ministry of Education has reiterated a need to strengthen the professionalism and quality of primary and lower secondary school teachers through the development of an accreditation process for all teacher preparation programmes. The colleges of education and the primary teacher-training colleges will be affiliated to the Kigali Institute of Education, whose staff will work with them and with principals to incorporate learner-centred pedagogical approaches into the teacher preparation curriculum (Ministry of Education, 2010).

Most principals, however, reported that there is no money for the teachers to enhance their knowledge and skills, and no set professional development days. They also reported that teachers hesitate in assuming middle-management positions since there is no longer any release time, or other benefits, associated with undertaking these more onerous responsibilities. The situation is compounded by the decimation of the principal and teacher workforce that took place as a result of the genocide. Consequently, there is a critical need to obtain qualified teachers.

The responsibility for recruiting principals and teachers resides at the district level and school principals are themselves thrust into leadership positions without training, mentoring or support. This is not to ignore their expressed desire to advance their knowledge and skills. The problem, however, is that they are often unaware of associated opportunities. They perceive the obtaining of a scholarship for further study through the Ministry of Education to be a somewhat mysterious activity, rather than one depending on the choice, the knowledge or the ability of candidates. Some also see it as a matter of being well-connected to the decision-makers. In summary, then, a second major challenge for school principals is how to progress professionally and enhance their skills in the absence of monetary assistance, support and knowledge of clear pathways enabling this to occur.

Challenge three: meeting the Ministry of Education's goal of quality education, while the emphasis of schooling is on set examinations

The competitive nature of Rwanda's examination-driven curriculum places intense pressure on school principals, teachers and students, and fosters the promotion of a teacher-centered classroom. There is constant pressure to maintain high achievement scores, better the position of schools in national examination rankings, and improve student test results. Principals observed that teachers who are involved with examination classes are especially prone to this pressure. As a result of concentrating their attention on improving students' test scores, only very limited opportunities are provided for engaging in more enterprising approaches in the classroom.

School examinations are organised at the commune level in Rwanda and are controlled by the National Examination Board, resulting in the examination system being highly centralised. Ongoing internal assessment is not part of the grading process. Principals disclosed their concerns that the examinations promote rote learning and memorisation skills, and take precedence over extra-curricular activities. One principal summarised the situation as follows:

> My teachers who teach the examinations years intensively prepare the students, so that the students do well in exams. The students prepare by looking at questions in past papers. If needed, students come to school and are given extra tutoring even on Saturdays and Sundays. When students do well, the school gets a higher standing. Internal assessment is not part of the criteria at all.

In summary, then, a third major leadership challenge for principals at the school level is dealing with the emphasis in schooling on set examinations, while also attempting to meet the Ministry of Education's goal of providing quality education.

It would be remiss to move on at this point without also highlighting the associated challenge regarding the language of instruction. Kinyarwanda is spoken by all, and English and French are spoken by those who have been to school. French was both an official language of the government and a medium of instruction in schools before the 1994 genocide, and in the current national constitution there are three official languages: Kinyarwanda, French and English. Previously, a trilingual policy was adopted, with choice regarding the medium of instruction. However, with Rwanda's increasing involvement in international partnerships, including membership of the East African Community and the British Commonwealth, the government has considered it important to give priority to the development of literacy in English, which is seen as an important mechanism for trade and socioeconomic development, and as a gateway to the global knowledge economy (Ministry of Education, 2010).

Against this background, a new policy was implemented in 2009 to introduce English as the medium of instruction throughout the education system. This has led to a new configuration of languages: Kinyarwanda as the bedrock of initial literacy, the use of English as the new medium of instruction, and the teaching of French as the second language. The challenge for the education system is that current levels of English language proficiency amongst teachers are low and there is a shortage of textbooks and readers in English. All of this presents an additional complication for school principals, who have to find ways to improve their own English-language proficiency, both generally and in the specialist language of teaching and learning, and also to improve the proficiency of their teachers, since nearly all have themselves studied through the medium of French.

Challenge four: contributing to the design of a contextually relevant Rwandan curriculum

In 2006, when the new curriculum was being developed, principals were aware of what was happening, but had no preparation in the process of curriculum design and development that was used. Also, the majority of principals disclosed that they had no involvement in the process of curriculum design itself. Thus, while the new curriculum introduced notions of interdisciplinary and interactive teaching to schools, many principals considered the associated content to be of little relevance to the realities of post-conflict, land-locked Rwanda. On this, one principal, who was a survivor of the genocide, gave the following example:

> I would like the new history curriculum to discuss how the genocide affected and shattered people's lives and how the people of Rwanda have come to survive, reconcile and heal. I would like to explore and discuss local and national ethnic diversity, and for the curriculum to carry themes of national reconciliation.

Notwithstanding such concerns, there have been some encouraging developments. For example, in October 1996, two years after the genocide, the Ministry of Education added a subject known as *Civisme* (Civics) to the standard primary school curriculum. This subject includes education for peace, human rights and life skills. Furthermore, a project was undertaken in one region of rural Kigali aimed at recounting and constructing a memory of the genocide through reconciliation and democracy. In collaboration with the

Ministry of Education and the National Commission for Unity and Reconciliation, the project seeks to examine how the genocide can be used in teaching, and how survivors can meet with schoolchildren and relate their experiences (Aegis Trust, n.d.).

As principals of rural schools see it, it is also important that the curriculum be relevant to the local community and its circumstances. One principal commented on this as follows:

> It is important to connect the classroom to the community; this is a powerful concept that can work naturally for the villages in Rwanda. By connecting the classroom and community, principals, teachers and students can play a fundamental role in understanding one's community and can contribute to the appreciation of local culture, including the resolution of social issues that are excluded from the curriculum.

The curriculum is being revised to include new subjects, such as entrepreneurial skill development to enhance the employability of students once they leave school, as well as promoting positive attitudes towards gender equity, environmental issues, population and HIV/AIDS (Ministry of Finance and Economic Planning, 2007). Since joining the East African Community in 2008, the curriculum has also been reformed to align it with Kenya, Uganda and Tanzania, the other members of the Community. Currently, the National Curriculum Development Centre, in line with the education sector 2010–15 policy, is working towards forging a closer integration of curriculum development, quality assurance and assessment, improving teaching and learning, and establishing a system to monitor learning achievement and setting up district level 'schools of excellence' (Ministry of Education, 2010).

Principals, however, sometimes promote reform themselves. One especially visionary principal extolled the virtues of a particular initiative he had adopted entitled 'the compound approach', entailing engagement in projects that include schools, teachers, students and the community. An education specialist working for an international organisation commented on the efficacy of this initiative:

> I was one time at a school where the head teacher, working with teachers, had initiated a small scale rabbit rearing and hair salon project and the revenue from these income generating schemes was used to improve the feeding programme for afternoon lunches at the school.

The 'compound approach' links the students to the class, to the school compound, to their home, and then to the village in which they live. In this approach, a school can invest in nursery beds, a kitchen garden for growing produce, and poultry. Parents are encouraged to engage with the projects. In this manner, 'knowledge communities' can be established. Again, however, principals inclined to adopt such an approach face a fourth challenge, which is to exert more influence on the National Curriculum Development Centre in Kigali in order to make the curriculum as contextually relevant as possible for the students of Rwanda.

Challenge five: improving the status of the teaching profession and conditions of teachers

Fieldwork conducted over various periods in Rwanda has revealed that the average class size is over 55 students per teacher in primary schools, thus making the work of principals and teachers very demanding. As with school principals and teachers in several other post-conflict countries, they are also overworked, underpaid and regularly even unpaid for many months. Furthermore, the classrooms in which they teach are often overcrowded and under-furnished. For many principals, there is compensation in the provision of good housing. This is seen as an incentive, especially by those located in the rural areas and in schools with a boarding facility. However, they are then presented with the major challenge of having to provide, by some means, similar residential accommodation for teaching staff, recognising the influence it can have on teachers' motivation and morale.

Overall, living conditions for teachers in Rwanda leave much to be desired. As one principal commented:

> The government must pay teachers better salaries and improve our living conditions. Many teachers leave the profession or do other jobs to survive. Most of them take up tutoring after school to survive. In some ways their lives have worsened after the genocide, living conditions are expensive. We do not know what will await us tomorrow. We work day and night, yet we are totally dependent.

In reality, teachers have become the impoverished people in Rwandan society and many look for jobs in NGOs, or in the government ministries working as consultants. One teacher summarised the predicament he faced when he stated: 'by the time I finished my studies at the Kigali Institute of Education, everything had changed and being a teacher was not a profitable profession'.

A recent teacher motivation survey undertaken by the MOE reveals that teachers are increasingly concerned about job satisfaction and low motivation. This is attributed to poor remuneration and deteriorating standards of living compared to other professionals in the country with the same level of education. The government is currently engaged in a review with the objective of closing the increasing gap between the salaries of primary and secondary school teachers. Further, the Ministry of Education, through the Teaching Service Commission, plans to review minimum standards for teachers' work and living conditions, review workload and class sizes, encourage and promote public recognition of teachers and improve school and classroom facilities (Ministry of Education, 2010).

At the national level, a teachers' savings and credit scheme was established in 2009, with the Ministry of Finance providing a sum of 1 billion Rwandan francs (US $185,000) for teachers to get credit. The scheme has been opened to teachers across the country and is easily accessible to them. Teachers have also been provided with bicycles for transport. Much still remains to be done, however, including addressing the acute shortage of housing for most teachers, especially those in the rural areas. Clearly, the current rhetoric concerning the centrality of teachers to the country's development must translate into practical policies relating to the quality of pre-service and in-service education, teacher retention, salary incentives, and other types of support, if the profession is to attract and retain teachers.

Conclusion

Eighteen years after the genocide, Rwanda continues to rebuild itself, heal the wounds and address the basic rights to healthcare, education and security for Rwandan men, women and children. This chapter has revealed the challenges, resilience and hopes of principals as they struggle to succeed in their endeavours in the context of a transitional society. The challenges demonstrate that meaningful and sustained educational reform is interconnected with changes in the fabric of society. Examining the challenges has also revealed a powerful hope that rests on dedicated human agency (school leadership in this case). In spite of its difficulties, Rwanda today is more peaceful and prosperous, and its school leaders, teachers and students want it to improve.

The challenges identified in this chapter also have important implications for the pursuit of educational change and teacher development in Rwanda. Specifically, in bringing about sustainable leadership and development, the situation that confronts principals is the creation of a more fulfilling, successful and sustainable future in their schools. On this, they need to acknowledge the past and to learn from it, especially in relation to the enormous changes that have taken place in the education sector.

As illustrated by key informants, school principals in Rwanda fulfil important educational and community functions, the zone of their active involvement extending well beyond the classroom and the school. In the various contexts of their work and life (classroom, school, home and community), they exhibit different functions and operate as professionals within a complex social organisation. They need to pass on knowledge from one generation to the next through effectively-managed succession, and distribute this responsibility widely so that it is shared. The challenge for the Ministry of Education lies in initiating and implementing principal preparation, reorganising teacher preparation structures, creating more pedagogical institutes and improving remuneration of principals and teachers.

The challenges identified in this chapter can help facilitate reflection and discussion with personnel from the Ministry of Education. For example, one could highlight the necessity to create the space and capacity for generating the political will to empower principals. They need to ask: 'What can be done to engage and listen to principals' voices? Can we mobilise and empower principals to initiate change in their schools?' Answers to these questions can lead to the development of holistic and inclusive strategies aimed at improving schools and student outcomes. Finally, the challenges identified can stimulate thinking about the possibility of building better schools and offering quality education through dialogue, knowledge generation and action. It is acknowledged that there are gaps in our knowledge base, but by respecting and listening to the voices of school principals in the transitional nation of Rwanda, realistic goals can be set, and associated plans formulated and implemented.

Acknowledgements

I would like to acknowledge the invaluable contributions of a friend and colleague with first-hand knowledge of issues which have had an impact on education in Rwanda.

References

Aegis Trust (n.d.) *Nyamata Memorials Project: Education outputs.* http://www.aegistrust.org/projects/rwanda/pages/educate.htm (accessed 17 April 2003)

Bridgelenad, J., Wulson, S. and McNaught, M. (2009) *Rebuilding Rwanda: From genocide to prosperity through education.* Washington, DC: Hudson Institute.

Department of Health Services (2010) *Demographic and Household Survey.* Kigali, Rwanda: Department of Health Services.

Destexhe, D. (1995) *Rwanda and the Genocide in the Twentieth Century.* London: Pluto Press.

Earnest, J. (2003) Science education reform in a post-colonial developing country in the aftermath of a crisis: the case of Rwanda (unpublished Ph.D. thesis). Curtin University of Technology: Perth, Australia.

Eriksson, J. (1996) The international response to conflict and genocide: Lessons from the Rwandan experience. Report of the steering committee of the joint evaluation of emergency assistance to Rwanda. Copenhagen, Denmark: DANIDA.

Fullan, M. (2008) School leadership's unfinished agenda: Integrating individual and organizational development. *Education Week,* 27(31), 3–4.

Government of Rwanda (2002) *The 2002 Poverty Reduction Strategy Paper (PRSR) of the Government of Rwanda.* Kigali: Government of Rwanda.

Hargreaves, A. (2007) Sustainable leadership and development in education: Creating the future, conserving the past. *European Journal of Education,* 42(2), 223–33.

Mbabazi, J. (2012) *This is Your Time, Rwanda: The emerging story of a bold nation and its brilliant destiny.* USA: Mbabazi Rukeba.

Ministry of Education (1998) *Education Policy Statement.* Kigali: Ministry of Education.

Ministry of Education (2000) *Higher Education Sub-sector Policy.* Kigali: Ministry of Education.

Ministry of Education (2007a) *Education Sector Strategic Plan 2007–2011.* Kigali: Ministry of Education.

Ministry of Education (2007b) *Teacher Development and Management Policy.* Kigali: Ministry of Education.

Ministry of Education (2010) *Education Sector Strategic Plan 2010–2015.* Kigali: Ministry of Education.

Ministry of Education, Science, Technology and Scientific Research (2003) *Education Sector Policy.* Kigali: Ministry of Education.

Ministry of Finance and Economic Planning (2000) *Rwanda Vision 2020.* Kigali: Ministry of Finance and Economic Planning.

Ministry of Finance and Economic Planning (2007) *Economic Development and Poverty Reduction Strategy, 2008–2012: The Republic of Rwanda.* Kigali: Ministry of Finance and Economic Planning.

Obura, A. (2003) *Never Again: Education reconstruction in Rwanda.* Paris: UNESCO Institute for Educational Planning.

Walker, A. and Dimmock, C. (1999) Exploring principals' dilemmas in Hong Kong: increasing cross-cultural understanding of school leadership. *International Journal of Educational Reform,* 8(1), 15–24.

World Bank (2010) *Statistical Data for Rwanda: Country reports.* Africa Region. Washington, DC: The World Bank.

World Bank (2000) *Implementation Completion Report: First education sector project.* Rwanda: Human Development Unit, Africa Region. Washington, DC: The World Bank.

7 Kenya

School leadership and the 2007 post-election violence

Aqeela A. Datoo and David Johnson

Introduction

This chapter explores the role of school leadership in managing the effects of the 2007 post-election violence in Kenya that significantly altered the context of schooling. Although violence has been an unfortunate feature of Kenyan elections since 1991, the magnitude and impact of the episode in 2007 were unanticipated. Given the historical connection between politics and ethnicity in the country, the conflict further deepened the cleavages created between ethnic groups. For schools, the consequences of the post-election violence translated into a displacement of students and teachers, as well as the creation of an urgent need for trained counsellors, all in a context of very scarce resources. It also brought to the forefront the challenges of managing schools beleaguered by ethnic tensions, fear and prejudice. Notably, it created a perceptible shift in the role of principals and teachers. Traditional references to the 'climate of learning' were supplemented by terms such as 'peace' and 'conflict resolution', these becoming commonplace in the discourse used at teacher conferences and training initiatives run by churches, as well as in the implementation of life-skills education. Given the challenges that teachers and students continue to face years after the conflict and the increased demand for 'peace' and 'conflict resolution' in Kenyan schools, this chapter explores the nature of the leadership being provided at the school level to deal with the realities of post-conflict schooling.

In various studies conducted on improving the quality of education in developing countries, the role of leadership has been highlighted as essential for the improvement of schools. The ideal principal has been defined by his or her ability to provide teachers with adequate support in curriculum delivery as well as to manage the equitable allocation of resources in order to ensure equal access for all children (Dalin, *et al.*, 1994; Verspoor, 1989, 2008). The principal is envisaged as 'active, supportive, pedagogical and policy-oriented, who also communicates well with the community and the district office' (Dalin, *et al.*, 1994: 245). Ultimately, the main focus advocated for principals is to ensure that teachers 'do it right' and that they are supported and monitored appropriately.

In this chapter we argue that the unique context of post-conflict countries significantly alters the demands placed on school leadership. The climate of uncertainty in which schools function and in which school leaders operate calls for great flexibility on the part of principals. They are often seen as a source of stability and are expected to maintain the normal functioning of the school and an adequate flow of resources. Importantly, in contexts where communal relations are frail, the role of the principal can also be that of counsellor, mediator, negotiator; a rebuilder of severed interpersonal relationships. That is to say, the responsibilities of principals often go beyond their role as administrators, or instructional leaders, to one that calls for flexibility and receptiveness to the needs of the community, teachers and students.

The chapter draws on data gathered through semi-structured interviews with public secondary school principals and teachers in Nakuru and Kericho, both regions in Kenya that were affected by the conflict. Access to schools was established through a local NGO. In total, 90 interviews were conducted at 20 schools. These included an interview with each principal. An additional 30 interviews conducted with principals from Nakuru, Nyanza, Kisii, Bongoma, and Kericho have also informed the exposition presented in this chapter.

Exploring the context of Kenya

Kenya has maintained a unique association with violence since 1991, when a transition from a one-party system of government to multi-party democracy commenced. The widespread violence that was triggered became an almost staple feature during election periods. Yet, the magnitude of the violence witnessed in 2007 was unprecedented. Scholars on the politics of Kenya have offered numerous explanations for these waves of conflict. These are much too extensive to address within this chapter. Rather, we will focus briefly on some of the causes of the 2007 post-election violence, particularly the two most commonly cited root causes, namely, access to land and ethnocentrism/regionalism.

On 27 December 2007, the general elections began with the two main stakeholders being the Party of National Unity (PNU) headed by Mwai Kibaki and the Orange Democratic Movement (ODM) led by Raila Odinga. The electoral process was hotly disputed, as was the counting of votes. Nevertheless, three days later the Electoral Commission of Kenya announced Mwai Kibaki as the winner. Within hours violence broke out in areas that supported the opposition party, with demands for justice. Initially the violence remained spontaneous and the government responded by using security forces to disperse protestors. However, it soon spread and intensified in a shockingly systematic manner, while taking on ethnic undertones.

Kanyinga (2009: 340) asserts that politicians and business people planned and enlisted criminal gangs to execute violence. These gangs targeted Kikuyus and Kisiis in the Rift Valley for expulsion from the region. This was followed by revenge attacks by the Kikuyus, which saw the displacement of Kalenjins, Luhyas and Luos from Nakuru and Naivasha in the eastern region of the Rift Valley, as well as from Nairobi. Thus, while rigged elections presented themselves as an intense source of disagreement between both parties, the central causes of the intense violence must lie elsewhere given the strong ethnic undertones and systematic nature of the conflict. Several scholars have traced these back to historical disputes and the ethnocentric nature of politics in Kenya (Anderson and Lochery, 2008; Kanyinga, 2009; Roberts, 2009).

Access to land, specifically the rich farmland, tea estates and pastures for livestock in the Rift Valley, Western and Nyanza provinces, has been a relentless bone of contention between ethnic groups dating back to the colonial period. Before the British colonised the country, the Kalenjins, Maasai, Turkana and Samburu inhabited these fertile regions. However, British settlers ultimately seized these lands during colonisation. Prior to departing Kenya, a land settlement scheme was created in order to reallocate the land previously occupied by the British. The scheme was heavily criticised for favouring the Kikuyus, (Kenya's first president Jomo Kenyatta's own ethnic group), and the associated disparate distribution of farmland among Kenya's many ethnic groups (Klopp, 2002: 273). Decades of bitterness and rivalry regarding the rightful ownership of these fertile lands have not only bruised ethnic relations, but have also become an easy and fatal tool used by politicians to usurp power. For instance, in early 1992, Assistant Minister Kipkalia Kones, a Kalenjin, declared war on the Luo community, and declared Kericho District a KANU (Kenya African National Union) zone, warning any who opposed this development that they would 'live to regret it' (Oucho, 2002: 92).

Land continues to play an imperative role in politics in Kenya. Kantai summarises this affiliation well:

> Whoever controls land in Kenya can be said to control the nerve centre of political power. And if one group can wrest the control of land from the other groups and monopolise it, that group will dominate the other groups.
>
> (cited in Oucho, 2002: 111)

The constant tug of war between ethnic groups over fertile land in western Kenya, coupled with inciting comments by politicians, offer a credible rationalisation for a majority of the violence erupting in the Rift Valley. However, the nature of Kenyan politics has also rapidly deepened cleavages between ethnic groups. In the past, many politicians consistently turned to their own ethnic group, or other allied groups, to gain control over certain districts. Politicians then rewarded those who helped spread violence through illegal settlements on, or purchase of, non-Kalenjin owned land (Human Rights Watch/Africa Watch, 1993: 34).

Holmquist sums up the state of politics in Kenya well: 'the style of the leader [in Kenya]...is the ethnic and lineage-based constituency representative whose role is primarily as ambassador from a constituency and only secondarily as representative of government to the people' (Holmquist, 1984: 185) In 2007, the PNU party affiliated itself with the Kikuyus, whereas the ODM drew its loyalty from the Kalenjins, Luhyas and Luos. Preceding the elections of that year, the issue of land ownership was revived, with each party making declarations that favoured its own ethnic group. The ODM supported a federalist system (also referred to as Majimboism, which calls for the devolution of powers to each region of the country) in which devolution would be considered as a policy to enable administrative units to make decisions on their own regions (Kanyinga, 2009: 339). This position favoured the Kalenjins, who believed they would regain control of their land. PNU, however, was against this policy, stating it would lead to eviction and hamper national unity, thus indirectly favouring Kikuyus who were settled on those lands. The latter reasoning explains the methodical and forced displacement of ethnic groups from their homes and lands witnessed during the post-election violence. In terms of numbers, around 350,000 were internally displaced and roughly 1,200 were killed (IRIN, 2008). Ultimately, after 59 days of violence, the former United Nations Secretary-General, Kofi Annan, brokered a power-sharing deal that saw the creation of a coalition government, with Kibaki (PNU) as President and Odinga (ODM) as Prime Minister. By this time, however, the country's unity was strained and fissures in ethnic relations had intensified. These effects seeped into schools and not only presented challenges for their day-to-day management, but also altered the context of schooling in Kenya.

The effect of conflict on the context of schooling in Kenya

While the next section relates specifically to secondary schools, since they were the focus of the empirical study upon which this chapter is based, the issues raised apply equally to primary school education. Even though it was set up in 2008, free secondary school education in Kenya has yet to be fully established. While the government now shoulders students' fees and teachers' salaries, parents are required to pay for books, uniforms, food and school facilities. The decentralised education system, coupled with the role parents are meant to play in providing facilities, means that schools in lower economic regions struggle to provide the necessary resources for their students. Indeed, the role of principals in Kenya is most often defined by their need to acquire resources in order to assist teachers in examination preparation due to the emphasis placed both by parents and society more generally on examination results (Lydiah and Nasongo, 2009: 84).

The creation of numerous internally displaced persons (IDPs) because of the onset of conflict brought about an additional challenging situation when schools reopened in January 2008, following the post-election violence.

Owing to the influx of students, schools were either overcrowded, or under-staffed. This resulted in an imbalance in teacher–student ratios, as well as an increased strain on school resources. Teachers reported that it took anywhere from three to six months for many of the students to eventually return to their original schools. Also, many families chose to relocate permanently and often orphaned students remained in the schools to which they had escaped during the violence. As a result, a number of schools continue to labour under strained resources and a shortage of staff. Two principals in Nakuru provided statistics to illustrate the degree to which their schools were stretched:

> The IDP camp, it's not far from here, it's just around the corner. So you see, I had so many students coming in ... 90 IDPs and most of them girls. Now we still have 30 IDPs left, the rest slowly left and went back home.

> We had students who came from Eldoret, up in the north. Roughly around 80 students. On top of that, three of our teachers left. It was very difficult to manage the classrooms.

Also, most schools lacked sufficient professionally trained counsellors, with many having only one for the whole school.

A large number of students and teachers who experienced psychosocial trauma have continued to go undetected by the school system, particularly with regard to rape and sexual abuse. As one of the principals interviewed commented:

> Yes, I'm sure. In fact, I'm quite certain there are one or two [students who were raped during the violence]. But, you see, what can I do. If they don't come forward and tell us, what can you do. They don't talk you know. When they are ready, they'll tell us.

Given that schools are a reflection of the society in which they are located, they have not been immune to the penetration of ethnic tension, fear, aggressive behaviour and prejudice into their cultures. In interviews conducted with secondary school teachers in Nakuru and Kericho, many of them related their personal experiences of ethnic tensions and prejudice:

> I was at the supermarket and I bought four bags of groceries to stock up at home. When I was leaving, these people came and snatched away my bags, they took everything. I was so shocked. I have been living here most of my life and still they treated me this way. I ran for my car and locked the doors. Then this other man from my ethnic group came, and they went after him. I saw them stab his eyes with their knives ... it was so horrible, I will never forget that day.

I froze with horror. I couldn't believe she said those things when members of the other group from our school were standing right there. I couldn't even open my mouth.

Several teachers also mentioned how prejudiced behaviour and comments were commonplace in schools:

There's a lot of prejudice you see. People talk about certain groups in a certain way, and it's normal. Like those people are stupid, they don't know anything. You still hear such things in schools.

Moreover, fears between ethnic groups were still evident two years after the post-election violence and were heightened during the constitutional referendum elections in August 2010. The situation was described by one principal as follows:

I have a few teachers who experienced terrible things. They were so fearful when they came back. One eventually left and transferred to another school. The two that are left, I keep an eye on them to make sure they are ok. Now with the constitutional referendum elections coming, I see it already, they are fearful. They rarely come in the staff room and they've become quiet. It's like they're not completely here.

Because of such ethnic tension and fear, several teachers were able to obtain swift transfers from the Ministry of Education to different schools. This, however, created a further imbalance in teacher-student ratios.

Once the violence was quelled and schools returned to normal, directives offered by the Ministry of Education, churches and NGOs created a shift in discourses on learning in schools. NGOs and prominent members of society repeatedly stressed the inclusion of 'conflict resolution' in the curriculum. In 2009, the Minister of Education, Sam Ongeri, emphasised the need to implement peace education in schools in order to combat the effects of the post-election violence. This increased interest in 'peace' and 'conflict resolution' was accompanied by teacher preparation programmes organised by churches, and was aimed at preparing teachers to deal with the psychosocial effects of the conflict. Often these training sessions included a seminar on managing students who had experienced psychosocial trauma, as well as employing a learner-centred approach to teaching. The workshops also stressed the use of alternative methods of learning through the use of poems, stories, music and voluntary activities in educating students about peace, conflict resolution and unity.

This shift in the 'climate of learning' was highlighted when the Ministry of Education accelerated the implementation of a life-skills programme, initially begun in early 2007, before the outbreak of violence. The programme aims to equip students with skills to help them perform well academically, as well as in their personal life outside of school. The syllabus covers four main areas of skill building: entering teen years; building self-confidence and communication skills; managing emotions; and improving peer relationships. It requires that school subjects be taught using a learner-centred practical approach, with specific emphasis on role-play, discussion and reflection, and utilising such basic resources as newspaper clippings as well as the mandatory life skills workbook.

School principal responses to the effects of violence

As discussed previously, principals have continually struggled to obtain funds to equip their schools with the necessary resources in order to improve examination results. The displacement of families because of the post-election violence drained them of already scarce resources in this regard as most students were no longer able to pay the required fees. Initially, an official directive compelled schools to enrol displaced students. While this was understandable, as time passed the inability to pay fees became a serious cause for concern. In order to deal with this situation, a handful of principals created a barter system that benefitted both the families and their schools. As one principal commented:

> They couldn't give us the money because they lost so much. So, I told them to give me bricks. We wanted to build a kitchen at our school so we were getting the bricks and the child was able to come to school. Some other parents would give me maize. You see, they weren't able to sell the maize, so why let it sit and spoil . . . we can use it at the school to feed our children.

Not all principals who faced similar situations, however, were welcoming of this innovative approach. On being prompted as to why the barter system was unsuitable, most principals mentioned that schools simply did not function in a manner that supported its operation. As one stated:

> What could I do? He wasn't able to pay the fees. We need the money too. I sent him home. After two weeks he was back with a little money, so we let him stay for some time. Then again, we had to let him go.
> Paying with maize and beans? No this won't work, it just won't work. We also need the money – we're a school, we require fees and in return we give them a receipt.

To obtain such basic resources as clothes, desks, chairs, sanitary towels and food, principals sought out the assistance of local NGOs that were active and visible in the communities once the violence subsided. They also 'reached out' to community members for assistance, with many going door-to-door asking for help, a scenario described in the following comments.

Here we have a lot more girls and boys, so when I spoke to NGOs I was always asking for pads. The Red Cross provided me with so many boxes of just sanitary pads.

So many of them had no clothes. They lost everything. I used to go around the whole neighbourhood asking for clothes. Finally, I managed to fill up a whole room with clothes and distributed them to the students.

Resources were really stretched because we took in 155 IDPs on top of all the students we already had. Initially, the students used to be standing in the back of classrooms or sitting on the floors because there was no place to sit. Then, all of us [teachers and staff] gathered whatever resources and money we could manage with the help of local NGOs and our board of directors and built 60 benches. Each bench sat 8–10 students. It wasn't comfortable because they had to squeeze, but it was better than standing or sitting on the floor.

What was paramount for school principals was that they continued to be resourceful in order to keep their schools running in the aftermath of the violence.

Tackling the ethnic tensions, fear and prejudiced behaviour in schools has been particularly challenging for principals. Counselling sessions have been the preferred and primary response. Indeed, at each of the schools visited there was at least one session of counselling when the schools reopened. These were generally large group sessions consisting of all students and teachers. In rare instances, the sessions were conducted separately for boys and girls. However, very few one-on-one sessions were conducted due to the lack of trained staff.

In order to combat the lack of trained counsellors, many principals sent their school counsellor and a selected teacher for additional training offered by the NGOs and churches. However, as the following comments indicate, it was often the school counsellor rather than the principal who requested, in the first instance, more professional training to cope with the situation:

My counsellor actually hasn't had any training in counselling. When the violence happened and we were dealing with all these issues, the trauma, the fear, it was too much for her. So, I sent her and another male-teacher for training at the nearby church.

There were so many problems and the students were going through a really difficult time. I found out that my church was providing one-day workshops for teachers so I told my teacher to please let me go. At least we'll know how to handle this better. I even told him to send two more teachers with me. I can't handle all these students by myself.

A few principals did seek out the support and assistance of community members in dispelling tensions through parent teacher association (PTA) meetings, where they discussed how to deal with deteriorating ethnic relations. Two principals commented on this strategy as follows:

> You see, the parents, they are our eyes in the community. They tell us what is going on out there. At PTA meetings, we discuss these issues and we encourage the parents to continue working together and being there for us like we are there for them.

> My counsellor and I discussed how to deal with it. We then decided to speak to NGOs. She brought in this NGO called Youth Aid and they trained some of our students in peace and conflict resolution, and then these students went out and put on drama and songs for the community.

Such instances, however, were rare. Indeed, a great number of principals exhibited the notion that the school and community are separate entities, with each having little to do with the other.

The prevalence of tension was not limited to students and community members. It was also widespread and deep-seated between colleagues, creating an additional obstacle for principals as it impaired the efficient management of their schools. Most principals mentioned dealing with the issue through staff meetings. However, several of them also lamented that, given the gravity of the situation, the staff meeting was inadequate. This prompted a group of them to seek the assistance of professionally trained external counsellors, based on the rationale that their resident counsellors were ill equipped to manage the situation.

A number of principals also found themselves at the receiving end of written threats from staff. While only a small number of them were able to confront their teachers over these threats, most acknowledged, somewhat hesitantly, that they dealt with the issue passively. This they attributed to fears regarding their own safety, as well as to the lack of support from the Ministry of Education. On this matter, two principals expressed their feelings as follows:

> I told the teachers at the staff meeting about the pamphlet I received. Then I told them, 'We should live together in harmony. I am a Kenyan and I have a right to live in any part of this country. If you have a problem with me, then please come forward and speak to me personally.' None of them came forward.

> See, if I told the Ministry of Education to remove this teacher and send them somewhere else, I would have lost a teacher and when would I get the replacement? Already we have a shortage. It's a difficult situation.

The result, in many cases, was that the violence had a debilitating impact on the schools' internal culture.

During the constitutional referendum election in 2010, tensions and fears of violence began to resurface in communities. This caused some teachers to move to safer regions until the elections were completed and votes were counted. Several teachers noted an increase in heated political dialogue in schools and a few principals swiftly responded by barring it, as illustrated in the following comment:

> I was informed by my teachers that there had been some heated discussions. It's fine to talk about politics but when they bring in ethnicity into it, that your group does this and your group does that, it is not correct. I held a meeting and I warned them not to engage in such political talk. I won't have it, I don't need another post-election violence.

This tendency towards the politicisation of school culture represented a further challenge that school principals often encountered.

Along with the continued presence of ethnic tensions, fear and prejudiced behaviour, schools were also threatened by youth gangs, associated with the Mungiki terrorist group in Nakuru. A number of young male students joined these gangs during the post-election violence and while several admitted to leaving, many others remained affiliated. Some of these students continue to engage in hostile and aggressive behaviour at school. Most principals, in response, follow their school protocol. This often includes organising counselling sessions, involving parents, issuing suspensions and, in the event of continued aggressive behaviour, involving the police. Here, the experience of dealing with a particularly troublesome student is described:

> I had one student who my teachers kept complaining about. Some of these boys who are a part of the Mungiki, they go around threatening their classmates and teachers. I spoke to him, sent him for counselling but it didn't help so I suspended him for two weeks. When he came back, he had not changed. In fact, it was worse and the students had become really fearful. This time I called in the police to arrest him and then suspended him for the rest of the term. I allowed him back to take his KCSE [Kenyan Certificate of Secondary Education] but the police escorted him. I thought at least he'll have his KCSE, maybe he'll still have a chance.

However, this approach has been deemed unsuitable by a school in Nakuru located close to a stronghold of the Mungiki.

Several Form 4 boys in the latter school are members of the Mungiki and have threatened teachers when they attempt to break up fights between students. The principal at the school discussed the manner in which she handles the situation:

> One of my female teachers tried to break up a fight and this boy turned around and threatened her instead. What could she do? She just quietly

left. We try to calmly get the boys to see it our way but I don't like my female teachers getting involved. I tell the men to handle the situation. We manage, we show them respect and they show us respect.

The life-skills syllabus also presented an alternative solution to dealing with the situation. Implementing it, however, has presented an exceptional challenge for principals, mainly because of the lack of resources, external support and direction. Some schools have reported receiving training with no materials, whereas others have reported receiving the life-skills books, but are yet to receive training. For these reasons, a number of schools in Nakuru that have not yet received training have implemented their own version of the life-skills syllabus as a 'peace club', or as a subject to be taught on Saturdays.

Most principals have also experienced resistance to the life-skills syllabus from their staff. Similarly, a school counsellor recounted opposition to her efforts to implement the programme at her school:

I was trying so hard to implement the life skills, but some teachers just did not want it or like it. Finally, I had to tell the principal, you create the schedule and assign teachers. Only then did we finally manage to start this programme. She had to tell them why we were doing this and what was good about it.

Furthermore, there are even principals themselves who remain apprehensive about life-skills education, highlighting, as in the following quote, both time and resource constraints as points of contention:

They gave us these books, but I don't know what I'm supposed to do with them. They're sitting in my office, I don't know how useful this will be. We've already got so much to deal with, exams are coming up soon too. The students are supposed to get these life skills books as well. I don't know.

Schools in Kenya continue to face such persistent difficulties and are ill-equipped to manage the associated challenges.

Many principals boldly admitted to the latter observation, conceding they had forgotten what little training they had received in counselling during their pre-service preparation years. As a result of their own lack of awareness regarding the psychosocial effects of conflict, coupled with the scarcity of resources, of government-sponsored workshops, and of support from the Ministry of Education, associated issues continue to go undetected, or are overlooked. In addition, because of their own fears and their mindfulness of the prevalence of ethnic tensions in the community, many principals strive to move on from the post-election violence and seek to forget the past, despite the fact that many underlying and unresolved issues remain in the school environment and continue to resurface during periods of political action.

Implications for the role of principals in Kenya

It could be concluded from the discussion so far that while principals are making efforts to manage the effects of the conflict, they remain largely unprepared to deal with such psychosocial effects as ethnic tension, fear and prejudiced behaviour. Often, they lack awareness regarding the magnitude and nature of psychosocial trauma that their students and teachers have experienced. As a result, they are unable to provide the necessary leadership. In addition, their own fears and prejudices hamper the nature of the role they play in post-conflict schooling and they increasingly leave it to their school counsellors to handle the effects of the conflict.

On the other hand, principals are more active and determined in managing the strain placed on school resources as a result of the conflict. Traditionally in Kenya, the role of the principal, as already pointed out, has been defined by the need to acquire the necessary resources to manage schools and maintain standards in curriculum delivery. The primary focus both prior to the violence, and since, has been the need to obtain those resources deemed appropriate for improving examination results, as well as ensure equitable access to schools. This has diverted attention away from other equally important issues brought about by the incidence of conflict. Most notably, it has prevented principals from adapting to the needs of the communities they serve.

The altered context of schooling demands that school leaders be more flexible and innovative in managing the new climate in schools. For instance, the strain placed on school resources arising from the conflict stemmed not only from the displacement of families, but also from parents' loss of their livelihoods. In these precarious situations, where the event of conflict has lured youth gangs out into the open, it is imperative that principals retain as many students as possible, thus ensuring they are not vulnerable to recruitment by the gangs. Some principals, as has already been pointed out, have demonstrated an ability to create innovative ways of gathering resources through a barter system. Others, however, continue to maintain the traditional approach of collecting school fees. A consequence of this is that students may have to leave a school until their parents are able to obtain the appropriate fees. The barter system, on the other hand, does create a unique opportunity for schools, guaranteeing that both parents and the schools involved are not at a loss. By enhancing the flexibility of school leadership in such ways, principals can maintain the flow of resources in a climate of uncertainty.

A majority of principals interviewed did not sufficiently involve the wider community in dealing with the challenges and obstacles occurring in the wake of violence. This is unfortunate since, in the event of conflict, when interpersonal relationships are frail, the support provided by community members for the maintenance and enhancement of schools can aid in countering the fear and prejudice that may seep into communities. Parents and family members can play a major role in reinforcing values and skills taught in schools. Similarly, schools can play a role in imparting knowledge regarding peace and conflict resolution to community members. On this, some principals did acknowledge that by strengthening the channel of communication between parents and teachers, it may be possible to increase a sense of unity and common purpose. They constituted a small group who were quick to note that their strong links to the community aided in safeguarding them and their schools during the conflict.

Principals in post-conflict situations like Kenya, it is arguable, must also place an increased focus on strengthening their ties with the churches and NGOs. Given the role churches play in Kenya and the importance of religion amongst the population, schools often enjoy a healthy relationship with them. It should not be overlooked that most principals send their teachers to workshops hosted by churches. Similarly, schools in Kenya maintain a relatively beneficial relationship with local NGOs. Indeed, it is evident that those principals who continue to maintain strong ties with NGOs are knowledgeable about, and committed to, peace and conflict resolution. They also often display an empowered attitude in relation to managing ethnic tensions and strive for a focus on national unity. To sum up, in situations where teachers are confounded by difficulties in comprehending and managing the psychosocial effects of violence, their ties with churches and NGOs can offer a valuable source of encouragement and support.

Conclusion

The research informing this chapter that was conducted with school principals in Kenya indicates the positive effect they can have on the culture of their schools. In instances where principals were motivated to engage in peace and conflict resolution, teachers were likely to follow suit, and displayed a sense of eagerness when discussing the relevant issues. Similarly, principals who were keen to create bridges with the community were likely to supervise teachers who encouraged projects that involved students displaying their songs and artwork about peace to the members of the community. All of this points to the importance of promoting endeavours aimed at improving the quality of school leaders to enable them to deal successfully with the effects of violent conflict.

Previous studies on the role of school leadership in improving the quality of education in 'normal' contexts ascribe an administrative and instructional role to principals. In other words, their primary focus is seen to be one of managing resource allocation, ensuring equitable access to schools, and maintaining standards of curriculum delivery. The context of post-conflict countries, however, requires us to rethink such roles and move towards a more flexible and innovative approach to enhancing the school climate in war torn, or conflict-affected, schools.

Of primary importance in both developing countries and conflict-affected and fragile states is the need for training in flexible and innovative approaches to the use of resources for maintaining schools. We have shown how principals have had to adapt to the altered circumstances of communities to acquire the necessary resources. Particularly instructive in this connection is the bartering system. It offers a plausible solution to the financial strains placed on both parents and schools. Parents can pay school fees through an exchange of such essential school materials as wood, bricks and food products for tuition, thus upholding their side of accountability guarantees relating to the education of their children.

Management of a climate of uncertainty by principals is also important. In countries affected by conflict, schools are often blighted by a lack of essential materials and, concurrently, by directives from the government to meet new expectations. In such contexts of uncertainty, it is essential that principals should be able to develop and work with the obstacles and challenges they face. For instance, recognising that life-skills education could not be implemented with fidelity, but then adapting it through the development of peace clubs outside of the formal school setting, was an innovative approach used by a number of principals when they were provided with the relevant books, but not training. While the adoption of such an approach does not aim to lessen the responsibility placed on governments, it does assist schools in providing the best possible education for their students while waiting for the government to make better provision.

It is also clear that principals in a country where ethnic tensions continue to fester, should play a part in countering fear and prejudice. Countless schools in Kenya reported a prevalence of ethnic tensions and fear between colleagues, yet little action was taken to diffuse this situation. Accordingly, fear and distrust continue to seep into schools during periods of political activity. It is imperative, therefore, that principals be assisted in building positive relationships between teachers and community members, and strengthening their unity. They also need to be equipped to manage interpersonal relationships in such a way that they develop a strong support network that can aid in enhancing the school climate. For instance, by strengthening ties with neighbouring schools, churches and NGOs, and exchanging skills and knowledge with each other, it is possible for principals to go some way towards filling the void created by a lack of resources and a lack of support from the District Education Office.

The culture of schools in post-conflict societies and the role of school leadership required for such schools are unique. Therefore, principals must be supported in gaining the knowledge, skills and dispositions to adapt accordingly. We do not argue that the focus of school leadership must be exclusively drawn away from ensuring equitable access, resource allocation and curriculum delivery. We do maintain, however, that because the immediate and persistent challenges principals face in post-conflict schooling are distinctive, their role in accomplishing such goals can be approached by reorienting their focus on adapting to the climate of post-conflict schooling. This can be achieved by increasing flexibility and innovation, building interpersonal relationships, and creating support networks.

References

Anderson, D. and Lochery, E. (2008) Violence and exodus in Kenya's Rift Valley, 2008: Predictable and preventable? *Journal of Eastern African Studies*, 2(2), 328–43.

Dalin, P., Ayono, T., Biazen, A., Dibaba, B., Jahan, M., Miles, M. B. and Rojas, C. (1994) *How Schools Improve: An international report*. London: Cassell.

Holmquist, F. (1984) Class structure, peasant participation and rural self-help. In J. D. Barcan and J. Okumu (eds) *Politics and Public Policy in Kenya and Tanzania*. New York: Praeger Publishers, pp. 171–97.

Human Rights Watch/Africa Watch (1993) *Divide and Rule: State-sponsored ethnic violence in Kenya*. New York: Human Rights Watch.

IRIN (Integrated Regional Information Networks) (2008) Kenya: Resettlement of IDPs begins in Rift Valley. http://www.irinnews.org/IndepthMain.aspx?InDepthID=68&ReportID=78060 (accessed 16 May 2010).

Kanyinga, K. (2009) The legacy of the white highlands: Land rights, ethnicity and the post 2007 election violence in Kenya. *Journal of Contemporary African Studies*, 27(3), 325–44.

Klopp, J. M. (2002) Can moral ethnicity trump political tribalism? The struggle for land and nation in Kenya. *African Studies*, 61(2), 269–94.

Lydiah, L. M. and Nasongo, J. W. (2009) Role of the headteacher in academic achievement in secondary schools in Vihiga District, Kenya. *Current Research Journal of Social Sciences*, 1(3), 84–92.

Oucho, J. O. (2002) *Undercurrents of ethnic conflict in Kenya*. The Netherlands: Brill.

Roberts, M. J. (2009) Conflict analysis of the 2007 post-election violence in Kenya. http://www.ndpmetrics.com/papers/Kenya_Conflict_2007.pdf (accessed 20 July 2009).

Verspoor, A. M. (1989) *Pathways to Change: Improving the quality of education in developing countries*. Washington, DC: World Bank.

Verspoor, A. M. (2008) The Challenge of learning: Improving the quality of basic education in sub-Saharan Africa. In D. Johnson (ed.) *The Changing Landscape of Education in Africa*. Oxford: Symposium Books, pp. 13–44.

8 Solomon Islands

Adaptive leadership strategies in schools

Jack Maebuta

Introduction

Solomon Islands, a developing nation comprising an archipelago of 922 islands, is a sovereign state in Oceania and a member of the British Commonwealth of Nations. The archipelago is made up of six large islands and many other smaller islands and atolls. The total land area is 28,369 square kilometres (Stanley, 1993). A Spanish navigator, Alvaro de Mendaña, was the first European to arrive in the islands, in 1568, and he christened them *Islas Salomon*. In 1893, the United Kingdom established a protectorate over the islands. Fierce fighting between the Americans and the Japanese took place here during the Second World War. Self-government was achieved in 1976 and two years later Solomon Islands became an independent constitutional monarchy.

Given the geographical isolation of the islands, accessibility is a major obstacle to development, and isolation and remoteness make it difficult for rural dwellers to gain access to efficient education and health services. In 2004, the latest year for which statistics are available, it was estimated that the population had exceeded 500,000 (Moore, 2004) and it was expected to double in the following 25 years. The increasing population growth has already outpaced economic output, exerting escalating pressure on the economy and government resources. This has created major problems for the government in its capacity to meet the needs of the poorer sectors of society as equitably as possible.

There are also problems associated with ethnic conflict. If not accustomed to staying abreast of developments in the South Pacific, one could be excused for assuming that the archipelago reverted to being a sleepy tropical backwater after the Second World War and has continued to be so until now. To make such an assumption, however, would not be correct because towards the end of the twentieth century Solomon Islands became embroiled in turmoil once again, though this time because of internal forces. The outcome has been terrible damage to the people, to their economy and to national cohesion. Schooling has also suffered.

This chapter opens with an outline of the recent ethnic conflict that has taken place in Solomon Islands. It goes on to describe some aspects of schooling during the period of conflict, before examining current challenges for school leaders arising out of this context, as well as strategies being adopted.

The ethnic conflict

Since independence, Solomon Islands has experienced many political, economic and social changes. For some time prior to the late 1990s, there were indications that community relationships were breaking down, crime levels were rising, certain sectors of society were experiencing alienation, unemployment was rising and significant disparities were appearing between income levels. The strength of local community ties was also coming under threat as a result of increasing urbanisation. Furthermore, as environmentalists began to point out, the nature and scale of the exploitation of the country's natural resources and the degradation of the environment were emerging as major problems.

Tension and discontent materialised, in particular, on the island of Guadalcanal, the location of Honiara, the national capital. From colonial days, this island has hosted wave after wave of migrants from other parts of Solomon Islands, especially from the densely-populated island of Malaita. One result was that ethnic tensions between local Guadalcanal people and settlers from Malaita built up over many years, with the locals being very concerned about the impact on their culture of the 'outsiders'. These tensions eventually spilled over in 1998, when a militant Guadalcanal group, which termed itself the Isatabu Freedom Movement (IFM), began a campaign of violent intimidation of settlers from Malaita.

As the campaign escalated, at least 15 people were killed and over 20,000 Malaitans fled their homes in rural, semi-developed parts of Guadalcanal. Some returned home to their own island, others moved to Honiara, and others, yet again, sought refuge in the interior of Guadalcanal. They then retaliated, forming themselves into the Malaita Eagle Force (MEF). They raided police barracks to seize arms, took control of Honiara, and engaged in combat with the IFM around the city, across Guadalcanal and in neighbouring islands. Between June 1999 and July 2003, a number of peace initiatives were undertaken. These included a government-funded public reconciliation feast, a Commonwealth-initiated Honiara peace accord, the Buala peace accord, the Townsville Peace Agreement (TPA), the Anglican Church of Melanesia's peace negotiation and the Australian-led multilateral Regional Assistance Mission to the Solomon Islands (RAMSI – mentioned in more detail below).

In 2000, the Australian and New Zealand governments assisted in negotiating a ceasefire between the militant groups. Following meetings in Townsville, Queensland, between the various parties, the provincial governments of Malaita and Guadalcanal, and the central government, the Townsville Peace Agreement (TPA) was signed. This Agreement established the framework for working towards peace by establishing the Solomon

Islands' Peace Monitoring Council (PMC) and an International Peace Monitoring Team (IPMT) of police and civilians from Australia, New Zealand and Pacific Island Countries. Progress, however, was limited since the militants held on to many of their weapons, lawlessness continued around Honiara and the industrial economy was at a standstill.

In 2003, the Australian government, invited by the newly-elected Solomon Islands' government, tried again by leading the multilateral Regional Assistance Mission to Solomon Islands (RAMSI). A consequence of this initiative was that more than 2000 police and soldiers from many member countries of the Pacific Islands Forum landed in the country and set about restoring law and order. Of all the peace initiatives undertaken, this was the one that hastened the return of the rule of law. Investor confidence was then restored and donor activity recommenced. The other initiatives were either partly successful or not successful at all because the adversaries in the conflict, particularly the militant leaders, had not been involved in them.

Schooling during the ethnic conflict

During the conflict I was serving as a deputy principal in one of the secondary schools in Honiara. Therefore, like many other school leaders, I experienced the effects of the conflict in my day-to-day work. In my school, as in many others, particularly on Malaita and Guadalcanal, access to education during the conflict was severely constrained. In Malaita, the mass influx of children from Honiara stretched an already struggling education system beyond capacity. Many of the extra children could not be accommodated in the rural schools. Indeed, a survey carried out in September 1999 (Kudu, 2000) showed that 41 per cent of children on Malaita were not in school. Also, at the time of the conflict, primary and secondary school enrolments in Guadalcanal and Honiara declined as students were harassed and intimidated by militants (Kudu, 2000: 1).

In some parts of Honiara, schools continued to function normally. In other parts of the city the school day occasionally finished early. There were also temporary closures because of outbreaks of violence. However, beyond the capital, in the surrounding rural areas, the conflict was more dramatic. In these areas considerable physical and emotional violence was experienced. Schools closed for long periods and, in some cases, closed altogether. Away from the battle areas it was perhaps the length of the conflict rather than its intensity that made an impact. Continual uncertainty about what would happen next and how long the conflict would last produced fear among school leaders, teachers, students and parents. One principal in Honiara reported that his school was experiencing the presence of armed militants around the school compound. The militants allegedly told him that they were providing security for the school's protection. In reality, however, they were using the school compound as a meeting place. Eventually, the school was closed until the militants moved out of the area.

Many teachers continued teaching, but were fearful for their personal safety. Most fears stemmed from where they were teaching, and whether their particular ethnicity put them in danger. In the schools, many felt the need to remain neutral in order to reassure the children that all was well. One teacher commented on this as follows:

> I really pretended to the children that everything was ok. But, you know, the children kept telling me, 'Teacher, I'm scared'. They were telling me all sorts of things and I said, 'No, nothing will happen to us'. I just tried my best to tell them all the good things.
>
> (cited in Burnet and Dorovolomo, 2008: 13)

Sustaining children's motivation in their learning under such conditions was also difficult. Some teachers claimed they developed creative learning activities to keep the children interested. On this, one teacher stated:

> Even though we were going through the conflict, I tried to do things that would attract students – interesting things. Because if you just stand in front of the blackboard and talk they can't listen, they can't concentrate so I have to get them doing things [playing educational games] to stop them looking outside.
>
> (cited in Burnet and Dorovolomo, 2008: 13)

Such observations highlight the adverse impact of conflict on schooling, particularly in terms of the suffering and psychological effect on the students, teachers and communities, as well as in the deterioration of the education system and its infrastructure. Some students suffered such psychological trauma that they refused to attend school. Consequently, student enrolments dropped drastically and there was an increase in the numbers failing in the national examinations. It is to these matters that attention is now turned.

Student enrolment

It is estimated that during the conflict the total student enrolment in primary schools was 83,000 (Pollard, 2005). Pollard further noted that 33,650 children between six and fifteen years of age were not attending school. At the secondary school level, it was estimated that in 2001 the enrolment stood at 23,000. Analysis of students' enrolment data reveals that at the height of the conflict 42 per cent of primary school students were unable to continue on to secondary school. Of those entering secondary school, 60 per cent progressed to year 10 and 11. After year 11, only 27 per cent were able to progress to year 12. A number of education reports pointed to the fact that less than 10 per cent of students completing primary school education were likely to proceed to the end of secondary school education.

Two key factors contributed to the varying participation rate in schooling. First, much of the upward mobility in the education system depends on students' success in public examinations at different levels. As a result of the conflict, students at school in Honiara, Guadalcanal and Malaita were not allowed to sit the national examinations. Those students who had moved from the conflict-stricken areas to the outer islands were able to sit for them, but because they had been psychologically traumatised they did not perform well. As a result, the Ministry of Education gave permission for schools throughout the country to allow students who failed their exams between 2000 and 2003, to repeat them.

Second, there was the impact of physical isolation. For many children, attending primary school involves waking up early in the morning and walking long distances. This situation is demotivating for young primary school children at the best of times. For some, it may mean leaving home and residing with friends or relatives in the village where the school is located, an arrangement that has proved to be a difficult challenge for young children who still need the close attention of their parents. These circumstances, however, were greatly exacerbated during the conflict. Indeed, most parents in the conflict zones refused to send their children to school as it was considered that their safety would be at risk in attempting to walk there.

Furthermore, some boarding schools on Guadalcanal, especially those outside of Honiara, were required to close to ensure the safety of their students. For instance, one school in West Guadalcanal was targeted by militants because students from the conflicting parties were in attendance. The militants set up a roadblock so that access to the school became impossible. This prompted the government to evacuate the students to Honiara, under the protection of an Australian naval boat.

Difficulties in teaching and learning

Despite the difficulties noted already, many school leaders persisted in ensuring that the education of the students would not be completely abandoned. One of the difficult tasks most schools faced at the time was dealing with disruption to the teaching of the curriculum, especially as various topics on the syllabus tended to be inadequately covered. The difficulty arose as most teachers left their schools for their home islands because they feared for their personal safety. Schools were instructed to monitor the situation and to advise students and teachers to leave voluntarily should they feel at risk. This situation left most schools in the conflict areas with very few teachers. As a result, affected schools were forced to suspend many classes and concentrate their attention on teaching the examination groups.

For those schools that were closed completely, examination classes were taught in another location. For instance, the students who were evacuated to Honiara from West Guadalcanal were accommodated in a Honiara school and their teachers continued to teach those who were preparing for their examinations. The priority in teaching and learning at that time was to coach the students by going through examination papers from previous years. I remember one teacher in 2000, speaking to me as follows:

> I gave my Form Three (Year 9) students a lot of practice on the past years' papers because there is a possibility one of them will be used again this year as the Ministry of Education has been distracted by the conflict and does not have the time and resources to write a new exam for this year.

For those schools in the outer islands, the conflict also resulted in the unavailability of many curriculum materials.

At the time of the conflict, a new English language curriculum was being implemented, but there was a misappropriation of government funds caused by the demands of the militants. This resulted in all of the basic services in the country, including those of education and health, being under-resourced. As a consequence, the implementation of the new curriculum, particularly the financing of curriculum workshops for teachers' professional development, was affected. In fact, curriculum materials were often sent to schools without any induction taking place and teachers were confused as to how to use them.

Teachers

As schools continued in a determined manner to manage the adversities generated by the conflict, they were also confronted with the human realities of survival. While teachers continued teaching, they became very demoralised by the non-payment of their salaries, being forced, in some instances, to pursue other means of earning an income. Unfortunately, the Ministry of Education has also not been able to keep accurate data on teacher demand and supply. The conflict disrupted the normal posting of teachers to schools, which resulted in inconsistent teacher mobility (in 2001 it was estimated that about 4,000 teachers were in the field). The conflict determined that the delivery of teachers' fortnightly salary became irregular and many had to leave school to visit their provincial education office to obtain their money. The non-payment of teachers' salaries mounted up (Burnet and Dorovolomo, 2008). It became evident that the problem had arisen because the government introduced a compensation fund to compensate people who had lost their property in the conflict. Many people made false lost-property claims and the economy became crippled. Consequently, the government was unable to provide basic social services, equip hospitals and clinics with essential medical supplies and pay its employees' wages.

Teachers who failed to receive their salaries saw no prospects in teaching, so a number of them left the profession in search of employment in the private sector. The worst hit were those female teachers who were the only income earners in their family. It was common for teachers to turn up at a bank only to be told that there was no pay. In my own school, the school committee decided that teachers should take over the management of the school canteen so that profits could be shared among teachers to help them when their salary was not paid.

In some of the worst affected schools the situation was even more severe. Again, Burnett and Dorovolomo, have reported:

> In some cases life became impossible and teachers were forced to find alternative means of income, particularly those with families. Some insisted that children bring in money, others turned to fishing or garden-ing to support their families. Sometimes classes were dismissed early to enable teachers to engage in other activities.
>
> (2008: 26)

Such was the demoralisation of teachers caused by the non-payment of salaries that some joined the militia groups. Burnett and Dorovolomo have cited the comment of one principal on this issue:

> The Malaitan male teachers got involved in the tension, they joined [the militia] groups, because of the salary problem, it was like six fortnights, if I can remember, we didn't get our salary.
>
> (p. 26)

As the conflict continued, the situation became unbearable for school prin-cipals. In particular, schools were unable to solicit advice from the Ministry of Education and their provincial education authorities. Instead, they made their own decisions within the constraints presented by limited resources.

Management and administration

Managing a school during any period of major conflict is difficult as schools invariably become dysfunctional (Bretherton, Weston and Zbar, 2003). In the case of Solomon Islands, management of finances has been a longstand-ing problem in many schools. As the non-payment of teachers' salaries continued, a good number of school leaders opted to loan school funds to teachers, with the intention that after they received their salary they would reimburse the school. Some schools allowed their teachers to make repay-ments by instalments. While this arrangement seemed to work well, principals and senior teachers in several schools were suspected of misappro-priating school funds, while blaming the situation on teachers who had left teaching without fully repaying what they owed.

The management and administration of the individual schools within Solomon Islands is vested in school principals. When it comes to infrastruc-ture development, the principal has to consult with the community through the school committee so that community-based decisions are made on school development projects. School leadership teams do not have full autonomy to manage schools. They can only make decisions on routine issues, while the major decisions are made in consultation with the provincial education office. During the conflict, this line of authority was disrupted and the Ministry of Education and Provincial Education Authorities offered little advice to schools. Decision-making relating to the conflict, therefore, tended to take place at the school level, thus giving individual schools greater autonomy. Also, some schools advised their teachers 'not to mention anything about the conflict' (Burnet and Dorovolomo, 2008: 23).

Given the absence of support from central authorities, some school communities began to work together much more than had been their practice previously. For instance, teachers and communities supported each other by donating food and money. This indicated that the schools could continue to function in difficult situations without bureaucratic support. On the other hand, communities in districts with multi-ethnic schools were fearful that ethnic violence might break out if community-organised activities such as a school fundraising drives were held, and so they put a stop to such community gatherings.

Schooling in the post-conflict environment: leadership challenges and strategies

The education system in Solomon Islands is largely examination-driven. Because a school's performance is judged mainly by students' pass rates in the public examinations, teachers spend most of the available instructional hours coaching students to pass; an approach to teaching that has forced many students to drop out of school. The most disadvantaged by the system are girls. A recent report released by the Ministry of Education demonstrates that while girls' access to education at all levels has improved, their dropout rate remains high (Puia, 2011). The most notable attrition takes place at the secondary school level. Of the total enrolment in the junior secondary level, 46 per cent are girls, while in the senior secondary level, 39 per cent of the total enrolment is girls (Puia, 2011).

Because the number of students dropping out of the system every year is on the increase, the government has attempted a number of reforms. The main thrust of what is taking place is to make education more relevant to the needs of students and the country. At the same time, it is important to note that there is nothing new about these initiatives; reform along such lines was influenced by the *Education for What?* report of 1973 (Bugotu, 1973), in which Bugotu recommended a vocational-based curriculum for self-reliance. This reform, however, was not successful because parents still favoured an academic-based education for their children.

As the educational challenges of Solomon Islands continue, so too does the search for alternatives to established practice. After the conflict, a national education reform was undertaken resulting in the adoption of a national education framework in 2008. The framework specifies outcome-based education (OBE) as one of the guiding philosophies for Solomon Islands' curriculum (Ministry of Education and Human Resources Development, 2008). It is envisaged that by using an OBE approach, the curriculum and syllabus of all subjects will lead to a realisation of the expected outcomes. Emphasis is placed on the learners learning and achieving the expected outcomes. In particular, it is emphasised that learners should acquire knowledge, understanding, skills, values and attitudes that will be useful for them in later life. It is too early, however, to judge the effectiveness of the OBE approach and the extent, if any, to which it is helping to overcome the problems inherent in an educational system still dictated by examinations.

Currently, the education system in Solomon Islands consists of primary schools and three different categories of secondary school, namely, the community high school, the provincial secondary school and the national secondary school. Most resources are devoted to the national secondary schools, followed by the provincial secondary schools. The community high schools, which constitute the majority of secondary schools, continue to have few qualified teachers, as well as having to contend with a dearth of resources, and generally have a lower status than the national and provincial secondary schools (Ministry of Education and Human Resources Development, 2005). The primary schools have the lowest level of resourcing of all.

The ethnic conflict, while under control, also continues to have consequences for schooling. They include low and uneven access, high levels of school dropouts, low standards of achievement, problems associated with lack of curriculum relevance and an examination system that pushes students out of the school system. The government has responded to these challenges by means of an education sector investment and reform program and a framework to guide policy strategies until 2015. The remainder of this chapter now examines the realities of the post-conflict challenges and the strategies adopted for dealing with them, particularly with regard to the curriculum, student enrolment, staffing, resources, management and administration, and community support.

School curriculum

There have been several improvements in the curriculum in each type of school to make it relevant to the post-conflict context. Many Solomon Islanders believe that the conflict could be repeated if peace is not built on a strong foundation (Ministry of Education and Human Resources Development, 2008). The school curriculum is seen as being one contributor to building such a strong foundation. This has led to the inclusion of a peace strand within the junior secondary school social studies curriculum. The strand in question is focused on community conflicts and peace building, with the aim of helping students to understand the dynamics of conflict and peace building in their own communities. According to Danesh, 'the notion of peace-based curriculum demands a total reorientation and transformation of our approach to education with the ultimate aim of creating a civilisation of peace' (2006: 62). It is now time, he argues, to introduce radical change into our curriculum approaches if the world is to move away from a culture of war. Principals in Solomon Islands are endeavouring as best they can to make this a reality. Given the cultural diversity in the nation, the challenge they face is to help each school to contextualise the teaching of peace in its own community so that learning becomes more meaningful to students, and helps them to understand conflict and work out non-violent resolutions (Adele, 2009; UNESCO, 2003).

A particularly interesting initiative has been instigated by the government and the Solomon Islands Football Federation (SIFF) in trialling a 'Learn and Play Project' in three secondary schools in the country. The project aims to provide secondary school education and football training for disadvantaged rural boys and girls. Currently there are 360 rural students who are primary school dropouts and do not have an opportunity to further their education in the formal system. Through the project, they are able to continue their secondary school education, while also undertaking football training and coaching.

As part of national extra-curricular activities, schools have also been participating in national peace festivals aimed at creating a culture of peace among school children. This initiative is organised under the aegis of a 'national kids football, cultural exchange, and education festival'. Along with playing soccer, schools are engaged in cultural exchange by way of showcasing their traditional dances and arts. In the case of students attending most provincial schools, this gives them their first opportunity to visit the capital city, Honiara. It is deemed educational for them to visit the government ministries, the national parliament and other national institutions and organisations. Schools have applauded the festival and commented that it has inculcated in students a sense of national identity and social cohesion (Maebuta, 2011).

Though such strategies are crucial for making the curriculum relevant in the post-conflict era, the vocational options within the school curriculum are not given the priority they warrant by those living in a rural and primarily subsistence-based society. Many students treat the vocational subjects as options applicable only to those with a low academic performance. Furthermore, teachers continue to concentrate their efforts on coaching students to pass examinations. This practice is likely to continue producing school leavers who lack necessary life skills (Pollard, 2005) and contradicts the OBE-based prescribed curriculum, in which the emphasis is placed on acquiring skills, knowledge and values related to living in the local community.

Student enrolment

Another post-conflict educational challenge is presented by increasing student enrolments. Internally displaced persons and returnees are flocking into the urban centres, resulting in substantial congestion in urban schools, especially in the capital city. This trend commenced after the arrival of RAMSI to restore peace and maintain law and order. Many people are confident that RAMSI's presence means they are now safe living in Honiara.

The challenge of increasing student enrolments has placed particular demands on educational planning at a time when organisational capacity and resources are constrained, necessitating flexible approaches to planning and greater reliance on local initiative. However, on-going disputes over the land on which many schools are built have made it difficult to construct more classrooms. In dealing with this matter, some schools use community church buildings as classrooms during school hours. Others have built temporary classrooms in whatever little space they have in the school compound.

In community high schools, those in the lower primary school classes finish at 12:00 noon, enabling some upper primary school classes and secondary school classes to then start the school day in the vacated class-rooms, and they finish around 5:00 pm. For those schools where these strategies are not feasible, the number of teaching periods per day has been reduced. In secondary schools, the number of contact periods has typically been nine per day, each of 45 minutes duration. Thus, to accommodate the increasing enrolments, the periods have been shortened to seven, each of 30 minutes duration per day. A major challenge for school principals is to try to maintain educational standards while working within such restrictive param-eters.

Staffing

In 2005, it was estimated that 20 per cent of all secondary school teachers were unqualified (Ministry of Education and Human Resources Development, 2005). Vacant secondary school teaching positions, particu-larly in community high schools, are being filled either by primary school teachers who are not appropriately qualified, or by untrained teachers (Ministry of Education and Human Resources Development, 2005). Also, in one study of rural secondary schools in Solomon Islands, Maebuta and Phan (2011) reported that 41 per cent of the teachers were not qualified.

Achieving a full complement of qualified teachers is one of the biggest challenges facing all schools. As student enrolment rapidly increases, so too does the demand for more teachers. The number of trained teachers gradu-ating annually cannot meet the demand. The conflict has further exacerbated this staffing issue for schools. The financial crisis at the time of the conflict prompted the Ministry of Education to restrict appointments and to halt recruitment of new teachers.

As a result of the teacher shortage, some subjects in secondary schools are not taught:

> Home economics [was not] taught until ... 2010. However, it is only taught in Forms 1 and 2. Technology and design (industrial arts) has never been taught. These subjects need specialised teachers, tools and equipment plus their own specialised building and these are lacking in our school. The school [does] not also have the prescribed curriculum materials for these subjects.
>
> (Maebuta and Phan, 2011: 173)

In some cases, schools resort to requiring teachers to teach subjects in which they have not specialised. For example, in one community high school, a teacher of agriculture was also teaching social studies and maths. It was concluded that, coupled with the unavailability of teaching resources, this teacher found it extremely difficult to teach those subjects which were not in his area of specialisation (Maebuta, 2011).

While one can think of long-term strategies to alleviate this problem, some initiatives that could be taken almost immediately also suggest themselves. For example, it is desirable that the government gives equal recognition to all teachers, irrespective of their teaching specialisations. Teachers should be remunerated according to their positions. The current practice, however, is for vocational education teachers to be paid lower salaries compared to their 'general education' colleagues (Ministry of Education and Human Resources Development, 2005). The vocational education teachers consider that there are no prospects in teaching unless discrimination of this kind is removed.

One possible way to deal with the problem would be to pay teachers according to their qualifications. For instance, a Diploma in Education (Industrial Arts) could be seen as being of equal status to a Diploma in Education (English). Both sets of teachers could then be paid at the same level and irrespective of whether they are teaching in junior, or senior secondary school classes. Also, it would be helpful for a national teacher supply-and-demand survey to be undertaken so that workforce projections can be made.

Resources

The problem of inadequate resources has been a vexed issue for a number of years. Many schools are in a poor financial state. School fees and government grants can meet the recurrent costs of teaching resources, but not the recurrent maintenance and repair of school buildings and other infrastructure. To ease the financial burden on parents, the government introduced a 'free education' policy in 2009 for basic education (years 1–9), which was funded by the Taiwanese government. However, the grant made available under this policy was not adequate to finance the total needs of the schools. Indeed, for most schools, the policy has drastically reduced their income compared to when full fees were paid by students. To cover the shortfall, schools began to require students in years 1–9 to make an annual financial contribution. However, parents were so angered by this development that the policy was withdrawn in 2010 when a new government was elected.

Providing proper school infrastructure is a government priority in the post-conflict period. Accordingly, considerable donor assistance has been allocated to schools for this purpose. While this assistance is intended to provide a boost for schools, a number of rural schools still do not have adequate textbooks for most subjects. In some schools, they have no textbooks at all, making it necessary to borrow materials from elsewhere. Teachers collaborate with their colleagues in nearby schools and share whatever resources they have at their disposal. Science subjects and vocational subjects such as industrial arts, agriculture and home economics are the most affected. They require laboratory-designed classrooms, which are lacking in many rural community high schools. Problems associated with the teaching of science and vocational subjects are further compounded by lack of equipment and tools (Maebuta, 2011). Hence, most schools concentrate on teaching the theory component of the subjects and leave out the practical aspects. In the case of senior secondary examination classes, some schools collaborate with others nearby that have science laboratories, in order to conduct practical work over mid-year school break periods.

School management and administration

The management and administration of schools lack an effective and efficient coordination mechanism. Most schools are under the jurisdiction of a provincial education authority and it is a common criticism among communities, school leaders and teachers that these authorities have provided ineffective management. The problem arises because the bureaucratic line of decision-making in the education system is burdensome.

At the school level, the complexities of managing teachers, resources, curriculum, students, and school communities are challenging. The school is regularly the victim of bureaucratic delays in decision-making. In the hope of obtaining speedy solutions, the school leadership personnel, teachers and the community often try to bypass their provincial government offices and consult directly with the Ministry of Education. For example, school principals in rural areas will travel to Honiara to sort out their school grant when there is a long delay in receiving it through the provincial government. Discrepancies in salaries are also a common issue brought to the attention of provincial education authorities. When results are not forthcoming, individual teachers deal directly with the Ministry of Education.

Such management issues are rooted in the dysfunctional coordination that characterises the interrelationship between the Ministry of Education, individual education authorities and schools. For this reason, it is necessary to find ways to coordinate the management and administration of schools more effectively. With this in mind, the notion of community empowerment and support is discussed in the next section.

Community support

Community support is an important component of the management of individual schools, particularly the community high schools. The concept of the community high school was initiated on the understanding that education is an integral part of the community and that the community should take a leading role in running the schools. Schools have attempted to involve their communities in the implementation of their projects, but have gained little support. There is expertise within the community, but it can be very expensive to harness because members of the community always expect to be paid. This is attributable to the impression held within the community that the receipt of school grants and payment of school fees means that the schools are prospering.

The concept of community empowerment can be conceptualised in various ways (Hur, 2006; Watts and Serrano-Garcia, 2003), but may be best defined as follows:

> A group-based, participatory, developmental process through which marginalised or oppressed individuals and groups gain greater control over their lives and environment, acquire valued resources and basic rights, and achieve important life goals and reduced societal marginalisation.
>
> (Maton, 2008: 4)

This definition relates to the process and outcome of community empowerment as perceived by key authorities (Mondros and Wilson, 1994; Speer and Hughey, 1995). Others contend that empowerment is a participatory-developmental process occurring over time, involving active and sustained engagement, and resulting in growth of awareness and capacity (Hur, 2006; Watts, Williams and Jagers, 2003). Ideally, such a participatory approach should drive engagement of the community in rebuilding schools in post-conflict Solomon Islands. This implies that if decentralisation of education is to work effectively, all levels of management and administration need to be resourced and empowered.

After the conflict, an AusAID-funded Community Peace and Restoration Fund (CPRF) was established to help rebuild and resource schools that were damaged. Money from the fund is provided directly to the school communities. One of the conditions of the CPRF is that the community should supply unskilled manual labour for such projects as providing a school building and water supply. If this condition is not met by the community, those projects that have been approved may not be funded. This arrangement has rallied community support, enabling many of the school projects under

CPRF to be successfully implemented in collaboration with the community. Also, through this initiative, communities connected with the conflicting parties have been able to work together and to rekindle broken relationships. The engagement of the community in such projects has strengthened its ownership of schools.

Conclusion

School leaders face enormous challenges in Solomon Islands. Some of these, as has been shown in this chapter, are as a result of the recent ethnic conflict. The situation is not helped, however, by the largely dysfunctional nature of the decentralised education system in the country. Provincial governments were established to facilitate decision-making through the devolution of powers and delegation of decision making. This applied to education as to other sectors of society, with provincial education authorities being established to oversee the effective management of schools in the provinces. However, while some administrative functions were devolved, others were not. The latter include decision-making with regard to curriculum, employment of teachers and some other key functions. This restricts the extent to which principals can take a leadership role at the school level. The expectation is that their role is largely one of maintaining daily routines.

Ironically, the period of ethnic strife presented principals with the challenge of seizing leadership opportunities to deal with the circumstances they faced. Some rose to the challenge and, as this chapter has pointed out, demonstrated both the resilience of their schools and the fact that they themselves were capable of initiating innovative responses in the interest of maintaining the education of their students. Having been released in this way, this potential should be developed in post-conflict Solomon Islands. This brings to mind Goddard's (2004) point that in order for schools in post-conflict settings to drive change, principals and senior teachers need to incorporate a rigorous social agenda in their leadership and management. To facilitate such an agenda, steps should be taken to ensure that bureaucratic controls of education do not present obstacles.

In other words, principals and senior teachers need to be empowered to initiate change in their own schools. For this to happen it is necessary for school and community leaders to work together. External aid, however, is also needed, especially from the country's nearest powerful neighbour, Australia, since Solomon Islands is too poor to provide the finances it needs to meet the challenges it faces, not just in education, but on several other fronts. Solomon Islands experienced severe economic contraction and stagnation over the period of the ethnic tensions (1998–2003) and while RAMSI assisted economic recovery, the country was badly hit again by the global recession and a drop in log exports. Furthermore, the majority of the population continues to be involved in subsistence/cash crop agriculture, with less than a quarter being employed in paid work. Australia recognises this situation and also that Solomon Islands has regional significance as part of an 'arc of instability' along Australia's northern edge, comprising other nations experiencing conflict, including Papua New Guinea and Fiji. It will be interesting to see how it responds in the future in providing assistance for the development of educational leadership at the school level in the country and contributing to the promotion of peace and harmony across the nation.

References

Adele, J. (2009) Curriculum and civil society in Afghanistan. *Harvard Educational Review*, 79(1), 113–22.

Bretherton, D., Weston, J. and Zbar, V. (2003) Peace education curriculum development in post-conflict contexts: Sierra Leone. *Prospects*, 33(2), 219–30.

Bugotu, F. (1973) *Education for What? British Solomon lslands protectorate education policy review committee report*. Honiara: Government Printer.

Burnet, G. and Dorovolomo, J. (2008) Teaching in difficult times: Solomon Island teachers' narratives of perseverance. *Journal of Peace, Conflict and Development*, 12, 1–34.

Danesh, H. B. (2006) Towards an integrative theory of peace education. *Journal of Peace Education*, 3(1), 55–78.

Goddard, J. T. (2004) The role of school leaders in establishing democratic principles in a post-conflict society. *Journal of Educational Administration*, 42(6), 685–96.

Hur, M. H. (2006) Empowerment in terms of theoretical perspectives: Exploring a typology of the processes and components across disciplines. *Journal of Community Psychology*, 34, 523–40.

Kudu, D. (2000) *Impact of the Ethnic Unrest on Social Development and Disadvantaged Groups in Solomon Islands*. Honiara: Ministry of National Planning and Human Resource Development.

Maebuta, J. (2011) The role of education in peacebuilding: Integrating peace education into secondary school social studies curriculum in the Solomon Islands (unpublished Ph.D. thesis). University of New England: Armidale, Australia.

Maebuta, J. and Phan, H. P. (2011) Determinants of quality learning in rural community high schools in Solomon Islands. *The International Journal of Learning*, 18(1), 164–80.

Maton, K. I. (2008) Empowering community settings: Agents of individual development, community betterment, and positive social change. *American Journal of Community Psychology*, 41, 4–21.

Ministry of Education and Human Resources Development. (2005) *Education for Living: Approved policy on technical, vocational education and training*. Honiara: Ministry of Education and Human Resources Development.

Ministry of Education and Human Resources Development. (2008) *National curriculum statement*. Honiara: Curriculum Development Centre.

Mondros, J. B. and Wilson, S. M. (1994) *Organizing for Power and Empowerment*. NY: Columbia University Press.

Moore, C. (2004) *Happy Isles in Crisis: The historical causes of a failing state in Solomon Islands, 1998–2004*. Canberra: Asia Pacific Press.

Pollard, B. (ed.) (2005) *Solomon Islands Education and Donor Assistance in Post-*

conflict Period. Wellington: He Parekereke Institute for Research and Development in Maori and Pacific Education, Victoria University.

Puia, M. (2011) Rate of female school dropouts high. *Island Sun*. http://www.islandsun.com.sb/index.php?option=com_content&view=article&id=2335:rate-of-female-school-dropouts-high&catid=36:latest-news&Itemid=79 (accessed 1 December 2012).

Speer, P. and Hughey, J. (1995) Community organizing: An ecological route to empowerment and power. *American Journal of Community Psychology*, 23, 729–48.

Stanley, D. (1993) *South Pacific Handbook*. California: Moon Publication Inc.

UNESCO. (2003) Education in situations of emergency, crisis and reconstruction. Division of Policies and Strategies of Education. http://unesdoc.unesco.org/images/0013/001323/132305e.pdf (accessed 10 March 2005).

Watts, R. J. and Serrano-Garcia, I. (2003) The quest for a liberating community psychology: An overview. *American Journal of Community Psychology*, 31, 73–8.

Watts, R. J., Williams, N. C. and Jagers, R. J. (2003) Sociopolitical development. *American Journal of Community Psychology*, 31, 185–94.

9 Lebanon

Post-civil war implications for schools

Nina Maadad

Introduction

Lebanon has a long and renowned tradition of education that was created through local institutions, international influences and foreign religious groups such as the French Jesuits, other Catholic orders and American and British Protestant missions. In recent years, however, it is mostly political and religious influences that have shaped the character of the education system in the country. Like other countries with ethnic, religious and political tensions, civil unrest and a fractious and volatile past have influenced how Lebanon's education system has been led and managed (Harrison, 2011. This chapter examines the situation by focusing on the following major themes: history and background, nature of the country's education system, post-civil war developments and challenges that school leaders face.

History and background

The rich history of Lebanon spans 7,000 years, when it was part of the maritime Phoenician culture during the period *c.* 1600–800 BC. It was subjected to invasions by the Egyptians, Assyrians, Persians, Greeks and Romans in the ancient period, and then fell to the Crusaders for a short period in the late eleventh century, before being occupied by the Ottomans in the early sixteenth century (Embassy of Lebanon, 2002). During 1832–41, the Egyptians occupied Syria and Lebanon. In order to support their political and economic affairs they often used armed Christian Lebanese against armed Druze Lebanese to fight their battles. These battles led to an onslaught that compelled British and French forces to intervene in 1840–41 and free Lebanon from Egyptian rule.

Lebanese prosperity was destroyed and the country experienced intense and widespread hunger after the Ottoman Empire joined the Central Alliance during World War 1. Anglo-French forces again had to intervene. It was only in November 1946 that Lebanon assumed independence when the last French troops withdrew.

In the early 1970s, approximately 300,000 Palestinian refugees migrated to Lebanon from Israel. To prevent a civil war from erupting, the Lebanese government signed the Cairo Accord with the Palestinian Liberation Organization (PLO) on the 3 November 1969. This treaty gave the PLO the right to establish military bases in southern Lebanon in order to defend its members. Soon after, they launched sporadic incursions into Israel. These raids caused retaliations and in May 1975, targeted villages were attacked by the Israeli army, resulting in the death of many innocent Lebanese people. The Christian rightists accused the government of failing to deal with the problem and feared being taken over (Cervan, 2011), while the Muslim leftists were defended by the Palestinians. The prospect of a civil war between Christians and Muslims led both factions (rightists and leftists) to form their own private militias. This development institutionalized violence over subsequent generations.

There are 18 religious groups in Lebanon and each of them has supported one of the country's two major political parties. During the early months of 1975, irregular violence between the two parties erupted, precipitating a civil war that lasted 16 years until the establishment of the Ta'if Agreement. This accord called for the elimination of political concessions and requested the Israeli and Syrian troops to withdraw from Lebanon. Israel withdrew its military forces in 2000 and Syria departed in 2005. The country's economy was irreparably damaged, its infrastructure was obliterated and the resentment between its religious sects was exacerbated. The number of people killed was approximately 150,000 and at least 600,000 people were displaced (Baroudi and Tabar, 2009).

Since the migration of the Palestinians, southern Lebanon has suffered tumultuous instability and has been subject to political violence. Regularly, attacks back and forth between the Palestinians and Israel resulted in severe retribution and it has often been the case that Israel expanded its strikes beyond the south (Cervan, 2011). In 2005, Prime Minister Al Hariri spent billions of dollars re-building the country, yet cross-party support was insufficient to prevent his assassination. This marked a major setback to the economic, religious and political stability of Lebanon and had significant implications for education.

Despite its history of wars, occupation, colonisation, battles and many contingent hardships, nothing has fatally undermined the positive nature and resilience of the Lebanese people. They have continued with their daily lives and rebuilding their country whenever possible. Because of the large number of tourists visiting Lebanon, it was, and still is, referred to as the 'Paris of the Middle East'. It was also once known as the 'Switzerland of the East' due to its long history of financial diversity and power. For such a small country with a surface area of 10,425 square kilometres and an estimated population in 2010 of 4,125,247 people, there was, in 2001/2, a surprisingly large number of 2698 private and public schools located in Lebanon (The National Centre for Educational Research and Development,

2009). The large number of schools compared to the size of the actual country and its population, reflects the importance placed by the Lebanese people on education.

The Lebanese education system

Lebanon enjoys one of the highest rates of literacy in the Arab world (97 per cent). It was estimated that in the late 1980s the number of students in schools was over 80 per cent (Library of Congress, n.d. Regrettably, the civil war had a catastrophic effect on educational standards and the country's literacy rates. Amongst the factors contributing to the decline in academic standards, one of the most important has been the destruction of over 150 schools by Israeli raids, and many families had to relocate to the remaining schools because their homes had been destroyed and they had nowhere else to go. The country also lost many teachers, professors and educators because of their migration overseas. Furthermore, some schools were pressured by certain militias to enrol unqualified students. Concurrently, many students lost their parents, their homes and access to schooling for a length of time, even though they were allowed to return to achieve a designated level of education when much of the infrastructure had been destroyed. Finally, many schools were used as distribution centres for humanitarian aid (Mikdadi, 1983), or as centres for the dissemination of propaganda and the recruitment of young soldiers to various militias (Brett and McCallin, 1996).

There are three systems of schooling in Lebanon: public schools, privately subsidized religiously affiliated schools, and privately non-subsidized schools. Most Lebanese wish to enrol their children in private schools in the belief that they provide better education, discipline and etiquette. However, the poverty caused by the civil war ensured that many people could no longer afford private schooling. When the number of people demanding education rose, the government was forced to open more public schools to accommodate their needs (Harrison, 2011).

Private schools depend heavily on numerous religious communities that have been long established in Lebanon and have created a variety of educational institutions and systems. The diversity in religious schools varies from Western clerical institutions, to the Jesuits' schools that have existed in Lebanon since 1625, and those of the Presbyterian missionaries who started to work in the country in 1866 and competed with the Catholics. Finally, there are the Makasids, or Islamic, schools, funded by the Gulf countries and Saudi Arabia. The Palestinians were not provided with public education in Lebanon until the United Nations Relief and Works Agency for Palestine Refugees in the Near East (UNRWA) was established and registered all Palestinian refugees in Lebanon, Syria, Jordan and Palestine (Ministry of Education and Higher Education, 2005). By 1975, the diversity of educational institutions in Lebanon was well entrenched, a situation that contributed to the divisions and barriers that erupted into civil war.

Most parents stretch their budgets to the extreme in order to keep their children in private schools. This practice is influenced by Lebanon's religious and internationalised culture, since most public schools are the object of criticism from Lebanese families. Yet, the education system in Lebanon is, to a reasonable extent, centralised and the same curriculum is taught in both private and public schools. Primary school education is almost universal and covers grades 1–8, with an enrolment ratio of 95.4 per cent of the population. In secondary school education the ratio reached 81.5 per cent in 2007 for grades 9–13 (UNESCO, 2008), while the adult literacy rate reached 88 per cent (UNICEF, 2004). Of the total number of students attending schools in the country in 2009/10, 30.29 per cent were in public schools and the remaining number were in various types of private schools.

The Lebanese Ministry of Education and Higher Education has long controlled the education system through its licensing of private schools by enforcing requirements and regulations for graduates to comply with the Brevet Diploma (for those graduating from middle school) and the Baccalaureate Diploma (for those graduating after completing the final year of high school). An extra examination beyond the Baccalaureate, however, is required for entry to most of those institutions of higher education where there is a concentration on language competency, science and mathematics (Aljarida Alrasmiya, 1997).

In 1998, a reformed curriculum was launched with a focus on social, economic and national perspectives. To teach the curriculum, 16,000 teachers were trained for public school delivery and 6,000 for private school delivery. The curriculum was based on the assumption that students should spend twelve years in school. One year was added to primary schooling, while one year was removed from the middle years' cycle. History, geography, literature and civics are taught in Arabic, while all other subjects are taught in either English or French, depending on the school's educational and religious background.

Post-civil war developments

Notwithstanding the reform of the curriculum, improvements in teacher preparation and development in most areas of education, many aspects of Lebanon's education system remain problematic and continue to compromise students' results and their future success. In 2004, UNICEF (2004) documented that at least 15 per cent of students in Lebanese schools were dropping out and another 11 per cent were repeating their year level. Research shows that the war left public schools with inadequate equipment and facilities to support students, while private school fees increased to facilitate rebuilding and restocking. This left large numbers of parents struggling financially and resulted in many students having to drop out. These circumstances were confirmed by the United Nations Human Rights Council (2006), which stated that as a consequence of the loss of over 180 school buildings in southern Lebanon and the southern suburbs of Beirut as a result of Israeli air strikes, more than 300 schools needed major repairs. It was emphasised that teachers needed to take account of the psychological effects of the war on children and their parents (UNICEF, 2007).

The Lebanese people are segregated by the education system itself. According to Hajjar, the three different sectors of schooling – French, British and American – have led to community division where there should be unity at a time when relationships between the communities have been deeply scarred by the civil war (Hajjar, 2002). History, with its variegated interpretations, is still taught in different versions within different school sectors, with the civil war being interpreted along sectarian lines (Euro News, 2011), even though the Ministry of Education formulated an agreement whereby all school sectors use a common history book. Unfortunately, and to the detriment of children who study the subject, Lebanese politicians and community leaders continue to disagree and refuse to compromise (European Neighbourhood and Partnership Instrument, 2006). The latest attempt at reconciliation was a meeting to release a new book titled *Learning and teaching history: Lessons from and for Lebanon* (Gussaini *et al.*, 2012) at the Ministry of Education and Higher Education, where most school sector leaders and university history advisors, as well as representatives from UNESCO, assembled to discuss the possibilities of writing a new common school history book (Ministry of Education and Higher Education, 2005.

Schools also have their own 'hidden curriculum' (Toronto and Eissa, 2007: 28), which is reflected in their ethos, teachers, community services and religious activities. A study undertaken by Abouchedid, Nasser and Blommestein (2002) contended that prototypes of political socialisation strongly influence the religious agenda in Lebanon, including that of schools. Their study focused on the teaching of history in the different school sectors and reported that seven different history textbooks were used. Each presented elements of the country's history that interpreted past events in terms that were politically acceptable to one section of the community. Also, political propaganda is often prevalent in private, subsidised-private, and public schools, being related to the ideas of the particular party, or militia, that provides them with support, protection and finance (Cervan, 2011). The only schools in which political topics cannot be discussed are the Hariri schools.

Challenges for leaders at the school level

This section presents an overview of four challenges that school leaders face in Lebanon. While these are not discussed in any order of priority, they illustrate shared views of principals, teachers, parents and students. Furthermore, the challenges mentioned are by no means the only ones that the schools, curriculum and leadership must overcome in Lebanon. They are as follows:

poverty, trauma, reform of the curriculum, and school culture. The exposition is based on data gathered in 2012 in five private and four public schools located in different parts of the country. Thus, a broad geographical perspective is represented. Some of the interviews were conducted through email, others in face-to-face situations. Additional information was obtained from newspaper reports and journal articles.

Poverty

Poverty in schools, especially in southern Lebanon, affects schools' management and the students. The lack of basic classroom materials such as seats, desks and blackboards plays a major role in undermining students' ability to learn. According to *Al Arabiya News*, these basic tools are not available in many schools because 'the state cares little . . . and there is no political will to change things' (Zablit, 2011). Principals and teachers describe the situation in public schools as being 'catastrophic, horrible and sad' (ibid.), but also refer to it as being not that unusual for the public sector.

In 2006, the Ministry of Education and Higher Education launched a series of reforms led by Minister of Education, Kabbani. These were triggered by low scores in mathematics and sciences in the Trends in International Mathematics and Science Study (TIMMS) conducted in 2003. The major factors contributing to such poor performance were identified as follows: socio-economic status of students and their families, geographical position and the schools' population, language used to teach the content, teachers' qualifications and experience, and the availability of resources and funding (The World Bank Group, 2006). A face-to-face interview with one public school principal in southern Lebanon supports the view that poverty was a fundamental cause of deteriorating educational standards and indicates that the situation does not seem to be improving:

> We need to beg again and again for support with appropriate staffing; resources and teaching materials and unfortunately it may take a very long time to get someone to look at our requests, if ever. Parents blame public schools for not providing the best for their children and this is not acceptable. We have top graduates in our school here but we don't get the support from home. Most parents here don't have the qualifications or the time to help the kids and I often suggest to parents to get a private tutor to help their kids at home, but they keep telling me that they can't afford it.

One especially passionate school principal spoke with confidence about her staff members and their ability to teach professionally and proficiently, and she criticised the lack of support they receive from the government. She also stated that dysfunction in the public school system is attributable to the Ministry's lack of control of the situation as a whole:

In general teachers in public schools have better qualifications and have subject specialisation, while in private it is mostly not the case, it is who you know to give you the teaching position. Parents don't seem to understand or maybe they don't want to understand, it is all about the image and competition with their friends and neighbours.

Another principal stated:

Unfortunately, parents in public schools don't put much effort into participating in decision-making about their children's education. I suppose because there is no cost so it does not worry them. We have many advantages here in our school, one very important factor is that 90 per cent of our teachers are local, they know the families, the history of the place and are involved in the community.

In similar vein, a few parents, when interviewed, talked about their struggle with financial difficulties:

My kids froze during the day and the teacher told them to wear more clothes because the heating system at school is not working and there isn't any money available for fixing it.

I could not buy the books required for my son's schooling and the ones he used were borrowed from his teachers. I was told that the school couldn't afford to buy books for the children.

Parents, in addition, mentioned that in certain schools trained teachers in particular subjects are lacking and those who are trained prefer to work in the private education system because facilities and opportunities are much better:

My daughter's class missed out for 5 weeks on science lessons because her teacher left and they couldn't get anyone to replace her. This could be due to the lack of material and resources available in the school and also the low wages these teachers receive. I can understand when they say that they prefer to work in private schools and pity for our children whose parents can't afford to pay such high tuition fees.

It is a fact that teachers in the public sector are more subject-trained than those in the private sector but there will always be this assumption that having a private education will open up greater opportunities for the future of the children. All our children sit for the same examination at the end of the day; it does not matter what school they have attended.

Teachers interviewed agreed with these sentiments. One teacher summarised the general view as follows:

Putting your children in private schools will determine a better education and a better future. You are lucky if you have the money, otherwise
you need to be willing to struggle and miss out on other necessities to
survive to provide them with good schools. If you are poor your kids will
miss out on such opportunities and pay the price for the rest of their lives
because of certain decisions made by the government and the financial
opportunities allocated to education.

Such comments illustrate how poverty can affect the choices that parents
have to make. There is also evidence that decisions made about some public
schools can be politically motivated:

A school not too far from us had six teachers for one Brevet student and
here we are begging for a teacher for a subject specialty and we are not
given one. That school was kept open until after the election to keep the
good image of the politician.

Indeed, it would seem that politics is still very influential in determining
when to keep a school open and when to shut it down.

Trauma

The civil war may be over in the eyes of the world, but the Lebanese people
and, in particular the children, are still traumatised (Wolmer *et al.*, 2011). An
entire society still lives in denial. Some do not talk about what happened,
some are afraid to return to their villages and original homes and some are
disabled physically and scared. Others are still grieving the loss of family
members, friends and neighbours, and others yet again are refusing to even
step outside of their homes.

School leaders are faced with many related challenges such as simply trying
to retain students and encourage them to achieve academically. The number
of 'drop-outs' has risen and in many cases it is only a matter of time before
children leave school (Zablit, 2011). Professor Kobeissi at the state-run
Lebanese University, has highlighted that 20–30 per cent of primary school
children are failing, or dropping out, that teachers are not always qualified
and that they are often underpaid (ibid.). Teachers have also commented that
it is necessary for them to engage daily in behavioural management of traumatised children, as illustrated by the following comments from two of them:

A few students in my school have lost everything, and I mean everything. They have lost family members, friends and their homes but they
still come to school and try to act normal when I know that they are
fighting depression all the time. These kids need all the love and attention they can have to come out of their sadness and start enjoying life
before they start learning.

Some students are tougher than others and this is a positive thing for us. They probably did not face the same challenges and fear that others did or maybe they handle things differently. Nonetheless, this is fantastic because they help their peers in their own way and support our mission to create a healthy and safe environment for all our students.

Many parents have commented in similar vein:

We are doing it tough now since my husband was killed a few years ago. Still, this does not mean that my children need to suffer forever. I am always trying to keep them safe and make them happy.

Ellie keeps to himself all the time and says that he does not like to go to school. He is worried that something might happen quickly and stops him from getting back to his family on time.

It is impossible to erase the many years of war and brutality in a short period. Our children will take a long time to forget what happened and move on.

They went on to make the following comment when asked about counselling support:

School counselling? What do you mean? We don't have anything like this at all. If our students need anything they can talk to us teachers.

Public schools are not financially covered for counselling costs by the government and students often talk to teachers with whom they feel comfortable, or to other students. I wish we had counselling for students and for teachers too. We need this badly after what we have all been through.

In our Christian environment here, the nuns provide the support for our students. This is not a professional service that we provide as most of our nuns are not qualified or trained as psychologists, but they can talk to the students and communicate with their parents to comfort and support them.

We have individual counselling for spiritual and orientation purposes but other than that we suggest that the parents take their children to specialists like psychologists or psychiatrists.

Such evidence suggests that counselling does not play an important role in schools in Lebanon. Indeed, many teachers have not even heard of the possibility of having counselling programmes included within the school curriculum to provide the support needed for their students. At the same time, many staff members feel that it is their obligation as teachers and mentors to provide counselling for the students as well as an education. The religious and private schools do place a small focus on counselling in their spiritual and educational programmes, but they direct parents to professionals when they deem that particular students need individual attention.

Teachers at one public school in northern Lebanon declared that a happy school environment provides support for their students and gives them a sense of belonging, safety and comfort. They encourage their students to contribute by decorating their classrooms and school with their artwork, displaying their ideas and their vision for their future. While most of the work witnessed was bright and cheerful, sadness and fear were also apparent in many of the displays. 'Students produced posters that make you cry', said one of the school principals. She was referring to posters of grieving families at funerals, posters of children running scared and posters of lost children in space. Such situations create challenges for everyone involved in the school, and not just the principal. It is the responsibility of the teachers, parents and students to provide support and care, and protect the children, and to ensure that they can learn in a safe environment they deserve. This is a formidable task, especially when teachers and other staff members are not really sure about what constitutes safety, or about the appropriate strategies by which it can be provided.

The curriculum

The Lebanese education system is in a state of convalescence after the war and civil unrest. The standard of primary and secondary school education, especially in public institutions, needs to improve (European Neighbourhood and Partnership Instrument, 2006). As already pointed out, schools in Lebanon lack subject-oriented qualified teachers in various disciplines. The fact that there are low ratios of students to teachers at both primary (17 to 1) and secondary levels (7 to 6) contributes to financial restraints and resource cutbacks (The World Bank Group, 2006). Also, the National Centre for Educational Research and Development indicates that the construction of the new school curriculum must cater to students' need for knowledge, values and attitudes, as well as developing their life skills. Such an approach is not new, having been emphasised in the following eight learning areas that were identified in the 1990s to help develop and educate Lebanese students (National Centre for Educational Research and Development, 1995: 10):

1   ensure that Lebanese students develop into cultured citizens;
2   identify and reinforce individual abilities;
3   educate students with knowledge and skills and train them in values of citizenship;
4   increase/supplement students' social, environmental, cultural and health education and provide opportunities to discuss contemporary issues to develop objective reasoning;
5   strengthen linguistic communication skills leading to creative expression and improvement in literary ability;

6 develop computer literacy and the use of technology as an education medium and source of information;

7 acquaint students with manual activities to develop positive attitudes toward work and prepare them for the future;

8 enhance students' self-esteem as independent and social individuals able to balance freedom and responsibilities.

In 1996, reform of the curriculum in line with these learning areas was planned to take place in three stages. The first stage was termed 'constructing the educational ladder', the second involved designing the curriculum and organising textbooks, and the third involved implementation and the provision of associated preparation for both private and public school teachers.

BouJaoude and Ghaith (2006) state that few concerns were expressed when the reform was evaluated in 2003. The requirement for a focus on strengthening the connection between schools, colleges and universities in order to link academic needs to the social needs of the country was emphasised. A comparison between the old and the new curriculum also indicated that the former, if it had persisted, would be outdated and limited to traditional subjects only. Nevertheless, some problems were identified in relation to special education, extra-curricular activities and the content of textbooks. Particular attention was drawn to the fact that teachers were not familiar with the prescribed 'student-centred teaching methods' as they had not been exposed to them in their teacher preparation programmes, or in the training they received on implementing the new curriculum (BouJaoude and Ghaith, 2006: 198–200).

More recently, various practical problems have also been highlighted by individual principals. One public school principal stated that with the reform have come new subjects that require additional, but unavailable, resources and spaces in the schools. He went on:

> It is chaos and an absolute nightmare for the teachers to be able to implement something that is so different without any preparation or training. This is not all, we are expected to teach science when we have hardly any resources in our laboratories, computers and IT and we have hardly any resources, our buildings are so old, our rooms are so small, we hardly have any materials and not enough financial support.

He then laughed and said:

> Maybe we need to train magicians not teachers! Well, in this country when you request things and no one wants to do something about them they get filed and put away in a place never to be found.

In contrast, private schools seem to be dealing better with the problems. They have the advantage of receiving more funds to provide special training for teachers and to prepare them for the new teaching methods. A principal of one private school stated:

> I have to agree that it is a lot easier when you work in the private sector. You can make your own decisions and have your own budget and funds. I feel sorry for my colleagues in the public sector and I know that this causes them headaches and difficulties to manage your staff and support them with the little funds that you have.

Another principal commented:

> When the parents are paying lots of money for the education of their children, they expect the best. This is what we have to provide and our teachers will have to be up-to-date with it all. The one positive thing that supports us in the private system is that parents get so involved and want to help in any way they can.

A teacher in a private school, currently working as a mentor and training other teachers since attending a government-provided 'how to train the trainer' programme, added:

> I am not sure how I would have handled the change and the expectation of performing under the new reform without the vigorous training and support that we have received in our school. This would have not been achieved without the principal's support, the parents and the community.

At the same time, there is a view that the problem will eventually disappear as newly-prepared teachers will acquire the necessary skills on entering the workforce since they are now being introduced to them in their teacher preparation programmes. In the meantime, however, current principals, teachers and parents continue to grapple with a fear of the unknown and to experience stress in having to face extra challenges and having to deal with lack of information and guidance on how to master the new curriculum. Their situation is not helped by the centralisation of all decision-making in the public school sector by the Ministry of Education and Higher Education and the concurrent restriction on the power of the school principals.

School culture

Foreign missionaries have played a major role in education in Lebanon since the sixteenth and seventeenth centuries when they used their languages of origin in establishing schools and in their teaching. In more recent years, all private schools have used both French and Arabic. English, however, started to appear after Lebanon became independent of French governance in 1943 (Bacha and Bahous, 2011). Currently, while Arabic is the main language, teaching and learning requirements are such that the teaching of a minimum of two languages is compulsory in all Lebanese schools, whether private, or public (ibid.).

Traditionally, what happened in the Lebanese classroom was the responsibility of the teacher alone. Teachers were viewed as the source of knowledge and their authority could not be questioned or challenged. Similarly, students were seen as passive participants who mostly followed instructions and obeyed the teacher's requests (Kibbi, 2003). However, the principal of one public school situated in Beirut emphasised that there seems to be some change in line with the globalisation of education and the multicultural nature of Lebanon. He stated:

> Our students are now confused, on one hand, they want to stick to their community and their families' traditions and values; and on the other, they are starting to realise that unless they are open to the world and its changes they will not get far in life.

Another principal commented:

> We can't close our eyes and pretend that the world is not changing around us. We have always been a nation of progress and modernisation in the Arab world and why should we stop now? Our education system should evolve with the rest of the world.

One mother also mentioned how her son is representative of a generation that queries aspects of its culture:

> My son is often questioning his culture. He keeps asking about its history and how it evolved. When I start to explain I get confused myself. Where do you really start? And how do you end? Maybe us parents now need an update on how to handle these situations and not confuse our children.

The emergence of such cultural awareness, according to one principal, is seen as a positive move and may be enabling the new generation to be more open to the outside world.

Yet, it is important not to forget the neglect in the teaching of history of the many events that took place in Lebanon over recent years. According to one teacher:

> I once was a history teacher, telling the children proudly the truth about our country, our ancestors and the wars we fought that led to our freedom. I am not allowed to mention any current history to them.

Another stated:

> How can we tell our children about the Lebanese culture when our system (all of it) especially the education system is based on the French, American or the British systems and their values?

This situation reinforces living in denial and makes the children ignorant of their heritage.

Another aspect of school culture having a negative effect on teaching and learning relates to the lack of teacher motivation and security, especially in public schools. On this, the principal of one private school stated:

> The difference between motivation and security in public and private schools plays a major role. We reward our teachers and have incentives to show them how grateful we are when they excel. We give out letters of appreciation, extra hours of preparation, extra time for professional development. While in the public sector there is little motivation and no rewards.

The relationship between the principal and the staff also differs between the two sectors. The principal of one public school commented thus: 'We have to make all the decisions. It is not a joke and a mistake cannot be fixed. We get the blame.' On the other hand, when asked how the school system works and who runs the meetings at his school, this principal said:

> Our policy is to be collegial in all our decision-making. The meetings in our school always include the board of directors and not only the principal but also the teachers from the department responsible are included in the meetings and take part in the decisions. If there is no need for the meeting we often cancel it. Teachers have plenty to do without having to waste time in a meeting that was not needed.

Furthermore, while private schools have their own resources, are independent of any government subsidies, do not have to wait for external approvals and can make their own decisions, financial requests in the public system are handled at central government level. The culture in public schools is totally bureaucratic, with the principal playing the role of an administrator or manager rather than of someone who can make decisions unilaterally.

Notwithstanding the support provided by UNICEF, there are other challenges confronting Lebanese education because its structure is a product of either the American, British or French systems. In particular, the schools do not target the core, or heartland, of Lebanese culture. Diverse cultures and relationships exist within schools. It is feelings of alienation resulting from such differences that can contribute to hatred and civil war (Davies, 2005). Recognition of this issue highlights the need for multicultural education enabling students to learn about one another, and to accept, respect and tolerate each other's views regarding their religious backgrounds and core values.

The development of the new Lebanese education system and the support provided by UNICEF to the Ministry of Education in 2006, seemed promising to those working in the 1400 public and subsidised private schools in the country. UNICEF also provided specific training programmes for teachers, preparing them to deal with issues arising from the post-war landscape. Such issues related to the existence of depressed and distressed children, emotional instability, behavioural management issues in the classroom and psychological well-being (UNICEF, 2007). A number of teachers commented on these programmes as follows:

> All these programmes are brilliant and so useful but they are originally based on the Western style of education, they are not tailored 100 per cent for our students.

> We are expected to teach maths and science implementing the new methods but no support, guidance or even materials have been offered to us. Take a look around you in this classroom and you will know what I mean.

> The whole system is new and we have pressure on us to provide better students, prepare them for universities and the new world. There is so much competition now and we are all struggling.

The message seems to be that while teachers participate willingly in the available professional development programmes, any chance of putting what they learn into practice is seriously curtailed by lack of resources.

Another area in serious need of addressing is that of positive student–teacher interaction. Social collaboration, or interaction, tends not to occur between students and teachers in Lebanese schools. The general attitude was summarised by two principals:

> What would students really know about the curriculum or what needs to be taught in schools? Sometimes they come with good ideas and you want to embrace these ideas to make them feel supported, other times they act smart and try to show you that they know more than you, which can be humiliating.

> Having the students make decisions for the future of the school is not acceptable here. We listen to their requests and might make certain adjustments and influence minor things but they can't change rules or regulations.

Given such attitudes, it is not surprising that there are no student representatives on school boards, or councils. The school culture and tradition do not allow students to make decisions affecting teachers, or about subjects being taught. Teachers cannot be criticised, or changed, if students do not like them, or encounter problems with them.

If students have any matters to discuss they have to request a meeting with the principal via members of the school administration. This procedure was introduced initially to safeguard against political parties becoming involved in school elections, promoting their views and creating problems. The wider consequence, however, is that students are deprived of avenues for voicing opinions that might contribute to the organisational health of the school. Thus, they do not play a major role in decision-making at the school level and have no influence on the direction of education.

Conclusion

Lebanon is a country that has experienced many problems since the civil war and it battles to rebuild itself. There continues to be lingering resentment between communities, and deep and ugly wounds are yet to heal. Many children attending schools in the country are doing so after decades of war and civil strife. Many are also disabled because of injuries from bombs and land-mines. Others are often terrified, while some have lost parents and have been sexually and mentally abused. The impact of war on these children has resulted in anger and has accustomed them to violence. They deal with their own daily problems aggressively and tend to live in fear that war may break out again.

This chapter has highlighted the difficulties of being a leader in schools working in such conditions. Challenges emanate from the conflicting demands of government, churches, mosques and militias. Reforms occurring in the curriculum, teacher preparation, social conditions and management styles in both public and private schools are pursued in the shadow of a long civil war and against a history of different European cultures that have shaped the country's education system. The grip of the state's Ministry of Education and Higher Education also serves to restrict the authority of public school principals.

While they realistically cannot solve the problems of poverty or social trauma, school principals can influence the situation in subtle ways and make recommendations for improvement. For example, they could advocate for universities to contribute to pre-service teacher preparation, and to professional development, especially for the improvement of principal leadership and management skills. Principals could also advocate for multicultural programmes aimed at helping students to learn about other religious groups in Lebanon, as well as for the introduction of counselling courses for addressing pupil trauma. Finally, they could advocate for interaction and cooperation across school sectors to help improve the curriculum and teaching.

References

Abouchedid, K., Nasser, R. and Blommestein, J. (2002) The limitations of inter-group learning in confessional school system: the case of Lebanon. *Arab Studies Quarterly*, 24(4), 61–82.

Aljarida Alrasmiya of the Republic of Lebanon (1997) *Laws and Decrees Concerning the Pre-university Educational System*. Beirut: Sader Publications.

Bacha, N. and Bahous, R. (2011) Foreign language education in Lebanon: A context of cultural and curricular complexities. *Journal of Language Teaching and Research*, 2(6), 1320–28.

Baroudi, S. and Tabar, P. (2009) Spiritual authority versus secular authority: Relations between the Maronite Church and the State in post-war Lebanon: 1990–2005. *Middle East Critique*, 18(3), 195–230.

BouJaoude, S. and Ghaith, G. (2006) Education reform at a time of change: the case of Lebanon. In J. Earnest and D. Tragust (eds) *Education Reconstruction in Transitional Societies*. Rotterdam: Sense Publishers, pp. 193–210.

Brett, R. and McCallin, M. (1996) *Children: The invisible soldiers*. Stockholm: Swedish Save the Children.

Center for Educational Research and Development (1995) *El Haykalah el Jadidah Fil Taleem Fi Lubnan*. Beirut: Lebanon: Ministry of Education.

Cervan, D. (2011) Religion in education and conflict: Lebanon and Northern Ireland compared. http://www.ruor.uottawa.ca/fr/handle/10393/20006. (accessed 11 April 2012).

Country Studies, Lebanon (1987) Sectarian and clan consciousness – Lebanon. http://countrystudies.us/lebanon/40.htm, (accessed 10 April 2012).

Davies, L. (2005) Schools and war: urgent agendas for comparative and international education. *Compare: A journal of comparative and international education*, 35(4), 357–71.

Embassy of Lebanon (2001) Profile of Lebanon: Statistical data. http://www.lebanonembassyus.org/country_lebanon/statistical.html (accessed 10 April 2012).

Embassy of Lebanon (2002) Profile of Lebanon. http://www.lebanonembassyus.org/country_lebanon/overview.html (accessed 10 April 2012).

EuroNews. (2011) A class from the past. http://www.euronews.com/2011/06/06/a-class-from-the-past/ (accessed 20 April 2012).

European Neighbourhood and Partnership Instrument (2006) Lebanese Republic, Country strategy paper 2007–2013 and national indicative programme 2007–2010. www.trade.ed.europa.eudoclib/html/136439.htm (accessed 13 April 2012).

Gussaini, R., Karami Akkary, R. and Akar, B. (2012) *Learning and Teaching History: Lessons from and for Lebanon*. Beirut: Lebanese Association for Educational Studies.

Hajjar, G. (2002) *Aspects of Christian-Muslim Relations in Contemporary Lebanon*. Lebanon: Notre Dame University.

Harrison, K. (2011) Between politics and identity: The history and future of education in Lebanon. www.tuftsgloballeadership.org/files/between_politics_identity.pdf (accessed 23 March 2012).

Lebanese American Information Centre (2005) War in Lebanon. http://www.Lgic.org/en/history.php (accessed 27 March 2012).

Library of Congress (n.d.) Lebanon – The society. http://www.mongabay.com/reference/country_studies/lebanon/SOCIETY.html (accessed 13 April 2012).

Kibbi, I. (2003) Lebanese and American educational differences: A comparison. *Education*, 11(3), 411–19.

Mikdadi, L. (1983) *Surviving the Siege of Beirut: A personal account*. London: Onyx Press.

Ministry of Education and Higher Education of Lebanon (2005) http://www.crdp.rof/CRDP/Arabic/ar-statistics/STAT (accessed 8 March 2012).

National Centre for Educational Research and Development (1995) *Lebanese National Curriculum*. Beirut: NCERD.

National Centre for Educational Research and Development (2009) *Statistical Report Lebanon 2001–2002*. The National Centre for Educational Research and Development.

Toronto, J. and Eissa, M. (2007) Egypt: Promoting tolerance, defending against Islamism. In E. Abdellah and G. Starrett (eds) *Teaching Islam*. London: Lynne Rienner Publishers, pp. 27–51.

UNESCO (2008) Institute for Statistics database. www.uis.unesco.org (accessed 19 April 2012).

UNICEF (2004) The state of the world's children, 2004. www.unicef.org/sowc04. (accessed 16 April 2010).

UNICEF (2007) The humanitarian action report, 2007. www.unicef.org/har07/index.html (accessed 6 April 2012).

Wolmer, L., Hamiel, D., Barchas, J. D., Slone, M. and Laor, N. (2011) Teacher-delivered resilience-focused intervention in schools with traumatized children following the second Lebanon War. *Journal of Traumatic Stress*, 24(3), 309–16.

The World Bank Group (2006) The Republic of Lebanon, First quarter 2006. www-wds.worldbank.org/2006/20060620133407/ (accessed 3 May 2012).

Zablit, J. (2011) Public school students face uphill battle in Lebanon. www.alarabiya.net/articles/2011/10/09/170892.html (accessed 1 May 2012).

10 Kosovo

Transitioning school leadership from conflict to coherence

J. Tim Goddard and Osman Buleshkaj

Introduction

In October 2011, the Municipal Education Director (MED) for Prishtina, the capital of Kosovo, helped to establish a school principal selection committee. The committee had representatives from the municipal education office and from the central Ministry of Education, Science and Technology (MEST), along with some non-voting members from the school and parent councils. This committee interviewed a number of candidates. In 'the old days', before Kosovo achieved independence from Serbia, the decision would have been easy; the most senior local teacher who was politically affiliated with the government, whether professionally successful or not, would have been promoted.

The MED, however, was of a different mind. He began his career as an English language teacher, became an education consultant during the 'parallel system' of education, and was then selected as the head of the teacher training section at MEST. He had completed an extensive training programme in educational leadership as part of a Canadian-funded education development project and had taken a number of master's degree classes, although he had not yet finished his degree. He had also worked with educational experts from the World Bank and other donors, and had a good knowledge of new ideas in the fields of school management and leadership, curriculum, and policy development in post-conflict Kosovo.

The interview was comprehensive. Candidates were asked about their philosophy of education, their thoughts on student-centred learning, their knowledge of the differences between administration and leadership, and their understanding of the importance of community engagement in the school. They were also asked to articulate their main objectives and vision for developing the school at which the successful applicant would be employed. The senior local teacher, who had been a principal at the same school for a number of years, had no problem talking about these things because he had experienced a series of school-leadership training programmes offered in post-conflict Kosovo. However, a younger candidate, who held a higher degree, struggled. He had never really needed to consider such things because although he had advanced qualifications, he had only limited teaching experience and had never participated in any school leadership training programmes.

Once the interviews were finished the committee sat to discuss the performance of the candidates. An argument was made for the candidate who held the postgraduate degree, but the opinion of the Regional Education Office (REO) prevailed. It was reasoned that if Kosovo was to continue moving forward into the twenty-first century, the skills and attributes of its leaders must reflect new practices of school leadership promoted in the training programs, rather than the higher education degree itself, which was neither in education, nor within the field of school leadership. The decision was made, and a relatively old teacher experienced as a school director, rather than a university-trained graduate, was appointed. The unsuccessful candidates were thanked for their time and were encouraged to keep applying should other vacancies arise.

A few days later the MED was sitting in his spartan office. He had an early morning meeting with some international donors who were supporting education in Kosovo. After the meeting he was reviewing some documents when the door was pushed open and one of the unsuccessful candidates walked in. He pulled a handgun from out of his pocket and shot the MED seven times. He left the room and once outside the building walked up to the nearest police officer and confessed to the murder.

The incident described indicates that new post-war settings, including the education context, can still be very volatile and dangerous places. This, in turn, can present considerable challenges for education leaders, especially for those at the individual school level. The remainder of the chapter is concerned with this matter in the case of Kosovo. It is structured in three parts. First, it describes the historical context to the conflict in Kosovo. Second, attention is turned to describing the education system. Third, there is an exposition on the challenges encountered by leaders in their schools

Historical context

The Republic of Kosovo is located in the centre of the Balkan Peninsula, in southeast Europe. To the north and east lie the borders of Serbia, with Macedonia being to the south, Albania to the southwest and Montenegro to the northwest. The geographical area of Kosovo is 10,908 km². It is divided into 33 municipalities, with a total population of 2.18 million (Statistical Office of Kosovo, 2010). The country's ethnic composition consists of 92.0 per cent Albanian and 8.0 per cent other ethnic groups, most of whom are of Serbian, Bosnian, Turkish and Roma heritage. There is an uneven population pyramid, with 60 per cent of the population being younger than 25 years of age. Indeed, Kosovo is considered to be the youngest country in Europe (Pupovci, 2002; Statistical Office of Kosovo, 2010).

Socialist Federal Republic of Yugoslavia

Throughout most of the late twentieth century, Kosovo was part of the Socialist Federal Republic of Yugoslavia (SFRY). Before it was dissolved in 1991, the SFRY consisted of six republics (Serbia, Montenegro, Macedonia, Croatia, Slovenia and Bosnia and Herzegovina) and two autonomous provinces (Kosovo and Vojvodina). In 1974 the SFRY Constitution granted Kosovo and Vojvodina 'the status of the Socialist Autonomous Province[s] with rights equal to those of the nations of Yugoslavia' (Daskalovski, 2003: 17). They had their own parliamentary assemblies and seats in the Federal Parliament, and a separate constitution from Serbia. When the former SFRY republics left the federation in 1991, their respective independent status was recognized by the international community throughout the world. However, Kosovo and Vojvodina remained within Serbia and later, all three, along with Montenegro, formed what was termed the Federal Republic of Yugoslavia (FRY) (OECD, 2002).

Federal Republic of Yugoslavia

In 1989, the government of Serbia undertook steps to abolish Kosovo's autonomy and install a direct controlling system from Belgrade. On the one hand, a number of constitutional amendments, including 'some amendments that had not been in public discussion' (Daskalovski, 2003: 19), were approved by non-Kosovan Albanian delegates from the Assembly of Kosovo. On the other hand, the Albanian delegates gathered on 2 July 1990 and 'approved the Declaration of Independence of Kosovo', which was followed by the 'Constitution of the Republic of Kosovo' in September 1990 (p. 21). In the wake of these developments in Kosovo, and a number of demonstrations and protests led by the Kosovan Albanian population, the government of Serbia declared a 'state of emergency', which resulted in numerous repressive measures being pursued by the Serbian special police units, military and paramilitary forces, and the local Serb population.

This situation continued for a number of years. Leadership positions throughout Kosovo were placed in the hands of Kosovan Serbs and of Serbs originating from within Serbia itself. At the same time, Kosovan Albanian public servants, including professionals in different fields, all teachers in the public school system, doctors at the hospitals and clinics, and higher education academics, were removed from their posts. In the wake of oppressive measures against these public servants, many of them were forced to leave Kosovo. It should be emphasised, however, that this period of deterioration in the Kosovan Albanians' circumstances was characterised by a peaceful and non-violent movement led by a number of Kosovan Albanian intellectuals.

Following this non-violent movement, and as a result of constant oppression against the majority of Kosovan Albanians, the attitudes of many within the Kosovan Albanian population had changed significantly by late 1997. A period of violence now commenced when a paramilitary group, calling itself the Kosovo Liberation Army (KLA) initiated a number of attacks against Serb police patrols, police stations and other Serb targets within Kosovo's territory. The response was harsh and the consequences tragic for the Albanian section of the population. Serb forces organised and executed a series of actions against the KLA members. These actions, led primarily by the Serbian police and paramilitary forces, resulted in the deaths of many civilians, including women and children, and thousands of Kosovan Albanians were internally displaced.

The Kosovan conflict

The period of violence and oppression against the Kosovan Albanian population in Kosovo was closely monitored and observed by the international community. There were attempts to mediate and help resolve the conflict by raising the issue at the UN Security Council, which at one point approved a political and economic embargo against Serbia. Early in 1998, the Serbian government made an announcement that all police activity against the so-called Albanian terrorists in Kosovo had been completed. Following this announcement, the UN Security Council passed a Resolution that requested both parties to implement an immediate ceasefire and also arranged for the presence of the international Organization for Security and Cooperation in Europe (OSCE) monitors in Kosovo. However, the presence of monitors did not deter the Serb authorities, which continued with their campaign against what they described as the Albanian terrorists. This led to a NATO ultimatum, issued on 20 March 1999, demanding that the Serb forces respect the ceasefire. Four days later, NATO forces began the bombardment of FRY military and police targets in Kosovo and other parts of Serbia and Montenegro (OECD, 2002).

About 12,000 people were killed in the period from March 1998 to June 1999 and more than 3000 people were reported to be missing as a result of the conflict. In the final four months, from March 1999 to June 1999, more than 850,000 Kosovan Albanians were forced to leave Kosovo and find shelter in neighbouring countries, including Albania, Macedonia and Montenegro. Thousands more remained internally displaced, even during the NATO bombing campaign. On 10 June 1999 the NATO troops signed an agreement with the Serbian authorities to stop the bombing. Following this, the UN Security Council passed another resolution authorising an international civil presence, the United Nations Mission in Kosovo (UNMIK), which served as the interim government until the first local elections in 2002.

The UNMIK administration supported the development of local capacity to take over responsibilities and lead the country. At the end of 2011, Kosovan local government had assumed all responsibilities from the UNMIK administration. As a result, Kosovans now lead the country. Another international presence, the European Union Rule of Law Mission (EULEX), led by a coalition of EU countries, was installed in Kosovo after the local Kosovans declared independence from Serbia. A series of unsuccessful nego-tiations related to post-conflict technical issues took place between the Serbian government and Kosovan leaders. Eventually, however, the Kosovan Assembly approved a declaration of independence on 17 February 2008. To date, the Republic of Kosovo has been recognised as an independent country by 87 countries around the world.

The education system

In the last quarter of the twentieth century, the Kosovan education system faced many challenges. Throughout this period, education leaders and Kosovan society as a whole struggled to maintain educational endeavour, and its structural organisation and quality barely survived the challenges of the time. With the establishment of the Yugoslav Federation, Kosovo became one of the autonomous provinces with overall responsibility for organising and leading education independently. When the Serbian government imposed the constitutional changes by unilaterally abolishing Kosovo's autonomy, the province's education system was adversely affected (Daskalovski, 2003; Hyseni *et al.*, 2001). The new Kosovan education legis-lation had a direct impact on the system, with disastrous consequences. The Serbian authorities in Kosovo closed all Albanian language primary and secondary schools and higher education institutions. Also, more than 18,500 primary and secondary school teachers, and 862 university professors were prohibited from entering education facilities because 'they opposed the polit-ical discrimination led by the Serbian authorities' installed in Kosovo (Buleshkaj, 2009: 2).

The parallel system

Throughout the 1990s Albanian education leaders organised and operated an independent system of education, the so-called 'parallel system'. This independent education system constituted the main plank of the Albanian opposition to the repression imposed by the Serbian government. The responsibility for operating the parallel system was transferred to the school principals, teachers, parents, and the greater school community. Albanian communities, both in Kosovo and across the diaspora, organised an inde-pendent funding system for education, which was primarily supported by Albanians living and working elsewhere in the world.

Nevertheless, the ongoing professional learning of educators, as well as curriculum development, were considerably debilitated. This decade is considered to have been the decade of resistance and a priority for the Albanian community was that the provision of education should continue. The further development of education, however, was only possible once the conflict ended in 1999. At that point the international community, under

UNMIK administration, took over the running of education in Kosovo (VanBalkom and Buleshkaj, 2006).

The post-conflict development of education

Soon after the conflict ended, the development of education became one of the most important areas for investment in post-war Kosovo. During this period, Kosovo underwent dramatic changes at the political, cultural, economic and social levels of its society (Goddard, 2007). The process of rebuilding the education system brought together a number of international donors from across the world. Kosovan education leaders cooperated with their international counterparts and with a number of donor organisations to plan and implement those immediate changes in education that were required to bring the system up to European standards (Hyseni *et al.* 2001). These changes included rebuilding the school infrastructure, developing a new policy for education and introducing curriculum reform.

The new Kosovan education system that resulted from these changes may be classified as semi-decentralised insofar as many responsibilities are shared between the central Ministry of Education and the municipal education authorities. It is important to emphasise that in a number of countries located in the Balkans, the responsibility for school finances, policy development and implementation, setting and implementing quality assurance standards, school inspection and overall education reform policies and strategies, remain under the strong authority of the central Ministry of Education (Trnavčevič, 2007; Zgaga, 2006). A similar system prevails in Kosovo.

Challenges for leaders at the school level

This section now turns to the challenges for leaders at the individual school level. It does so under five headings: strategic planning directives, curriculum development, professional development, educational management and administration, and the selection of school principals. Each of these issues is considered with particular attention being given to their implications for leaders in schools.

Strategic planning directives

In 2002, the newly established Ministry of Education Science and Technology (MEST) in Kosovo developed a five-year strategy to guide the direction of initial reform and introduced the new educational structure which, amongst other changes, included five years of elementary school, four years of lower secondary school and three years of upper secondary school. A comprehensive pre-university education curriculum reform was also initiated, and an immediate in-service teacher and leadership training system was planned and implemented. This initiative was undertaken with the strong support of such international donors as the Canadian International Development Agency (CIDA)-funded Kosovo Education Development Program (KEDP), the German GTZ Project for Vocational Education, the Finnish Project on Special Needs Education, and the UNICEF curriculum reform project. The initiative comprised initial steps to upgrade the education system and support local leaders in taking ownership of the further development of education in Kosovo. In March 2007, the Council of Experts of Pre-University Education approved a strategy for the development of pre-university education in Kosovo for the period from 2007 to 2017 (MEST, 2007).

The current pre-university education system includes children between the ages of 6 to 18 attending school at one of three levels: the primary school (grades 1–5), the lower secondary school (grades 6–9) and the upper secondary school (grades 10–12/13). The first two levels are compulsory for all children. Hence, pre-university education constitutes the largest sub-sector within the education system and serves, on a daily basis, more than 400,000 beneficiaries, comprising almost 20 per cent of Kosovo's population.

The ongoing transfer of responsibilities from the central to the municipal level characterises the current reform. This process requires a careful coordination of efforts to ensure that expected changes in the classroom are appropriately supported by strengthening leadership capacity in the municipal offices and individual schools for implementing and sustaining the reform. The newly approved curriculum is competency-based, which represents a major challenge for teachers and school principals, who now recognise that overall quality assurance mechanisms are yet to be fully implemented.

Kosovo has also extended its compulsory education system from 9 to 13 years. This creates another challenge, particularly related to students' mobility in upper secondary schools. The physical distances between these schools, exacerbated by the social welfare system and the high level of poverty, have had a negative impact on student access. As a result of the high proportion of young children, a number of schools in Kosovo continue to operate a shift system to accommodate all of their students. In some of the larger communities, two, or sometimes three, shifts operate. The application of technology in teaching and learning is another aspect of curriculum reform that still requires to be nurtured among teachers and school principals (Pupovci, 2010).

The Government of the Republic of Kosovo, and specifically the Ministry of Education Science and Technology (MEST), have recognised the need for improved sector-wide planning to maintain those outcomes in education already achieved and to address key areas for further improvement. This sector-wide approach and the coordinated efforts of all partners, both local and international, serve as a catalyst for an improved sector-wide performance. Accordingly, MEST has developed the Kosovo Education Strategic Plan 2011–2016 (KESP), with the objective of linking life-long learning and inclusion initiatives in education. This plan adopts a learning approach that reaches out to all learners and aims to provide quality education based on the equal participation of all children (MEST, 2011).

In addition, in the Strategy for Development of Pre-university Education 2007–2017, MEST has outlined a vision aiming to guide overall development in the education sector. The goal here is to integrate the Kosovan education system with current trends in the democratic and developed countries of the European Union. As such, the vision defines Kosovo as 'a knowledge society, integrated in European trends with equal opportunities for personal development of all its members, who, in return, contribute to the sustainable economic and social development' of the country (MEST, 2007: 40). This consideration of strategic planning directives reveals the following challenges for leaders at the school level:

- managing the multiple changes to the structure of schooling which have taken place;
- acting as a 'gateway', or a 'gatekeeper', between municipal reform efforts and local communities;
- coordinating the continued impact of a shift system in reducing time for student learning.

Curriculum development

The first curriculum framework used in post-conflict Kosovo was developed in 2001 by the UNMIK Department of Education, with the support of UNICEF's project in the country. The aim of this framework was to set the foundation for the coherent and quality functioning of the education system based on the principles of learner-centred instruction, flexibility and inclusion. In April 2010, the Ministry of Education released a second draft of the new curriculum framework. This document was created in consultation with education stakeholders around the country. The new curriculum promotes a competency-based approach that is to be developed through practice-oriented teaching and learning. The major shift from a content-based to a competency-based curriculum aims to mobilise the potential of Kosovan youth to compete successfully in the labour market, handle the challenges of the digital age effectively and develop the knowledge, skills and attributes required for the twenty-first century world (MEST, 2011a: 16).

The goal of the new curriculum framework is also to find the most effective means to maximise the potential of the growing number of young educated children in a way that will bring about desired improvements in Kosovan society and align these improvements with the developments that are occurring in EU countries. It states the importance of, and the need for, an improved communication and cooperation system between schools and the wider school community, to enhance the quality of education services at different levels (MEST, 2011a). This consideration of curriculum development reveals the following challenges for leaders at the school level:

- implementing technology-based curriculum in a resource-free environment;
- supporting teachers to move from content-based to competency-based curriculum;
- moving schools from traditional 'factory-model' structures to more open environments conducive to learner-centred instruction.

Professional development

Before the war in Kosovo there had been a dearth of professional development opportunities for teachers for more than two decades. Soon after the conflict ended the Ministry of Education took a number of steps to restructure teacher development and education practice. The intentions of this restructuring were to enhance the quality of teaching and learning, adapt to the new curriculum requirements and respond to new teacher licensing agendas. International donor organisations such as CIDA, GTZ, UNICEF and local NGOs supported the Ministry of Education in organising a series of in-service teacher preparation programs to help teachers learn about, and be exposed to, different learner-centred teaching methods and critical thinking approaches to student learning.

During this period thousands of teachers were prepared and a number of professional development programmes for serving teachers were formulated. However, there was an urgent need to coordinate these efforts and institutionalise initiatives introduced by different providers so that all practising teachers had access to these training programmes. MEST has recently established some new structures and procedures to accredit the programmes and link these with the teacher licensing system, which is also related to the teacher salary system. Further to this, MEST is also developing a system for teacher performance evaluation, which will regulate teacher promotion and career advancement. The continuous professional development of teachers and the upgrading of teachers' qualifications to the equivalent of a bachelor's degree are prerequisites for successful implementation of the new curriculum and a better student learning experience (MEST, 2011b).

This consideration of professional development reveals the following challenges for leaders at the school level:

- assisting teachers to overcome a twenty-year gap in their professional knowledge base;
- advocating for the linking of continuing professional development programmes into the teacher licensing system;
- accessing NGO-led programmes and facilitating implementation in one's own school.

Educational management and administration

Parallel to other developments occurring in the Kosovan education sector, the management and administration of the system has undergone a number of changes, both in its structure and in terms of particular responsibilities. When the first Ministry of Education was established in 2002, it created seven Regional Education Offices (REO). Each REO was responsible for about four municipalities and had the duty to oversee curriculum reform and policy implementation at the school level. The division of responsibilities between the municipal authorities and the REOs, however, was unclear. This lack of clarity, in turn, often led to confusing situations occurring in the field.

In 2007, the Ministry of Education transformed the REO management structures into Regional Inspection Offices for monitoring the implementation of education legislation. As a result of this arrangement and the new trend towards decentralising the education system, the municipal education authorities perform a number of tasks to facilitate and support the provision of education from pre-school institutions to the upper secondary school institutions (Gowing and Saqipi, 2010). However, the process of decentralisation has also resulted in the creation of new municipalities to ensure that Kosovan minority-culture educators will lead education reform processes in those municipalities where minority community populations comprise the majority. This structural and legal change has raised concerns about the municipal education authorities' capacity to manage and administer education, and there is uncertainty as to the degree to which support for teacher professional development and curriculum implementation exists. This consideration of educational management and administration reveals the following challenges for leaders at the school level:

- managing expectations for the achievement of school improvement indicators;
- overcoming post-conflict community stressors (PCCS) to establish an inclusive school environment that integrates multiple ethnic communities;
- establishing vertical-flow relationships with other educational institutions in the pre-school to upper secondary structure.

The selection of school principals

From the 1980s until the introduction of the parallel system of education in 1992, school principals were selected on the basis not only of their teaching qualifications but, more importantly, for being 'correctly' affiliated with the politics and regime of the time. All teachers who had a two year High Pedagogical School degree were qualified to teach at the elementary school level. They were also qualified to become school principals at that level on the condition that they had gained a minimum of three years of experience. There was no stipulation that this experience should have been 'successful', nor was there a shared understanding of what being successful entailed. During the parallel system of education in the 1990s, teaching experience and teaching qualifications were not always mandatory for the selection of school principals. More importantly, perhaps, a principal needed a great deal of courage and commitment. Candidates tended to be educators who were aware that their lives and the lives of their families could be in jeopardy. Hence, in accepting an appointment one was also demonstrating a willingness to take risks in leading schools for Albanian children since the Serbian government was, simultaneously, using oppressive measures to prevent their schooling (Buleshkaj, 2009).

The selection of school principals is currently regulated by the Law on Pre-University Education in the Republic of Kosovo (Official Gazette of the Republic of Kosovo, 2011) and the Law on Local Governance (Official Gazette of the Republic of Kosovo, 2008). The practical selection procedures are regulated by an 'administrative instruction' (AI) that was issued by MEST (MEST, 2009) and is still used by selection committees across the country. This AI regulates selection procedures, the criteria for selection, the membership of the interview panel, other matters related to interview reporting and the final appointment of the school principal. Until the AI was issued, the central MEST had primary responsibility for the selection process, including the setting up of the interview panel and the hiring of new school principals.

Municipalities advertise vacancies in their respective jurisdictions. The advertisement is posted in a local newspaper for 15 days, during which time candidates must submit their applications. Amongst other things, it is a requirement that candidates are citizens of Kosovo, that they have graduated from MEST licensed and accredited university programs within the country, and that they have at least three years of teaching experience. Further, all candidates are required to provide a comprehensive curriculum vitae, including reference letters, certificates of attendance at professional development and training courses and a five-page organisational development plan for the school and/or education institution to which he, or she, is applying. It is important to highlight that the school development plan is publicly presented to an open audience. Once the MEST is in a position to issue teacher licenses, the new Law on Pre-University Education requires that all school principals be licensed teachers. However, the infrastructure for establishing teacher licensing is yet to be established.

Municipal authorities set up an interview panel consisting of three voting and two non-voting members. Two voting members represent the municipality and one represents the MEST, with the non-voting members representing the school board and the parent council. All candidates who have submitted completed applications are invited for an interview and are given the opportunity to present their school development plan publicly. Voting members cast their votes and the panel submits the final report to the mayor of the respective municipality, who then offers a four-year contract to the successful candidate. If performance in-post is deemed to be successful, the same school principal can be reselected at the end of the contract. Judging what constitutes 'successful' performance, however, remains problematic since there is no process in place to evaluate systematically the performance of school principals. This deficiency is sometimes misused for political reasons and is an area of school leadership recruitment and retention that requires further attention. This consideration of the selection of principals reveals the following challenges for leaders at the school level:

- contributing to the development of context-specific indicators of effective school leadership;
- engaging staff and community in the construction of a coherent school development plan;
- participating in professional development and further study opportunities whenever possible.

Conclusion

During the last quarter of the twentieth century, Kosovan education was in a state of inertia. First, this was a period when there was little access available to many of the new ideas sweeping through Western education systems. Second, this was the period of repression by Serbian authorities, resulting in the establishment of the parallel system of education, which existed outside the public sphere. Third, this was the period when a bitter conflict erupted that resulted in thousands of deaths as well as a great number of externally and internally displaced Kosovan Albanians.

The first decade of the twenty-first century, however, has seen extensive educational reform in Kosovo. In 2001 the system was in such disarray that multiple independent initiatives were welcomed. Funded by the international community, these initiatives were pursued in a policy vacuum and were, for the most part, uncoordinated. As a result, many teachers and school leaders appeared to spend more time participating in training activities than working in their schools. This observation was highlighted in 2003 by the then REO of Prizren district, who complained: 'No more training! All my schools are being filled with unqualified substitute teachers because the government teachers are away being trained. Let my teachers teach!' (Milhaim Elshani, personal communication, 23 March 2003).

The incoherence of the policy agenda in the early twenty-first century has now been replaced by a more coordinated approach to educational reform. The coordination is provided by the Ministry of Education, Science and Technology, with power being devolved to the municipalities through the Regional Inspection Offices. Overcoming generations of tradition is, however, a difficult task. As illustrated in the introduction to this chapter, not all Kosovans are comfortable with the new direction of educational reform. The reduction of power and authority as acquired according to age and political connection, and its replacement by the need for professional knowledge, experience and aptitude is a bitter pill for many. Nevertheless, the demographics of the country are driving such change. As some 60 per cent of the Kosovan population is under 25 years of age, the majority of them have little or no memory of the dark days of the late twentieth century. The idea of students walking to classes located in a teacher's house, or travelling alone, or in pairs, to avoid the security forces, has become the stuff of legend rather than lived experience. The use of cell phone technology and the internet are now part of the daily lives of over half the population. Social media sites are actively embraced and virtual communities of youth span not only the country, but also the diaspora. As with many other countries, knowledge is no longer the domain of the old and experienced members of Kosovan society. This socio-demographic transition bodes well for the continued success of educational reform in Kosovo.

Dedication

This chapter is dedicated to the memory of Remzi Salihu, 1956–2011.

References

Buleshkaj, O. (2009) Building capacity for effective leadership in post-conflict Kosovo (unpublished master's thesis). University of Calgary, Alberta, Canada.

Daskalovski, Ž. (2003) Claims to Kosovo: Nationalism and self-determination. In F. Bieber and Ž. Daskalovski (eds) *Understanding the War in Kosovo*. London, UK: Routledge, pp. 13–30.

Goddard, J. T. (2007) The professional development needs of educational leaders in post-conflict Kosovo. *The Educational Forum*, 71(3), 200–10.

Gowing, E. and Saqipi, B. (2010) Report on capacity building needs assessment of the municipal education directorates in Kosovo (unpublished report). Phrishtina, Kosovo: Ministry of Education, Science and Technology.

Hyseni, H., Pupovci, D., Salihaj, J. and Shatri, B. (2001) *Education in Kosovo: Figures and facts*. Prishtina, RKS: KEC.

MEST (Ministry of Education, Science and Technology) (2007) *Strategy for Development of Pre-university Education in Kosovo 2007–2017*. Prishtina: Druckart.

MEST (Ministry of Education, Science and Technology) (2009) *Administrative Instruction No. 03/2009 on Procedures for Selecting Directors of Education and Training Institutions*. Prishtina: MEST. http://www.masht-gov.net/advCms/documents/3-2009-UA_Zgjedhja_e_Drejtorve.pdf [Albanian language] (accessed 2 February 2011).

MEST (Ministry of Education, Science and Technology) (2011a) *Curriculum Framework for Pre-university Education of the Republic of Kosovo*. Prishtina, RKS: Grafika Rezniqi.

MEST (Ministry of Education, Science and Technology) (2011b) *Kosovo Education Strategic Plan 2011–2016*. Prishtina, Kosovo: Ministry of Education, Science and Technology

Official Gazette of the Republic of Kosova (2008) *Official Gazette of the Republic of*

Kosova, Pristina (No. 30/15). http://www.kgjk-ks.org/repository/docs/GZK-17-ANGLISHT_545882.pdf (accessed 28 November 2008).

Official Gazette of the Republic of Kosova (2011) *Official Gazette of the Republic of Kosova, Pristina* (No. 17/16). http://www.kgjk-ks.org/repository/docs/GZK-17-ANGLISHT_545882.pdf (accessed 15 February 2012).

OECD (Organisation for Economic Cooperation and Development) (2002) *Thematic Review of National Policies for Education: Kosovo.* http://www.oecd.org/officialdocuments/publicdisplaydocumentpdf/?cote=CCNM/DEELSA/ED(2001)6/REV1&docLanguage=En (accessed 2 February 2011).

Pupovci, D. (2002) Teacher education system in Kosovo. *Metodika,* 3(5), 125–45.

Pupovci, D. (2010) Background report on pre-university education in Kosovo (unpublished report). Pristina, Kosovo: Ministry of Education, Science and Technology.

Statistical Office of Kosovo (2010) *Kosovo in figures 2009.* Prishtina, Kosovo: Statistical Office of Kosovo.

Trnavčevič, A. (2007) School leadership and equity: Slovenian elements. *School Leadership and Management,* 27(1), 79–90.

VanBalkom, W. D. and Buleshkaj, O. (2006) Parathënie. In M. Fullan (ed.) *Forcat e Ndryshimit: Vazhdim.* Prishtinë: Ndërmarrja Gazetare Botuese ADEA Publishers, n.p.

Zgaga, P. (ed.) (2006) *The Prospects of Teacher Education in South-east Europe.* Ljubljana, Slovokia: Tiskarna Littera picta d.o.o.

11 Timor-Leste

The now in the not yet of school leadership

Margie Beck and Silvanio Araujo

Introduction

School leaders in Timor-Leste work in conditions that would make those occupying similar positions in more developed countries despair. In every aspect of school administration school principals face almost insurmountable problems to keep their schools functioning. Indeed, without their commitment and dedication the doors of the schools would be unlikely to be kept open on a daily basis. This chapter describes the background to the situation. It looks at the history of Timor-Leste and the reconstruction of the education sector after independence in 1999. It goes on to describe the reality of school leadership, placing the experiences of school leaders in the wider context of education in a developing nation. The chapter also reflects on the particular difficulties being faced by leaders in the education sector in trying to build a system that will help its citizens to reduce poverty and achieve human development for the future.

Context

In the nine years since achieving formal independence, Timor-Leste has undergone substantial growth and development. Those in government since 2002 have had to rebuild the whole country from virtually nothing, with every sector needing complete restructuring. This has been no simple task and national goals and planning are being realised at a much slower rate than first anticipated, in spite of the huge influx of aid money, in addition to funds derived from fuel reserves.

Timor-Leste is located in Southeast Asia, on the southernmost edge of the Indonesian archipelago, northwest of Australia. It is a very small country comprising a land area of 15,000km, with a population of 1,066,409 according to the 2010 census (Republica Democratica Timor-Leste, 2010). The country includes the eastern half of Timor island, as well as the Oecussi enclave in the northwest portion of Indonesian West Timor, and the islands of Atauro and Jaco. The mixed Malay and Pacific Islander culture of the Timorese people reflects the geography of the country at the confluence of where Malay and Pacific Island cultures meet. Traders from China, Malay states and India all preceded the arrival of the Dutch and Portuguese in search of spices, sandalwood and other resources. This contact has resulted in a diverse racial and language mix.

Portuguese influence during the four centuries of colonial rule has resulted in a substantial majority of the population identifying themselves as Roman Catholic. Some of those who consider themselves Catholic practise a mixed form of religion that includes local animist customs. As a result of the colonial education system and the 24-year Indonesian occupation, approximately 13 per cent of East Timorese claimed to speak, read or write Portuguese, 43 per cent to speak Bahasa Indonesia and 6 per cent to speak English, according to the 2004 census. Tetum, the most common of the local languages, is spoken by approximately 90 per cent of the population, although only 46 per cent speak Tetum Prasa, the form of Tetum dominant around Dili, the capital city (Republica Democratica Timor-Leste, Census, 2005). Mambae, Kemak and Fataluku are also widely spoken. This linguistic diversity is enshrined in the country's constitution, which designates Portuguese and Tetum as official languages and English and Bahasa Indonesia as working languages.

The conflict

East Timor was first colonised by Portugal in the sixteenth century and remained colonised until the Portuguese revolution in 1974 prompted decolonisation. In late 1975 it declared its independence, but later that year was invaded and occupied by the Indonesian military. East Timor was declared Indonesia's 27th province the following year.

During the 24 years of Indonesian occupation from 1975 to 1999, Indonesian became the official language and young people were indoctrinated in state ideology. In order to garner support from the Timorese people, roads, water, communication systems and other basic infrastructure were provided by the Indonesian government. Indonesian military rule established many schools at primary and post-primary level. The Indonesian curriculum was also introduced, and was promoted throughout the various islands that made up the nation, as was the ethical code, 'Garuda Pancasila'. This code identified the five precepts that were deemed necessary to follow in order to live as a 'good' Indonesian citizen. These ideological and material programmes were used as strategies to quell the resistance of the East Timorese people. However, freedom fighters who were members of FALIN-TIL (*Forças Armadas da Libertação Nacional de Timor-Leste*), continued to wage a guerrilla war against Indonesian occupation from their mountain jungle hide outs. According to Soares, the freedom fighters employed 'hit and run' tactics and even managed to infiltrate the Indonesian army intelligence (2000: 59). In this way, they were able to set up contact with sections of the army for information and the acquisition of weapons.

The Indonesian army, however, continued to brutalise the population and from the early days of Indonesian occupation until its end, over 200,000 East Timorese died. The local economy was controlled by Indonesians and by some East Timorese who were loyal to them. According to Amnesty International, women were systematically raped by Indonesians, especially by soldiers, until the late 1980s. This constituted a form of ethnic cleansing. McCloskey provides a cogent summing up of the situation:

> The massive human rights violations in East Timor which followed Indonesia's invasion included random massacres, extra-judicial killings, starvation, deaths from preventable diseases, torture, forced movement of populations, coerced sterilisation of women, rape and imprisonment without legal redress.
>
> (McCloskey, 2000: 4)

In late January 1999, the Indonesian government suddenly announced that it would be prepared to relinquish East Timor. However, the new President, Habibie, had no real plan for independence. Neither had he consulted with the United Nations, Portugal or the pro-independence leaders of East Timor, on the efficacy of this proposal. In spite of this, a plan was rapidly developed to enable the people of East Timor to vote in a referendum to decide their future. This plan was accepted in May 1999 by Indonesia and Portugal, and the Secretary-General of the UN was authorised to conduct a referendum on independence. In turn, the Indonesian armed forces were given the responsibility for security before, during, and after the referendum.

In reality, since November 1998, elements within the armed forces had begun 'Operasi Sapu Jagad' or 'Operation Global Clean Sweep', which involved using paramilitary units to instigate engagement in violence in order to portray East Timor as being racked by civil war and incapable of self-government. It was hoped that this strategy would undermine the referendum, while death squads would focus their attention on eliminating pro-independence leaders. The plan ran counter to the agreements made with the UN, but in Jakarta the main political parties campaigning for the June assembly elections were all pushing a pro-unity line, and were unhappy that what they regarded as an integral part of Indonesia could potentially become independent. In this political climate, the armed forces became relatively unaccountable for their actions. Consequently, paramilitary violence escalated during the first eight months of 1999, with between 5000 and 6000 people being killed and thousands fleeing from their homes.

The small United Nations electoral team (UNAMET) that conducted voter registration, and then the poll, was largely spared direct violence against itself, but still found it difficult to operate. There were also doubts as to whether voters would be too intimidated to turn out on polling day and the referendum was postponed twice because of problems created by the violence. However, on 30 August 1999, over 98 per cent of registered voters turned out to cast their ballots and it was announced on 4 September that 78 per cent had voted for independence, instead of favouring the alternative of remaining an autonomous province within Indonesia (United Nations Security Council, 1999).

The Indonesian military was stunned by the vote and stood by as pro-Jakarta paramilitary units proceeded to scorch Dili and drive hundreds-of-thousands of people into either the mountains or refugee camps in West Timor. Dili itself became a ghost town and over 80 per cent of East Timor's infrastructure was destroyed, including almost all of its electrical grid system and other essential public utilities. As one East Timorese put it to the present authors: 'If the Indonesians could have rolled up the roads and taken them also, they would have.'

In the education sector, the majority of the teachers who had been working in East Timorese schools were from Java and they left East Timor. Up to a quarter of a million Timorese were displaced from their homes, resulting in thousands of children losing up to two years of schooling. Also, for those schools now unroofed, the coming rainy season threatened to destroy whatever educational resources were left in them.

Resolution of the conflict

The United Nations Transitional Administration in East Timor (UNTAET), which took over responsibility for rebuilding the education sector during 1999–2002, had a complicated relationship with the Timorese with whom they were trying to work. The matter of which language to use became a difficulty everywhere, because English, Indonesian and Tetum were all being spoken. Also, there was often little interaction between the international staff and East Timorese, other than through their working relationships with counterparts (Nicolai, 2004: 117). UNICEF's João Pereira pointed out: 'the complexity of change and its demands, particularly on newly appointed and often inexperienced East Timorese decision-makers and administrators, constrained...program planning and implementation' (cited in Nicolai, 2004: 83). However, an immediate priority was to get children back to school. Thus, at least in the short term, the restoration of infrastructure took precedence over teacher-preparation and capacity-building.

At the same time, a large number of non-government organisations were trying to help the new nation. Nevertheless, because there was no overall coordination of their efforts, projects often overlapped. Furthermore, funding was often distributed inequitably, with emphasis being placed on rehabilitation in Dili and other major population centres, while rural areas, where the need was often greater, were relatively neglected.

The achievement of independence was formally celebrated on 20 May 2002. The new nation, Timor-Leste, supported by many international groups and agencies, including a United Nations transitional administration, emerged as one of the poorest in the world. The war had destroyed most of the country's infrastructure and there was limited economic development to provide for a growing population characterised by low life expectancy and high levels of illiteracy.

The country's future was to be partly shaped by its past, especially by its traditional culture and values, but also by its inherited colonial legacies, first from centuries of Portuguese, and more recently Indonesian, control. Its prospects were also to be influenced by its educated elite returning from exile and holding differing views on development. In addition, international agencies occasionally sought to impose predetermined policies upon the new nation, often without consulting the local population as to their appropriateness. The result was sometimes conflicting advice, creating problems for those charged with making policy.

In the months following the vote for independence, Timor-Leste was described by the United Nations as being:

> ...a strange land. There was no government, no official language or currency, no system of law, no media and no shops or schools. Not only was the country physically plundered and raped, but also no former structure existed which could be used as a base for re-building.
>
> (United Nations, 2000: 18)

In the early days after the crisis, UNICEF served as the *de facto* Ministry of Education since there was no national education authority. It worked with UNTAET district officers to assist with the practical responsibilities of registering those who wanted to become teachers and disbursing teacher financial incentives, paid for by UNICEF (Nicolai, 2004: 75). Portugal, Australia, Germany and Brazil, together with the World Bank, USAID, UNICEF, JICA and other aid agencies, all contributed to the rebuilding of the education sector. This work ranged from rehabilitating schools, to providing water and toilet facilities (Nicolai, 2004: 102).

Birdsall, Ross and Sabot have stated:

> Education is one of the major means of reducing poverty and achieving successful human development in a country. It leads to improvements in health and nutrition and is widely thought to reduce inequities and discrimination. Indeed, education is seen as a driving force towards achieving the entire set of Millennium Development Goals.
>
> (1995: 1)

Taking cognisance of such a position, the Ministry of Education (MoE) started to implement a strategic plan for universal primary education in 2005, aiming to create the opportunity for every child to complete a 'quality' primary education. This plan was further developed by the Law for Basic Education (MoE, 2008), by which compulsory education was extended to nine years.

Overview of the contemporary educational situation

The key priorities in the national education strategy were constructed around three core concepts: improving access to education, enhancing the quality and relevance of primary education, and advancing school management. The aims of schooling in Timor-Leste were developed from these concepts. They are designed to promote and increase the quality of education in the country by:

- personal and community development of the learning of individuals, through the full development of their personality and the shaping of their character, enabling them to reflect conscientiously on ethical, civic, spiritual and aesthetic values, as well as providing them with a balanced psychological and physical development;
- ensuring the cultural, ethical, civic and professional training of children and youngsters, enabling them to be critically reflective;
- ensuring equal opportunities for both genders, namely by way of co-education practices and school and professional guidance, raising the awareness of the stakeholders in the education process;
- contributing towards the defence of national identity and independence and to the strengthening of identification with the historic matrix of Timor-Leste, raising awareness as to the cultural legacy of the Timorese people, by way of a growing interdependence and solidarity among peoples;
- developing work capability in individuals, and providing them, based on a solid general training, with specific competencies in terms of knowledge and initiative, enabling them to occupy a fair position in the labour market, contributing towards the progress of society according to their interests, skills and aptitudes;
- decentralising and diversifying education structures and actions, so as to provide an appropriate response to local realities, a high sense of participation among the people, an equitable implementation in the community and efficient decision-making;
- contributing towards the correction of regional and local asymmetries, achieving equal access to the benefits of education, culture, science and technology throughout the whole country;
- ensuring the public service of education and teaching, through a network of central and local administration offices, as well as private and cooperative entities, meets the needs of the entire population;
- ensuring the organisation and operation of public, private and cooperative schools, in order to promote the development of specific education projects that respect national curricular directives, as well as growing standards of operational autonomy, through accountability for the pursuit of pedagogic and administrative objectives, subject to the public evaluation of results against public funding

based on objective, transparent and fair criteria that encourage good operational practices;

- ensuring freedom to attend the school of choice;
- contributing to the development of democratic spirit and practice;
- ensuring a second-chance education for those who seek professional development.

(Translated by the authors from Portuguese) (MoE, 2007a: 27)

These aims have been pursued in Timor-Leste since independence in seeking to improve and transform the education system that was inherited from the 24 years of Indonesian occupation and its aftermath. In 1999, after the massive burning and destruction of property throughout the country, nearly 90 per cent of schools were damaged or destroyed. Also, as has already been mentioned, the majority of Indonesian teachers had left the country. A further compounding factor was that the school curriculum and its associated Indonesian textbooks were no longer considered to be relevant for either the new political situation, or the requirements of Timorese education.

Another crisis emerged in 2006. It started as a conflict between sections of the Timorese military over discrimination within the armed forces, and escalated to a coup attempt and to more general violence throughout the country. During this crisis, schools were again victims of vandalism and destruction. Once more, rebuilding had to take place. The current situation is that the education system has expanded considerably, with extensive efforts having been made by the Ministry of Education to recover and reconstruct the sector. Nevertheless, there is a long way to go to achieve the nationally and internationally set goals (UNESCO, 2009). Some of the challenges and the extent to which they are being met will now be considered in relation to the curriculum, teaching and learning, and management and administration.

Curriculum

In Timor-Leste, there are three cycles of basic schooling: primary school classes 1–3, primary school classes 4–6 and junior secondary classes 1–3, thus making nine years of basic education. At the time of writing, the curriculum for the third cycle of basic schooling is being released into schools. This means that for the first time since independence, schools in the basic education sector will have access to a curriculum that has been specifically designed for Timor-Leste. It remains to be seen how long it will take for teaching materials that accompany the curriculum for the third cycle of basic education to reach the schools.

The basic education curricula have been produced in both Portuguese and Tetum, although from 2012 Portuguese has been mandated as the language of instruction. This mandate has been legislated despite the ongoing difficulties faced by both teachers and students in using Portuguese. In reality, many teachers have to employ three or four languages when they are introducing new concepts in the classroom. These are Portuguese, Tetum and Indonesian in secondary school classrooms, and the mother tongue with younger children. When the Presidency of the Council of Ministers openly criticised the problems associated with the official teaching language and of the teaching of other languages, including the national languages, and English and/or Indonesian as working languages, it became clear that the language issue had been placing a huge burden on those directly involved in the teaching and learning process. Research conducted by Quinn (2007, 2008) on realising language and literacy goals in the country's schools further highlighted the difficulties faced by teachers in their everyday work.

The prescribed aims of the curriculum state that it is 'certified, child-centred with clear rules. It is democratic, flexible, inclusive and focussed on the local context while meeting individual and social needs; supported by team organisation' (MoE, 2007a. p. 26) (translated from Tetum by the authors). Each of the curriculum documents and supporting teaching materials distributed by the Ministry make this same claim. However, in reality, most schools do not have the supplementary texts available for students to use during their lessons, meaning that it is often only the teacher who has access to a single copy of the student text. Consequently, most of the time during a typical 100 minute lesson is spent engaging students in copying information from the blackboard, which the teacher has written out from the textbook.

The curriculum has been devised by both Portuguese and Brazilian curriculum specialists, many of whom have never visited Timor-Leste and are unfamiliar with the conditions encountered by schools in this setting. Their brief was to provide a curriculum that would be relevant for the children of Timor-Leste using Portuguese as the language of instruction. The textbooks to accompany the curriculum come from Portugal. While these textbooks are now being written specifically for Timor-Leste, they were originally designed for the Portuguese context, and were simply transferred from Portugal to Timor-Leste, ignoring the special circumstances of the emerging country and its needs.

Teaching and learning

The curriculum exhorts teachers to use child-centred teaching and learning strategies appropriate to the development of the child. Strategies such as group work, individual learning and discovery learning are recommended in each curriculum for each subject area as being the ideal approaches to be used by teachers. As the *Estudo do Meiu* (Studies of Society and its Environment) curriculum document states:

> First, students should feel, from their experiences in this subject, that they are able to:

- share with others their knowledge and experiences when working in groups;
- understand from their contact with other students, their families and communities where they live about how the physical world continues to evolve;
- complete activities through their interaction with each other working in groups;
- apply their knowledge and experiences in the areas of Society and its Environment, Social Science and Natural Science;
- access and utilise partly from the students themselves and partly from methodology, approaches to real life in different areas, according to their development;
- use assignments such as activities and projects to help students' development and learning;
- use resources that will allow students to participate, work together and develop the skills to do this;
- use examples from the planning activities to complete evaluation of learning, and develop good work and behaviour patterns, through activities in the classroom.

(Translated by the authors from Portuguese and Tetum)
(MoE, 2007b: 29)

Management and administration

There are continuing constraints that hinder the realisation of the aims of education and schooling in Timor-Leste. These include the lack of clear and consistent policies, particularly in the area of early childhood and pre-school education; the lack of infrastructure to meet the needs of increasing numbers of students who now have access to compulsory education; the lack of resources, textbooks, and ongoing teacher preparation; and the lack of qualified teachers throughout the whole education sector. Administrative practices across the system are also deficient, with frequent restructuring debilitating 'on-the-ground' capacity to manage the four regions of educational administration. One school principal with whom we spoke described his relationship with the local regional office of the Ministry of Education in this way:

It is very hard to work with the leaders of education in the district because sometimes they make decisions and don't consult with the teachers. As leaders of the school we face many challenges because sometimes it's very difficult to lead the teachers because they might not be willing to follow the suggestions made by ourselves or by the Ministry. We have teacher meetings every month and try to find solutions to our problems.

As the principal of a school, he was particularly keen to highlight issues for leaders working at the school level. It is to this matter of leadership at the individual school level that we now turn our attention.

Leadership at the individual school level

The reality in Timor-Leste is that the education system is still in the early stage of development. Despite the rhetoric, the process of rebuilding the sector has been difficult because of the enormity of the work involved. While millions of dollars have been poured into the sector, tangible results have been limited. Progress has been impeded by changes in government and even more frequent changes of leadership at district and regional level. There has also been a 'revolving door' of advisors and consultants offering differing recommendations to the Ministry and undermining the capacity of middle management. Frequently, decisions are slow in being made at all levels of the education system because of a lack of strong leadership, a situation that is compounded because decision-making is undertaken centrally in Dili. Furthermore, once decisions have been made, it takes a long time for a new policy to be communicated, let alone implemented. Indeed, decisions made by the Minister of Education often remain unknown, or fail to be enacted by the bureaucrats in the Ministry.

Schools are dependent on the Ministry of Education to supply every need, ranging from desks and chairs in classrooms, to chalk and blackboards. However, the supply of these resources is still deficient, especially in those schools located outside of the major urban centres. The further away from urban centres the schools are situated, the less likely it is that renovation, rehabilitation and resource building are taking place.

In a recent interview featured in *The Dili Weekly* (4th September, 2011) following Member of Parliament, Francisco de Araújo's monitoring visit to schools to assess the state of their infrastructure, he was reported as saying:

> We noted that many schools do not have a bathroom. They also do not have books, boards and the school feeding program still has many problems. There are no desks and chairs, teachers do not have curriculums. The Ministry's intensive course program is also problematic. Courses are very general and do not follow basic curriculums.

In addition, recent data indicate that over 70 per cent of children do not make it to grade 9 in school and fail to complete the full course of 'basic education'. It also takes children an average of 11.2 years to reach grade 6, which is more than double the time that is officially prescribed (MoE, 2010). Moreover, it has been suggested that a large proportion of families are enrolling their children in school at an older age than expected, not enrolling them at all or withdrawing them early because of community perceptions that what is taught is still irrelevant, or incongruent with their own beliefs and values (Caroll and Kupczyk-Romanczuk, 2007; Romiszowski, 2005).

High population growth only adds to the enrolment problem. It is forecast that the population in Timor-Leste will double in the next 17 years, with enormous pressure being placed on the education sector to provide resources for the increasing number of children entering school every year (Saikia, Hosgelen and Chalmers, 2011). Schools are already faced with overcrowding, making it necessary for principals to organise morning and afternoon sessions for the students. In one local school, three sessions are run daily, meaning that each student's learning is restricted to only 2 or 3 hours of class contact time in the day. No matter how much rehabilitation and school construction takes place, the number of students who require placements continues to outstrip the availability of schools.

Given such a large population of young people, it is a matter of great concern that, according to UNESCO, only about 80 per cent of children completed primary schooling in 2008. Furthermore, at least 20 per cent of children are not attending primary school at all (UNESCO Institute of Statistics, 2010), an estimate that must be regarded as conservative since the World Bank suggests the figure is closer to 30 per cent (World Bank, 2009: 3). These poor school attendance and retention figures have serious implications for future human resource and literacy development, employment prospects, poverty reduction, economic growth, social cohesion and overall global competitiveness. In short, the figures indicate a trend running counter to the country's aspirations to meet its national development plans and the UN Millennium Development Goals (Taylor-Leech, 2011: 3).

School leaders are often teachers with experience that goes back to Portuguese times. One of the consequences of the colonial administration, however, is that they have no experience of leadership. Without formal management and leadership training, it is the school leaders' belief in education that is the key to future development for the country and that drives them to maintain their efforts in creating functioning educational institutions. Nevertheless, teachers working in the schools often lack the same commitment. This is regularly reflected by their not turning up for work on time, not turning up at all, preparing lessons that are completely teacher-centred, or following the same lesson format day after day. Many of these teachers are waiting for the government to introduce a national pension scheme and are simply 'going through the motions' and waiting to retire.

School principals are frequently called to meetings at the regional offices. Many have no private transport and have to walk long distances to reach the main office. If principals are required to travel to Dili, schools are left for hours, or even days, without any supervision. Teachers have been known to take advantage of this situation by finishing school early and sending students home. Sometimes, on such occasions, teachers may not turn up at all, so classes are left unsupervised and no teaching takes place.

School leaders have found it difficult to work with these and other circumstances they encounter every day. One principal of an elementary school who spoke to us commented that he finds leadership very difficult because 'our school now has improvements, but it is hard for me to work as a responsible leader because I don't know how to manage the policies and the administration for the school'. Given that, as leaders, they may have had little teacher preparation and even less preparation for management and administration, they look to their local regional education department for guidance and leadership. Only by following a prescribed timetable comprising annual, through to weekly, programming are they enabled to function on a day-to-day basis and to feel confident in doing so. Very few leaders would risk deviating from this plan for fear that the children and teachers would be disadvantaged at national exam time.

At least one copy of the primary school curriculum is now available in most schools. Yet, teachers struggle with understanding the concepts that have been included and tend to use the general objectives listed in the curriculum documents as specific objectives because they are unable to refine them with the required level of precision. Also, most teachers employ a prescribed format for their lesson plans and write them in Portuguese. They do so because the main emphasis of requirements is on precision of language use in the lesson plan, rather than on the appropriateness of the content and strategies to be used in teaching the lesson.

The Ministry of Education has published an annual, trimestral and weekly programme for each curriculum area, and schools tend to follow this document to the letter, while ignoring the reality that often students do not learn according to a programmed timetable. In most cases, lessons remain limited to the teacher introducing the lesson, students copying notes from the blackboard, students reading the content in Portuguese and teachers giving explanations of the Portuguese language content in Tetum, the local language, or Indonesian, to help students understand what has been written. Students are then required to answer three knowledge questions related directly to the material on the board. Each lesson tends to follow the same format. Even when textbooks are available for student use, they are often stored away in case the students might get them dirty. Frequently, schools have only one or two copies of the textbooks, so the material is copied for the students to learn according to the methods described above.

One school principal interviewed said: 'As a leader my greatest difficulty is to carry out the requirements of my position because the facilities in the school are not good enough so I can't do a good job to manage the administration nor to implement the school policies.' He went on to add that the government did not provide resources for him to use with his teachers, so often he resorts to his own private materials to assist his staff and students. Such problems are intensified in those schools situated in the more remote areas of Timor-Leste. The distance from the regional offices means that principals struggle with effective communication. Often the telephone network does not reach rural areas and there is no postal service away from the main towns. If principals need to attend meetings they could be out of the school for at least a week. Resources are often non-existent. One school, located in the outer reaches of a particular district, never received copies of the curriculum, textbooks, planning information or the calendar for the teaching year. The conditions in which these schools operate are also extremely poor. For example, chairs and tables for the students may be broken, or be unsuitable for the age group being taught, living quarters for staff have not been refurbished since Indonesian times, floors are packed with dirt and windows are non-existent. During the wet season, staff and students are unable to reach their schools because of localised flooding. Also, teachers have little or no pre-service preparation and are unable to gain access to professional development opportunities.

Conclusion

The education policies that have been implemented in Timor-Leste since independence have comprised major reforms intended to transform the educational system that was inherited from the 24 years of Indonesian occupation. Supported by aid from Portugal, New Zealand and Brazil, and by multilateral agencies such as UNICEF, there has been a steady growth in the level of schooling provided for the people of the nation. However, in spite of these policies, the injection of aid funding, the provision of resources for schools and the availability of teacher professional development during every school holiday, there remain many deficiencies across the whole spectrum of the education sector that have implications for school leadership. For example, there is a lack of clear and consistent policies and practices for supporting school leaders in their daily decision-making. They are also constrained by inadequate sanitation, lack of even basic furniture, poor playing areas and an absence of technological resources that would help them to provide a more holistic education for their students. Furthermore, insufficient curriculum support documents, as well as inadequate continuous professional development in curriculum implementation, impede progress in every classroom.

Difficulties encountered with teaching in two or three languages, the lack of clear policy on the role of the teaching language for promoting national unity, and the shortage of written texts available for teacher use, mean that school leaders may ignore the policy in order to provide support for teachers and students. For example, it is not unusual for teachers to write some material in Portuguese on the blackboard, with the students copying it into their exercise books, and then continue the lesson in Tetum or the local language. Teachers have not been taught how to teach Portuguese (or Tetum) as a second language and tend to teach language in isolation without even building vocabulary lists that would help students to develop bilingual thinking. Although it is claimed officially that Portuguese is the only language of instruction in the classroom, this is far from being the reality.

For leaders, 'inadequate decentralisation of regional education services with responsibilities for management, teacher training, library/resource centres, budgetary matters and school inspections' (Presidency of the Council of Ministers, 2011, np) leaves them resorting to their own experience and commitment to education to forge the future of Timor-Leste as a developing nation. Inspectors have been appointed for each region and sub-region, but the effectiveness of this arrangement is yet to be evaluated, particularly as frequent changes in Ministry personnel at the regional level have delayed the drawing up of inspectors' job descriptions. Often, these new bureaucrats move into the office without the benefit of a handover or briefing, so months can be spent finding out what they are supposed to be doing and where things are kept. Even something as simple as the distribution of new curriculum documents becomes problematic because no one knows where the documents are located.

Basic leadership development as well as school management and administration training would help school leaders to assume their responsibilities more effectively. At present, school principals and teachers receive a salary which is determined by years of service and qualifications, but there is no recompense for holding leadership positions. Some financial recognition would help them to be more respected within the school and the community, and encourage younger teachers to seek promotion. Currently, promotion tends to be awarded to the most experienced person in the school (often a male as the women have had careers interrupted by child rearing). While the Ministry controls what is provided by way of professional development, there is no opportunity for school leaders to develop their own management capability. Teachers and principals attend the same courses for professional development, regardless of their individual skills and experience. In the more remote areas, teachers from elementary to senior levels are accommodated together, causing resentment when the courses do not meet individual needs and interests. For example, teachers of mathematics who were delivering professional development courses during one holiday period were catering for senior secondary school teachers, while the primary school teachers were neglected. When they requested a different programme these primary teachers were informed that the programme had been set by the Ministry and could not be changed.

The government's Strategic Development Plan for 2011– 2030 states:

> Despite challenges, we have made enormous progress in terms of access to basic education and now need to focus on quality of education. The quality of much of the teaching in Timor-Leste remains poor, with an inevitable flow-on effect on student learning. More than 75 per cent of teachers are not qualified to the levels required by law. The curriculum is also inadequate to deal with the development needs of our nation. School administration remains inefficient and does not encourage participation by families or communities.
>
> (Republica Democratica Timor-Leste, 2011: 16)

While such comment from the government may seem to be pessimistic, it actually assists those involved in planning. The admission of deficiencies in the education system encourages a focus on improvement that, it is hoped, will be maintained. The road to reconstruction in any developing country recovering from conflict is not one that can be achieved quickly, particularly when its whole infrastructure has been destroyed. In ten years, the education sector in Timor-Leste has come a long way in spite of the difficulties encountered in 2002. It is important to acknowledge the progress that has been made: schools have been rebuilt, teachers are receiving some useful on-going professional development, regional administration offices are operating and the Ministry of Education continues to develop its capacity. For school leaders, much remains to be done to support them in their work, and to provide them with management skills. Perhaps in another ten years the reality will finally match the rhetoric.

References

Birdsall, N., Ross, D. and Sabot, R. (1995) Inequality and growth reconsidered: Lessons from East Asia. *World Bank Economic Review*, 9(3), 1–21.

Caroll, G. and Kupczyk-Romanczuk, G. (2007) Millennium development goals and Timor Leste. In M. Clarke and S. Feeny (eds) *Education for the End of Poverty*. London: Nova Science Publishers, pp. 65–82.

McCloskey, S. (2000) Introduction: East Timor – from European to Third World colonialism". In P. Hainsworth and S. McCloskey (eds) *The East Timor Question: The struggle for independence from Indonesia*. New York: I. B. Taurus, pp. 1–16.

MoE (Ministry of Education) (2005) *Strategic Plan for Universal Primary Completion by 2015*. Dili: Ministry of Education.

MoE (Ministry of Education) (2007a) *National Education Policy 2007–2012: Building our nation through quality education*. Dili: Ministry of Education.

MoE (Ministry of Education) (2007b) *Estudo do Meio. Curriculum*. Dili: Ministry of Education.

MoE (Ministry of Education) (2008) *Education and Training: Priorities and proposed sector investment development*. Dili: Ministry of Education.

MoE (Ministry of Education) (2010) *National Draft Strategic Plan 2011–2030, 2nd Draft*. Dili: Ministry of Education.

Nicolai, S. (2004) *Learning Independence: Education in emergency and transition in Timor-Leste since 1999*. Paris: UNESCO International Institute for Educational Planning.

Pereira, J. (2001) Education section annual review, East Timor: UNICEF. In S. Nicolai. *Learning independence: education in emergency and transition in Timor Leste since 1999*. Paris: UNESCO International Institute for Educational Planning, pp. 80–90.

Presidency of the Council of Ministers (2011) Programme of the 4th Constitutional Government (2007–2012). Republica Democratica Timor-Leste. Chapter 3, section 1. http://www. timor_leste.gov.tl (accessed 16 August 2011).

Quinn, M. (2007) The challenge of realising language and literacy goals in East Timor's schools. In D. Kingsbury and M. Leach (eds) *East Timor: Beyond independence*. Clayton: Monash University Press, pp. 251–68

Quinn, M. (2008) Choosing languages for teaching in primary school classrooms. In J. Earnest, M. Beck and L. Connell (eds) *Education and Health Rebuilding in Post-conflict Transitional Society: Case studies from Timor-Leste*. Rotterdam: Sense Publishers, pp. 23–38.

Republica Democratica Timor-Leste (2005) *Census*. Dili: Republica Democratica Timor-Leste.

Republica Democratica Timor-Leste (2010) *Census*. Dili: Republica Democratica Timor-Leste.

Republica Democratica Timor-Leste (2011) *Timor-Leste Strategic Development Plan 2011–2030*. Dili: Republica Democratica Timor-Leste.

Romiszowski, A. (2005) *Fundamental School Quality Project Consultancy Report on Teacher Professional Development and School-based Performance Management: Context; current situation; future strategies*. Dili: Republica Democratica Timor-Leste.

Saikia, U., Hosgelen, M. and Chalmers, J. (2011) Investigation into the population growth and its implications for primary schooling in Timor-Leste by 2020. *Asia Pacific Viewpoint*, 52(2), 194–206.

Soares, D. (2000) Political developments leading to the referendum. In J. J. Fox and D. B. Soares (eds) *Out of the Ashes: Destruction and reconstruction of East Timor*. Adelaide: Crawford House Publishing, pp. 57–76.

Taylor-Leech, K. (2011) Timor-Leste: Sustaining and maintaining the national languages in education. *Current Issues in Language Planning*, 12(2), 298–308.

UNESCO (2009) http://unesdoc.unesco.org/images/0018/001852/185239e.pdf (accessed 29 April 2011).

UNESCO Institute of Statistics (2010) UNESCO Institute of Statistics Data Centre. http://stats.uis.unesco.org/unesco/TableViewer/document.aspx?ReportId=143&IF_Language=eng (accessed 8 February 2011).

United Nations (2000) *Building Blocks for a Nation: Common country assessment for Timor-Leste*. Dili, Timor-Leste: United Nations

United Nations Security Council (1999, September 3) Press release SC6721. 4041st Meeting. www.un.org/News/Press/docs/1999/19990903.sc6721.html (accessed 11 June 2003).

World Bank (2009) *Timor-Leste: An analysis of early grade reading acquisition* (Working paper 56909-WPO). Washington, DC: Human Development Sector Unit East Asia and Pacific Region.

12 Northern Ireland

Some post-conflict challenges in education

Sam McGuinness, Lesley Abbott and Frank Cassidy

Introduction

This chapter is concerned with educational leadership and associated challenges at the school level in post-conflict Northern Ireland. It opens with a brief overview on the period of conflict. The contemporary educational situation is then outlined. This is followed by an account of contemporary leadership developments in Northern Ireland related to the principalship, many of which are similar to those occurring in countries throughout the Western world that have not had the same experience of conflict. Considerations then take a very different turn, with an examination of challenges for principals regarding post-conflict initiatives related to the sectarian aspect of the conflict.

Background

Northern Ireland (NI) consists of the six counties at the north-east corner of Ireland. It has a population of 1.7 million and occupies an area of 13,843 square kilometres. Fitzpatrick (2007) reported that, in the census of 2001, 1.7 million people were registered as living in NI. The population is relatively young, with 22 per cent aged under 15 (the same as in the Republic of Ireland (RoI)), compared to 19 per cent in Great Britain. In 2005, the NI birth rate at 12.9 births per 1,000 of population was the highest in the UK. The population level is expected to peak at 1.8 million around 2030 when it will be younger than that of most other industrial countries.

The history of NI has its origins in the seventeenth century when the north-east of Ireland was colonised by Scottish and English Protestants, establishing the area as different from the rest of Ireland, which was predominantly Catholic. During the eighteenth and nineteenth centuries, the standard of living rose in the north as industry and manufacturing flourished, notably ship-building, rope manufacturing and the production of linen, while in the south the unequal distribution of land and resources resulted in a relatively poor standard of living for the large Catholic population. The political separation of NI from the rest of Ireland did not come until early in the twentieth century, when Protestants and Catholics divided into two warring camps over the issue of Irish Home Rule. The British government passed the Government of Ireland Act in 1920, which divided Ireland into two separate political entities, each with some powers of self-government. The Act was accepted by northern Protestants, but was rejected by southern Catholics, who continued to demand total independence for a unified Ireland. Herein lay the essence of the unrest occurring decades later. Following a period of vicious guerrilla warfare between the nationalist Irish Republican Army (IRA) and British forces, a treaty signed in 1921 created the southern Irish Free State, while NI remained part of the United Kingdom.

Although armed hostilities between Catholics and Protestants largely subsided after the 1921 agreement, violence erupted again in the late 1960s. Bloody riots broke out in Londonderry in 1968, and in Belfast and Londonderry in 1969. Alan Smith has explained the background as follows:

> As the Civil Rights movement in the United States unfolded during the 1960s, a civil rights campaign emerged in NI focused largely on griev-ances concerning social injustices against Catholics in housing, employment and electoral issues. Protest, counter-protest and State reac-tion gave rise to civil disturbances and street rioting in the late 1960s.
>
> (1999: 1)

British troops were brought in to restore order, but the conflict intensified as the IRA and Protestant paramilitary groups carried out bombings and other acts of terrorism. The NI government was abolished and direct rule from Westminster was introduced in 1972. Repeated efforts were made to bring about a resolution to the conflict during the 1970s and 1980s, yet terrorist violence was still a problem in the early 1990s and British troops remained in full force. More than 3,000 people died over this period, includ-ing both civilians and security forces.

A determined attempt to resolve the conflict was made in 1985, when the British and Irish prime ministers, Margaret Thatcher and Garrett Fitzgerald, signed the Anglo-Irish Agreement, which recognised for the first time the RoI's right to have a consultative role in the affairs of NI. However, Unionist politicians opposing the Agreement blocked its implementation. Further talks between rival nationalist and unionist politicians and the British and Irish governments occurred during the early 1990s. Then, in late August 1994, the peace process received a boost when the IRA announced a cease-fire, making it possible for Sinn Fein, the political arm of the IRA, to participate in the offi-cial talks. The issue of IRA disarmament continued to be an obstacle to progress throughout the negotiations, yet in 1996 multi-party peace talks opened in Belfast. British politicians attended the talks, together with most of NI's feuding political parties, including Sinn Fein and the Ulster Unionist Party (UUP), the then largest Protestant political party in NI. The more extreme Democratic Unionist Party (DUP) refused to participate.

The historic talks finally resulted in the landmark Good Friday Agreement, which called for an elected assembly for NI, a cross-party cabinet with devolved powers, and cross-border bodies to handle issues common to both the RoI and NI. Under this arrangement, minority Catholics gained a share of the political power in NI and the RoI gained a voice in NI affairs. In return, Catholics were to relinquish the goal of a united Ireland unless the population of NI voted in its favour in a referendum. Hopes ran high, yet brinkmanship continued.

In the legislative elections of late 2003, the Ulster Unionists and other moderates lost out to what were then perceived as NI's extremist parties, namely, Rev. Ian Paisley's DUP and Sinn Fein. As a result, the prospect of power-sharing became unlikely. Nevertheless, shortly after parliamentary elections in March 2007 (with similar results), Gerry Adams, the leader of Sinn Fein, and Rev. Ian Paisley, met face-to-face for the first time and thrashed out an agreement for a power-sharing government. Local government was restored to NI in May 2007, as Rev. Ian Paisley, and Martin McGuinness of Sinn Fein, were sworn in as leader and deputy leader, respectively, of the NI executive government, thus ending direct rule from London.

The contemporary education situation

Before 1921 and Partition, almost all national (primary) schools in Ireland, both established and publicly funded, were denominational and controlled by the churches. In 1920, the Lynn Committee was created to advise on education in NI. With the Catholic Church refusing representation on the Committee, its report in 1922–3 formed the basis of the 1923 Education (Northern Ireland) Act, with recommendations being in accord with Protestant educational assumptions. Over the next two decades, the Protestant churches transferred control of their schools to the state, while the Catholic Church maintained control of its schools. Consequently, state schools became 'controlled schools' and the Catholic schools became 'maintained schools'. While teacher salaries in both categories were met by the State, maintained schools received only 50 per cent of capital costs. Nowadays, however, maintained schools receive 100 per cent of capital costs if they waive the right to majority religious affiliation on the board of governors (Osborne, 1993). Most maintained schools are regulated by the Catholic Church. In order to facilitate the management of these schools, the Education Reform (Northern Ireland) Order (1989) transferred responsibility for all Catholic maintained schools to a statutory body, the Council for Catholic Maintained Schools (CCMS). This council exercises certain responsibilities in relation to its schools, including advising on matters relating to this sector and the employment of teaching staff.

Fitzpatrick (2007) has provided a summary of the school types and populations in NI. The 300,000 pupils are educated predominantly on a segregated basis. In the primary sector there are 383 controlled (predominately Protestant) and 396 maintained Catholic schools, with only a further 42 schools classified as integrated (educating both Catholic and Protestant children together and considered later in this chapter). In the post-primary sector, there are 74 controlled (grammar and non-grammar) and 71 maintained non-grammar schools, with 29 Catholic voluntary grammar, 22 other voluntary grammar schools and 20 integrated schools. There are 8 Irish language schools supported by *Comhairle na Gaelscolaíochta* (The Gaelic Schools' Council), most of which are grant-aided from government, and 10 independent Christian schools associated with the Free Presbyterian Church, which do not receive government funds.

When direct rule was introduced in 1972, legislation for NI was by way of Order in Council at Westminster. This resulted in legislation in Westminster being largely mirrored in NI, with limited discussion, or debate. As a result of the MacCrory Report (1970), five Education and Library Boards (ELBs) (local education authorities) were established. These boards were 'quangos' (quasi-autonomous non-governmental organisation) with delegated power to supervise the allocation of budgets, transport matters, school meals and human resources, and to give curriculum support. The Education Reform (Northern Ireland) Order (Department of Education, 1989) established open enrolment, a statutory curriculum, the reform of governing bodies, and Local Management of Schools (LMS). Plans are currently well in train to replace the ELBs with one authority, the Education and Skills Authority (Education and Skills Authority, 2011), which will integrate with other bodies such as the Council for Curriculum, Examinations and Assessment (CCEA) and CCMS.

In the 1960s, 1970s and beyond, NI was the one portion of the UK that did not embrace a comprehensive education system, preferring to retain academic selection at age eleven (the 11+), with pupils proceeding either to a grammar or non-grammar school. With the establishment of the NI Assembly in 1999, the Minister for Education, Martin McGuinness, abolished the recently introduced school league tables and initiated the abolition of the 11+. Following publication of the Burns Report in 2001, he set up a consultation process on its recommendations. The responses from 200,551 households, including 162,000 parents and 21,000 teachers, showed that while the majority were in favour of abolishing the 11+, they also favoured the retention of academic selection *per se*. Political compromise among politicians around the implementation of the St Andrews Agreement (2006–7) permitted grammar schools to set their own tests if they so desired. The current situation is that there is diversity in testing, as the Catholic grammar schools and the state (mainly Protestant) grammar schools, cannot agree on a common test. With transferring pupils having to decide which test to take, and many choosing those of both sectors, feelings continue to be strong for and against selection at eleven on academic grounds, and there seems little chance of a solution that will satisfy both sides.

Regarding the curriculum, up until the end of the 1980s, schools had great freedom in choosing their students' curricular experience, which for the post-primary sector was aimed at success in the Ordinary-level and Advanced-level examinations. Since 1989, however, the CCEA has had responsibility for prescribing the compulsory NI curriculum and setting examinations. The traditional subject areas prescribed were art and design, music, English, Irish, geography, history, modern languages, mathematics, science, technology and design and physical education. In addition, information and communications technology (ICT), education for mutual understanding (EMU), cultural heritage (CH), health education and economic awareness were introduced as cross-curricular themes.

Following a major study by Harland *et al.* (2002), the curriculum was reviewed. While all pupils still study the broad base of subjects and the cross-curricular themes, the curriculum was reformed to place a powerful and challenging emphasis on such skills-based areas as self-management, working with others, critical and creative thinking, managing information, problem solving, decision making, communication, application of number, and ICT. This approach was compulsorily introduced to Key Stage 3 students (11–14), with associated teacher preparation provided by officers from the Curriculum and Advisory Service (CASS) of the ELBs, and was a clear follow-on from a revised primary school curriculum. However, it promises to present challenges to many teachers in terms of meeting the accountability imperative around examination results at GCSE and A-level. In particular, many fear the emphasis on skill development has reduced the content acquisition and subsequent knowledge base of students. There is also concern about the appropriateness of assessing the skills largely through paper-based tests. Furthermore, there are those like Perks (2007) who, while not disputing the importance of teaching transferable skills to cope with the changing demands of society, take issue with the interpretation by many that such skills can be taught in the abstract, separated from the subject matter to which they relate.

Leadership developments in education

The Department of Education of Northern Ireland (DE) states that it exists 'to ensure that every learner fulfils her or his full potential at each stage of development' (Department of Education, 2008: 12). The strategic framework it has developed to guide it has four themes: valuing education, fulfilling potential, promoting equality and inclusion, and resourcing education. Borrowing from Hopkins's (2007) publication, *Every school a great school*, it more tentatively coined the phrase 'Every School a Good School' (ESAGS) as a theme to assist in focusing improvement, and centred its policy on the following key areas: effective leadership and an ethos of aspiration and high achievement; high quality teaching and learning, tackling the barriers to learning that many young people face; self-evaluation and self-assessment, using performance and other information to effect improvement; support to help schools improve – with formal interventions where there is a risk that the quality of education offered in a school is not as high as it should be; engagement between schools, parents and families, recognising the powerful influence they and local communities exercise on educational outcomes.

A strong focus on accountability has emerged, with school inspections being carried out by the Education and Training Inspectorate (ETI). This body provides inspection services and advice on all professional education issues, as well as on standards of educational provision throughout schools, colleges and grant-aided institutions. In assessing the various features of provision, inspectors relate their evaluations to six descriptors, ranging from outstanding to unsatisfactory. Inspection systems have been modified to take less time and be less intrusive in schools that are providing a good standard of education. Inspections are carried out on a regular cycle, but at short notice, so that less time is taken preparing for them; a key element is the school's ability to become more aware of strengths and areas for development through its own self-evaluation. The DE has presented the document, 'Together towards improvement' (Education and Training Inspectorate, 2010) which drives the post-primary self-evaluation agenda, establishing a clear link between ESAGS and TTI, and providing a detailed list of indicators for school self-evaluation, so that schools can benchmark and assess themselves. Where the agenda is heading, however, is unclear, since the NI government's Committee for Education (2010) has expressed scepticism regarding the validity of the whole self-evaluation process.

Curriculum-specific leadership developments have also taken place. The aims and objectives of the NI curriculum show a strong connection to personal development, together with society and the economy. A central aim is to empower young people to achieve and to make informed decisions throughout their lives. At age 14, pupils select the subjects they wish to study for General Certificate of Secondary Education (GCSE) examinations. Currently, it is compulsory to study English, mathematics, science and religious studies. Most pupils elect to continue with other subjects and many study eight or nine. Taking the GCSE examination at age 16 marks the end of one's compulsory education. An increasing number, however, stay on at school to study Advanced Level AS and A2 level subjects, together with a growing range of more vocational qualifications. Many others attend Further Education (FE) Colleges to study vocational courses.

One of the greatest challenges for leadership through all of the innovations has been the implementation of an Entitlement Framework (EF), which became mandatory through the Education (NI) Order (2006). This framework places a requirement on schools to offer greater breadth and balance in the courses and pathways available to young people, and is a key contributor to the goal of raising standards within all post-primary schools and of improving educational achievement. It is designed to offer all post-primary pupils aged 14 and above greater choice by providing them, by

2013, with access to a minimum number of courses at Key Stage 4 (current target 24) and a minimum number of courses at post-16 (current target 27). In both cases, at least one-third of the courses must be general (academic) and at least one-third applied (vocational/professional/technical). This requirement has placed the onus on post-primary schools to engage in collaboration with others by forming a series of Area Learning Communities (ALCs) to provide the proposed range of courses.

The legacy of the competitive educational climate in the 1980s and 1990s is seen as an impediment to collaboration. Such a competitive climate, it is argued, is harmful to young people's academic progress and contributed to the formation of a 'long tail of underachievement'. While there is some contesting of this view (PricewaterhouseCoopers, 2008), Bradshaw, *et al.*, in a discussion of the NI results from the Programme for International Student Assessment (PISA), supports it, in stating:

> Northern Ireland, along with several other countries, displays wide variation around its mean: while some students performed very well, others performed more poorly, a phenomenon often referred to as 'the long tail of underachievement'. This may reflect the fact that NI has a selective education system.
>
> (Bradshaw *et al.*, 2007: 34)

The associated positive argument put forward by ALC supporters is that the development of strong learning communities will improve academic performance and that this will support those who are currently performing least well – the tail will shorten. This is in accord with Hopkins and Higman's (2007) argument about the need for the development of school principals as 'system leaders' who care about, and work for, the success of other schools as well as their own. Such an approach represents a massive challenge for school leaders in NI to move from competition to collaboration.

Special preparation is provided to help school principals acquire the necessary skills to meet such challenges. Leadership and management arrangements are enshrined in the Education Reform Order (NI) 1989. While schools' boards of governors have the legal obligation to determine an individual school's strategic direction, in practice the majority of governors take great cognisance of the guidance and advice of the school principal, who is responsible for the day-to-day organisation and management of the school. The Regional Training Unit (RTUNI) awards the Professional Qualification for Headship (PQH(NI)), drawing on the best leadership and management research and practice, and is underpinned by the following National Standards for Headteachers: shaping the future; leading learning and teaching; developing self and working with others; managing the organisation; securing accountability; strengthening community. While the qualification demonstrates readiness for the principalship, it is not mandatory. Nevertheless, there are now 1620 candidates who have gained it. This number comprises both practising principals and those who have taken up a principalship subsequent to gaining the qualification

The University of Ulster awards a Master of Education degree in Educational Leadership and Management, which provides a three-year developmental programme focusing on team-building, accountability issues, leadership focused on learning, and strategic development planning. It is underpinned by key research material and embedded in a blended learning setting, mixing face-to-face sessions with a robust virtual learning environment. Queen's University, Belfast, offers a similar qualification. Challenges, however, continue. For example, research by PricewaterhouseCoopers (2008) highlighted a strong message that many staff in NI schools did not feel engaged and involved, and concluded that there is a need for a form of leadership that goes well beyond the distribution of tasks by embracing distributed decision-making and autonomy.

Challenges for principals in relation to post-conflict initiatives associated with sectarianism

Considerations on leadership so far have centred on developments similar to those in countries throughout the Western world that have not had the same experience of conflict. This section of the chapter now considers challenges for principals pertinent to post-conflict initiatives related to the sectarian aspect of the conflict. These are examined under three main sub-headings, namely, integrated education, Area Learning Communities and the combating of sectarianism, and curriculum initiatives arising out of the conflict.

Integrated education

Following unrelenting political unrest from the late 1960s, amidst segregated schooling as well as divisive housing and employment, a group of concerned parents from the two main cultural traditions established All Children Together (ACT) in 1974. They perceived segregated education to be 'a contributing factor to continuing conflict and violence' (Abbott, 2010: 846), with children leading parallel lives in which being 'different' was seen as a threat or a challenge, and a 'culture of silence' prevented any meaningful opportunity to explore difference and contributed to 'a benign apartheid' (Wardlow, 2006: 2). The first integrated school was opened in 1981 with 28 pupils. It obtained government funding in 1985, and the 'dream took hold (ibid.: 1). Integrated education was recognised by the 1989 Order and in 2006, Russell (2006) reported that in spite of a demographic downturn, 5772 children and young people had been turned away due to a lack of available places. Currently, there are 62 integrated schools (42 primary and 20 post-primary) supported by the Northern Ireland Council for Integrated Education (NICIE), along with 19 integrated nursery schools, which are mostly linked to primary schools. In organisational terms, integrated schools exert control by determining enrolment patterns through admission criteria, employing teachers from both community backgrounds and ensuring a high level of parental representation on their governing bodies (Belfast Telegraph, 2011).

As well as the 'planned' grant maintained integrated (GMI) schools, a number of state (*de facto* Protestant) schools have 'transformed' to controlled integrated (CI) status, and comprise about one-third of the total in this sector (17 primary, 5 post-primary). Reasons for seeking to transform are pragmatic, or altruistic, or both, as schools may be faced with closure or falling enrolments, perceive a threat from an integrated school in the area or genuinely wish to embrace the integrated ethos. Transformation is 'a procedure [that allows] existing schools to convert to controlled integrated status and thus qualify for mainstream funding' (Lundy, 2000: 278). Transforming schools have to meet targets, which are legal (re-constitution of the Board of Governors) and numeric (obtain a reasonable balance of the two main traditions over two years). Initially, they have to demonstrate that they have a whole-school development plan, which is inspected after five years, and highlights how the school aims to move towards being fully integrated. In 1997, the policy document, 'A framework for transformation', required those schools wishing to transform to show that 10 per cent of their first year's intake, after conditional status was granted, came from the minority tradition (Northern Ireland Council for Integrated Education, 2005). Lundy states that, 'given the composition of the Board of Governors and general ethos in Catholic maintained schools, it is extremely unlikely that a Catholic maintained school will ever seek integrated status' (Lundy, 2000: 282).

The ethos of integrated education, whether planned or transformed, is child-centred, coeducational, accommodating of all-abilities and essentially Christian, but accepting children of all faiths, or none. It provides the statutory NI curriculum, while also offering religion, sport and cultural activities reflecting the main traditions. It aims to foster within children respect for difference and diversity and the capacity to welcome both. NICIE states specifically that, in supporting integrated education, it aims to prepare young people for 'life in a world where they can address conflict and controversy rather than avoiding them' (Northern Ireland Council for Integrated Education, 2008: 18).

Integrated education has not been pursued naively. For example, Marriott offered the following word of caution:

> In order to respect a point of view or a cultural or religious practice once first has to understand it and then to value it . . . respect does not mean agreement, indeed it may provoke fierce dispute, but it does mean taking other people and their beliefs and actions seriously.
>
> (2001: 8)

At the same time, research has shown that the essentially inclusive rationale that is fundamental to integrated education has the potential to 'enable a new interpretation of the concept, one in which inclusion ultimately emanates from the children themselves' (Abbott, 2010: 857).

The slow rate of take-up of education and of movement of schools towards integrated status is a source of frustration for those who support it, particularly as recent research indicates strong public support. For example, the Ipsos Mori Social Research Institute claims that 'the vast majority of people in Northern Ireland support schools sharing facilities, partnering or collaborating from different religious traditions' (Ipsos Mori, 2011: 1). The research further claims that even in the current period of financial austerity, the majority would choose the amalgamation of schools and the sharing of resources over cutbacks in other educational areas. Indeed, Peter Robinson (Belfast Telegraph, 2011), NI's First Minister, has recommended that a commission be set up to examine a way of bringing about integration of schools.

Consideration of the above matters suggests the following challenges for leaders at the school level:

- embracing aspects of the vision of the Integrated Education movement;
- sharing these aspects in a variety of challenging contexts;
- developing communication and negotiation skills for success;
- developing shared strategic plans for change.

Area Learning Communities and the combating of sectarianism

There is an imperative in NI to combat sectarianism by promoting intentional collaboration with schools across the sectarian divide. Research has indicated the effect of 'the troubles' on the academic performance of students. Curran described as follows the psychological disturbance to children emanating from atrocities: 'On the occasions of major bombings or shooting massacres, there was an increase in referrals of affected children and their families, approximating to 10 per cent of the workload at those times' (Curran and Miller, 2007: 1). Also, Daly (1999) found that prolonged exposure to the conflict and frequent reminders through the media, brought about an increase in symptoms of stress and a deterioration of academic performance.

There is value in examining closely the genesis of two of the ALCs, namely, 'Hightown Learning Together' (HLT) and the 'Lowlands Learning Community' (LLC), to provide insights into the leadership challenge in NI associated with overcoming cross-community tensions and meeting the needs of the EF.

Hightown Learning Together

A group of principals from the nine post-primary schools in Hightown, County Antrim, meeting since 2004, became a formal steering group in

2006, with elected officers and a coordinator. From the outset the group envisaged a cooperative, collaborative relationship between the schools that would embrace both cross-community and curricular issues. Following the murder of a schoolboy in the town through sectarian violence, the learning community was galvanised to demonstrate leadership for change. They adopted a view similar to that promoted by Bottery (2003), where he set out crucial factors for success in such a venture, namely, developing a values set founded on the beliefs of our cultures and social development, and challenging participants critically to analyse and question previously accepted practices, values and norms. Distributed leadership below the principalship level had to be created to manage the collaboration. Using good practice and shared expertise, a working party was set up to plan and direct the initiative. Baseline, computer-aided testing was used to define the scope of the problem and materials, and strategies were jointly agreed and developed.

A particular challenge to the success of the learning partnership is offered by the prevailing inspection practice. On this, it is helpful to consider that in England currently there is a focus on the inspection of compliance: 'Rather than Ofsted being independent and reliable in evaluating the work of schools, the teachers clearly state that there is a perceived need to comply with a set of predetermined criteria' (Dunne, 2010: 1). The same has been happening in NI, with inspections monitoring school development planning and self-evaluation processes oriented towards improvement in stipulated areas and in accountability. There are few incentives for school leaders to take risks, or be innovative with new, collaborative enterprises.

Collaborative decisions that principals make cannot compromise individual school success. In other words, there exists a potential clash of priorities for principals between school collaboration and school competition, whether that is competition for pupil numbers, or in league tables which, although discontinued in NI in 1999, still exist in the media. Some assert that such a tension may be reduced if reporting of combined results for the partnership of schools carries as much weight as the reporting of the individual schools. To move in this direction would encourage healthy competition between ALCs through the 'compelling scoreboard' phenomenon (Covey, 2004), the idea being that the continuing appropriate use of data can have a motivating influence on participants. Using an appropriate data set, it emerged that student literacy should be a priority for the HLT. Action plans were drawn up. Data-driven benchmarking and shared good practice now address the issue at an area level representing a new shared accountability for improvement by area, rather than by individual school alone.

The challenge then is for a new style of school leadership, one based on a system of values that include respect, trust and optimism, and that sees the concept of community as going far beyond the narrow confines of the individual school and into the community. This demands that leaders ask not only what they can do for their students, but what can they do to improve the lot of all students in their locale. More specifically, consideration of the

Hightown Learning Together case suggests the following challenges for leaders at the school level:

- moving from a culture of competition to one of collaboration;
- developing an inclusive vision for one's students and for all students in the locale;
- articulating and sharing that vision with stakeholders, significantly with staff and school governors;
- proactively planning for and implementing opportunities for increasingly significant collaboration.

The Lowlands Learning Community

This community of five schools and a FE college was one of the very first ALCs to be established in NI. In contrast to the HLT, it was formed out of the excellent cross-community relationships that epitomised the area, combined with the visionary stance of the principals involved. This vision was firmly founded on several of the points that Bottery (2003) presented as purposes for learning, including on the economic purpose of education.

There was a perceived imperative in the LLC for a focus on the economic needs of the area, and the principals had this to the fore in their discussions. Unemployment was high and the industries which did provide employment in the area were threatened by local economic challenges. As these industries gradually moved away, the principals discussed the need to focus on careers and employment opportunities.

Bottery (2003) has also written on the intellectual purpose of learning, namely, the need for students to build a portfolio of qualifications to provide a gateway to higher education or employment. This purpose occupied much of the initial and continuing discussion of the LLP principals. Alongside their positive tone existed tensions. There had been, for the two decades prior to 2002, a small but growing influx to the sixth form in the Lowlands Grammar School from the two non-grammar schools, one controlled and one maintained. This took place because of the steadily improving academic performance at GCSE level of the pupils and a lack of opportunity for them to study A-level subjects at these two schools, while the grammar school offered a choice of eighteen A-levels. During these years the Lowlands Further Education College (FE College) offered a main menu of vocational courses, selected mainly by those from the non-grammar schools in areas such as catering, motor maintenance and hairdressing. Very little useful discussion took place between the different providers for many years.

In November 2000, however, informal meetings took place between the principals of the main schools. These were formalised in September 2001 and a facilitator from the ELB was included. The latter had a significant impact on proceedings, with meetings becoming much more focused and a vision beginning to emerge in which the Lowlands' pupils were at the centre. A subject duplication issue was addressed as the non-grammar schools were enabled to introduce several new vocational subjects, one eventually becoming a specialist school in the performing arts. The FE College responded to the challenge by hosting meetings and providing expertise in the form of its principal, whose presence further galvanised progress, especially when it was announced that the College was opening up a centre specialising in engineering and construction. The model began to emerge of the town as a group of centres of learning offering distinct, but complementary, educational opportunities for young people.

As the community of principals became a team, confidence grew in raising issues affecting the success of the venture. With the original four centres, which became five as the special school joined the community, geographical location was not an impediment. All were within easy walking distance so transport and cost were of minimal concern. After a year, as a sixth school located ten miles away joined the ALC, the challenge was faced and dealt with in an imaginative way. The other schools offered to carry the transport costs to facilitate movement of students from the 'satellite' school. Development work continued apace on pastoral care arrangements between schools, service level agreements were drawn up and progress was evaluated through student and parent questionnaires. Links with the Lowlands community generally were developed and a community-based strategic plan was drawn up. An emphasis was placed on the career aspirations of the students across the LLC.

As the number of links grew, the need arose to address the key issue of quality assurance of classroom practice from school to school. The principal of Lowlands Grammar promoted Hopkins' view that 'a school head has to be almost as concerned about the success of other schools as he or she is about his or her school' (Hopkins, 2007: 109). He organised a series of developmental activities in his own school and with the other schools in the ALC, during which teachers engaged in co-construction of their understanding of best practice in the classroom. From these activities emerged an agreed approach to classroom activity to be implemented across the ALC.

Consideration of the Lowlands Learning Community case suggests the following challenges for leaders at the school level are to:

• overcome impediments caused by strongly embedded cultural mores;
• develop robust arguments for novel curricular initiatives such as the introduction of a range of vocational opportunities;
• involve experts from outside the locale to increase the skill set of the group and to develop its members as an effective team;
• focus on the quality assurance of classroom practice through leading focused on learning.

Curriculum initiatives arising from the conflict

It has already been pointed out that since 1989, the CCEA has had responsibility for prescribing the compulsory NI curriculum and setting examinations. Cross-curricular themes were also introduced. Two of these were education for mutual understanding (EMU) and cultural heritage (CH). This development represented a courageous move towards conflict resolution. However, Smith and Robinson (1992) reported that the inclusion of EMU in particular, caught schools unaware and unprepared in terms of policy documentation and skills. They later reported a less than enthusiastic approach to implementation due to several factors, including a perception of government meddling (Smith and Robinson, 1996). Nevertheless, the common curriculum provided the prospect of developing programmes of study such as history and religious education, which took cognisance of the two main cultural traditions in NI (Richardson, 1990). Over the following decade many schools of one tradition engaged in activities involving pupils from schools of the other tradition.

Smith and Robinson (1996) have argued that despite the intuitive nature of the notion that increased contact and interaction between groups would likely lead to a reduction in conflict, the empirical evidence to support this notion was limited. They stated that the difficulty of establishing causal links between inter-group contact and attitudinal change range from the lack of sensitivity in research instruments to the possibility that attitudinal changes only emerge over a long period of time. They suggested that there may be merit in adopting approaches to evaluation that track significant numbers of individuals who have participated in a variety of educational and reconciliation programmes over the past 25 years (Smith and Robinson, 1996: 77–8).

Pollak (2011), reflecting on a number of cross-border educational programmes, described one such programme, 'Dissolving Boundaries', as the single most outstanding example of mutually beneficial cross-border cooperation between schools anywhere in Europe, let alone Ireland. Dissolving Boundaries uses information and communications technology to link teachers and pupils in primary, secondary and special schools in NI and the RoI. The programme began in 1999 with 52 schools, growing to 180 in the 2010/11 academic year. Funding is provided by the Department of Education and Science in RoI and by the DE. The project is managed in the RoI by the Education Department, National University of Ireland, Maynooth and in NI by the School of Education at the University of Ulster, Coleraine. It aims to engage pupils in collaborative, curricular-based projects to promote mutual understanding on both sides of the border and to promote sustainability in the use of technology in schools

The group of academics at the two universities who manage the programme published a report in October 2011 entitled 'Dissolving boundaries through technology in education' (Austin *et al.*, 2011). In the report, Matthew Gould, British Ambassador to Israel commented: 'I want to congratulate you on the Dissolving the Boundaries Programme. I think it's a really fantastic programme...and you are real role models to others around the world who want to do the same. We should make sure you share your experiences with people in this region' (Austin *et al.*, 2011: ii).

Consideration of the 'Dissolving Boundaries' project suggests that leaders at the school level need to face the challenge of how to:

- align the school's vision to the broad goal of promoting intercultural education;
- use technology to facilitate collaboration and encourage and support staff to engage in intercultural education;
- articulate the benefits of engagement in school-to-school and cross border networking as a vehicle for cultural and social re-engineering;
- involve academics and other experts to open avenues of possibilities.

Conclusion

School principals, we hold, need to develop as 'system leaders' who care about, and work for, the success of other schools. This position has application to all countries, including those like NI that have emerged from sectarian conflict. The problem in the case of NI is that schools that for decades have been divided on sectarian grounds do not easily collaborate. This presents unique challenges for school leaders. The school vision must continually articulate with the promotion of intercultural education. School principals and senior managers need to ensure that teachers involved in such work are supported in terms of professional development. They also need to be imaginative in terms of the use of technology and of outside experts to achieve their aims. Furthermore, they need to ensure that there is 'innovation distraction', so that a focus can be kept on the core purpose, namely, to assure the quality of what happens in classrooms. More broadly, leaders in government departments of education need to ensure that overall strategic plans make provision for the widest possible uptake of such schemes, whether they involve curricular collaboration, or intercultural exchange, and to lobby for the necessary funds to ensure that the plans can be translated into practice.

References

Abbott, L. (2010) Northern Ireland's integrated schools enabling inclusion: a new interpretation? *International Journal of Inclusive Education*, 14(8), 843–59.
Austin, R., Smyth, J., Rickard, A. and Grace, A. (2011) Dissolving boundaries through technology in education. www.dissolvingboundaries.org/ download.php?id=15 (accessed 21 October 2011).
Belfast Telegraph (2011) Integrated education. *Belfast Telegraph*, 17 January.
Bottery, M. (2003) The leadership of learning communities in a culture of unhappiness. *School Leadership and Management*, 23(2), 187–207.

Bradshaw, J., Sturman, L., Vappula, H., Ager, R. and Wheater, R. (2007) Student achievement in Northern Ireland results in science, mathematics and reading among 15-year-olds from the OECD PISA 2006 study (OECD Programme for International Student Assessment). Slough: NFER. http://www.nfer.ac.uk/nfer/publications/NPC04/NPC04.pdf (accessed 24 October 2010).

Committee for Education (2010) Successful secondary schools. http://www.niassembly.gov.uk/record/committees2009/Education/100623_SuccessfulSecondarySchools.htm (accessed 21 May 2011).

Covey, S. (2004) *The 8th Habit: From effectiveness to greatness.* London: Simon and Schuster.

Curran P. S. and Miller, P. W. (2001) Psychiatric implications of chronic civilian strife or war: Northern Ireland. *Advances in Psychiatric Treatment,* 7, 73–80.

Daly, O. E. (1999) Northern Ireland. The victims. *British Journal of Psychiatry,* 175, 201–4.

Department of Education (1989) The education reform (1989 Order) (Commencement No 2) Order (Northern Ireland). http://www.DE.gov.uk/ed_reform_89_order_1990-34.pdf (accessed 21 May 2011).

Department of Education (2008) Every school a good school. A strategy for raising achievement in literacy and numeracy. http://www.DE.gov.uk/literacy_and_numeracy_strategy_-_english.pdf (accessed 20 November 2011).

Department of Education (2009) Every school a good school. http://www.DE.gov.uk/esags_policy_for_school_improvement_-_final_version_05-05-2009.pdf (accessed 21 May 2011).

Dunne, C. (2010) The role and performance of Ofsted. http://www.publications.parliament.uk/pa/cm201011/cmselect/cmeduc/writev/ofsted/101.htm (accessed 4 February 2011).

Earl, L. and Katz, S. (2003) Leading schools in a data rich world. In K. Leithwood, P. Hallinger, K. S. Louis, G. Furman-Brown, P. Gronn, B. Mulford and K. Riley (eds) *Second International Handbook of Educational Leadership and Administration.* Dordrecht: Kluwer Academic Publishers, pp. 1003–24.

Education and Skills Authority (2011) Convergence document. http://www.esani.org.uk/docs/convergence_delivery_plan_february_10.pdf (accessed 7 December 2011).

Education and Training Inspectorate (2010) Together towards improvement. http://www.etini.gov.uk/index/together-towards-improvement/together-towards-improvement-post-primary.pdf (accessed 20 May 2011).

Fitzpatrick R. (2007) Improving school leadership. Country background report for Northern Ireland. http://www.oecd.org/dataoecd/29/59/38752145.pdf (accessed 20 May 2011).

Harland, J., Moor, H., Kinder, K. and Ashworth, M. (2002) *Is the Curriculum Working?* London: NFER.

Hopkins, D. (2007) *Every School a Great School.* London: Open University Press.

Hopkins, D. and Higman, R. (2007) System leadership. *School Leadership and Management,* 27(2), 147–66.

Ipsos Mori. (2011) Attitudinal survey on Integrated Education. http://www.ief.org.uk/wp-content/uploads/2011/09/Attitudinal-Survey-Final-Report.pdf (accessed 24 December 2011).

Lundy, L. (2000) *Education Law, Policy and Practice in Northern Ireland.* Belfast: SLS Legal Publications.

MacCrory, M. (1970) Review body on local government in Northern Ireland. http://cain.ulst.ac.uk/hmso/macrory.htm (accessed 17 May 2011).

Marriott, S. (2001) *Polite Encounters: Integrated primary schools and community relations. A report for the Northern Ireland Council for Integrated Education.* Coleraine, NI: School of Education, University of Ulster.

Northern Ireland Council for Integrated Education (2008) *ABC: Promoting an anti-bias approach to education in Northern Ireland.* 3rd edition. Belfast: Northern Ireland Council for Integrated Education, International Fund for Ireland and the Esmee Fairbairn Foundation.

Osborne, R. D. (1993) Research and policy: a Northern Ireland perspective. *Environment and Planning C – Government and Policy*, 11(4), 465–77.

Perks, D. (2007) *What is Science Education For? The corruption of the curriculum.* Trowbridge: Cromwell Press.

Pollak, A. (2011) Bringing schools together in Ireland through ICT, A note from the next door neighbours. http://www.crossborder.ie/notes-from-the-next-door-neighbours/bringing-schools-together-in-ireland-through-ict/ (accessed 7 August 2012).

PricewaterhouseCoopers (2008) School workforce matters. Towards a modernization of the school workforce in Northern Ireland. http://www.DE.gov.uk/no_49-2.pdf (accessed 21 July 2011).

Richardson, N. (1990) *Religious Education as if EMU Really Mattered.* Belfast: Christian Education Movement.

Russell, D. (2006) *A Shared Future: Policy and strategic framework for good relations in Northern Ireland.* Belfast: Northern Ireland Council for Integrated Education.

Smith, A. (1999) http://cain.ulst.ac.uk/issues/education/docs/smith99.htm (accessed 18 May 2011).

Smith, A. and Robinson, A. (1992) *Education for Mutual Understanding: Perceptions and policy.* Coleraine: Centre for the Study of Conflict, University of Ulster.

Smith, A. and Robinson, A. (1996) *EMU: The statutory years.* Coleraine: Centre for the Study of Conflict, University of Ulster.

St Andrews Agreement. (2006–07) http://www.parliament.uk/documents/commons/lib/research/rp2006/rp06-056.pdf (accessed 21 June 2011).

Wardlow, M. (2006) In support of integrated education. http://www.nicie.org.uk/ (accessed 15 July 2011).

13 Educational leadership in post-new war societies

Insights from the field into challenges and possibilities

Simon R. P. Clarke and Thomas A. O'Donoghue

Introduction

Milligan (2010) has pointed out that interest in education after conflicts of the type considered in this book has grown considerably over the last decade. This might well be because such contemporary conflicts tend to be more deadly for children and more destructive of civilian infrastructure, including schools, than traditional wars (Mundy and Dryden-Peterson, 2011). As a consequence, conventional priorities in these contexts, including the provision of food, shelter and healthcare no longer take precedence over schooling, which is now recognised as being essential to maintaining communities, the psychological recovery of children and the general recovery of society. Milligan (2010) has also pointed out that although there is an emerging body of literature that considers the challenges and needs of students and teachers in post-conflict conditions, particularly those of the post-new war type, the area of educational leadership in these contexts has been neglected. We concur with this observation, while also emphasising that school leadership, specifically, is even more barren terrain from a research perspective.

The main purpose of this chapter is to contribute to rectifying the latter deficit by highlighting the ways in which school leadership is understood and practised between and among post-new war contexts, especially those featured in the overall content of this volume, though we should emphasise that the scope and complexity of the task means that our commentary is necessarily selective. By examining such a rich combination of contexts it is possible to reveal more clearly the issues and influences that school leaders face as they perform their work, the nature of the context within which these issues and influences arise, the strategies school leaders adopt to deal with the complexities of their work and the reasons behind these strategies. It is also possible to identify some implications presented by the specific needs, concerns, challenges and problems faced by school leaders in new post-war contexts for policy for practice and for research.

To this end, we refer back to the three main learning agendas outlined in Chapter 2 that exist within a school (Knapp, Copland and McLaughlin,

2003) as an orchestrating framework for portraying the complexities of school leaders' day-to-day work in the extraordinarily challenging circumstances that typify post-new war settings. In keeping with our focus on leadership in individual schools, we concentrate our attention on 'organisational learning', 'teacher learning' and 'student learning'. The agenda for organisational learning is primarily concerned with providing the appropriate conditions and opportunities for bringing to fruition the hidden capital of everyone associated with the school. The agenda for teacher learning is primarily concerned with building the intellectual and professional capacity of teachers in the school. The agenda for student learning is primarily concerned with building the academic and social capacity of all students in the school. These learning agendas, of course, are not discrete, but tend to overlap in extremely complex ways.

Organisational learning

Given the extent to which school leaders' work is influenced by the broader education system, as illustrated so powerfully in much of the commentary presented here, we have extended the meaning of the organisational learning agenda, as considered in Chapter 2, to embrace the ways in which a school orients itself to its external environment. As the education system is instrumental in determining many aspects of what leaders can and must do within their schools, especially within the turbulent circumstances that characterise post-conflict contexts of the post-new war type, we take this agenda as our starting point. It would have been equally appropriate, however, to have begun this discussion with students' learning and work backwards from there to organisational learning.

Consideration of organisational learning in its connection with the school's external environment raises the question of the extent to which principals and their staff have the space and inclination to exercise genuine agency in confronting the challenges with which they are faced. Although it could be argued that this question might be applicable to a diversity of education jurisdictions, it assumes far greater significance in the post-conflict settings of the type described in this volume. Indeed, there are many examples provided within the chapters that serve to illustrate the observation that school leaders are denied considerable operational discretion. For example, in the case of Solomon Islands, Maebutu refers to incompetence within the education system, the misappropriation of funds and the poor use of data as constraints over which a school leader has little control. In the case of Angola, Davies comments on the normality of corruption that undermines leaders' efforts to develop the capacity of their schools and communities. And in relation to Kenya, Datoo and Johnson contend that the role of principals is most often defined by their need to acquire resources in order to assist teachers in examination preparation as determined by the emphasis placed both by parents and society more generally, on examination results.

All of these examples, of course, relate to developing-country settings. The case of Northern Ireland, by contrast, serves to illustrate that while the problems noted above seem to exist in many post-new war societies, they do not necessarily exist in all.

The situation depicted in most of the cases mentioned above, it may be argued, suggests that in many post-new war settings, school principals encounter problems well beyond their control and are attempting to lead schools and improve children's education in much more challenging situations than education authorities acknowledge (Tanaka, 2012). The somewhat dysfunctional nature of the organisational learning agenda as it often relates to the external environment of post-new war schools illuminates the true role that school principals are able to exercise on a day-to-day-basis. Milligan, commenting on the predicament of principals in the southern Philippines, who are detached from the centre of formal educational authority in a highly centralised system, describes the situation as 'marginalised leadership' (2010: 39).

In similar vein, we find it instructive to consider the intriguing concept of 'bastard leadership' (Wright, 2011). This concept has been used to portray the ways in which school principals in Britain are purported to be denied the full scope of authentic leadership by policy imperatives. It is a portrayal of principalship that seems especially poignant in its relevance to the exercise of school leadership in post-conflict settings of the type reported here because education authorities, as well as influences within the broader environment, may provide little basis for effective leadership in schools. In these circumstances, a key challenge, it would seem, is to enable principals to balance the impact of potentially detrimental external pressures on school improvement against what they consider to be in the best interest of the children in their charge. The Northern Ireland case, for example, is illustrative of a number of ways in which school principals can take initiatives for this purpose while still working within system parameters. Also, the Lebanon case shows how parents who have the means may choose the option of private schooling if it is available and where principals of these schools have a reputation for promoting the interest of children in spite of the trying circumstances that prevail.

It might be contended that the impact and reach of leadership are also constrained at the more school-specific dimension of the organisational learning agenda, which relates to providing the appropriate conditions and opportunities for bringing to fruition the hidden capital of everyone associated with the organisation. In this connection, the overall culture of the school is critical in its potential to either foster, or debilitate, school improvement initiatives. Indeed, MacBeath (2012) makes the point that the pre-eminent task of leadership is to foster a 'culture' in which learning is the day-to-day norm, built into the fabric of school life. Here again, however, school leaders in post-conflict situations such as those considered here face enormous challenges. As Datoo and Johnson emphasise in their chapter, schools are a reflection of the society in which they are located. It often follows, therefore, that in post-conflict circumstances, they are not immune from the penetration of ethnic tension, fear, aggressive behaviour and prejudice into their organisational cultures. Indeed, it is not unusual for these cultural norms to extend into the school's community, undermining its willingness and ability to support leaders in enhancing the performance and vitality of schools.

In the case of Solomon Islands, for example, Maebutu comments that in multi-ethnic schools especially, it was often feared that ethnic violence might break out if community-organised activities were held and, for this reason, community gatherings were avoided. In similar vein, Barakat and his colleagues (2012) describe how communities in comparable environments take time to overcome local grievances and perceived injustices associated with identity, faith and ethnicity that had originally prompted an intra-state conflict. McGuiness, Abbot and Cassidy have also drawn attention to an imperative in Northern Ireland to combat sectarianism and describe how progress can be made by intentional collaboration with schools across the sectarian divide. These examples serve to illustrate that while the overall culture of schools in post-conflict settings can be fractured by deeply embedded cultural and tribal priorities, which debilitate the effectiveness of the organisational learning agenda, education can continue to play its part in alleviating the situation.

The provision of a productive organisational learning agenda for many school leaders is further compounded by a lack of basic infrastructure. The dilapidated conditions in which schools are often forced to function are epitomised by Beck and Aroujo's description in their chapter on Timor-Leste, which mentions the frequency of ramshackle classroom furniture, floors packed with dirt and the absence of windows. Similarly, with reference to Sri Lanka, where conflict-affected schools have also had to contend with the impact of a tsunami, Earnest draws attention to buildings that are frequently deprived of latrines, water and sanitation. In these examples, limited resources are placed under further pressure by demographic shifts occurring in the wake of the conflict, which have considerable ramifications for the functioning of schools. Consequently, it is not unusual for the daily operation of a school to be characterised by multiple shifts and shortened class periods. To sum up, if it is accepted that leading learning is not only an intellectual investment, but also a physical one, the combination that is often apparent in post-conflict schools of damaged organisational culture and depleted infrastructure can have a tremendously stultifying impact on the capacity of leaders to initiate, implement and sustain school improvement.

Teacher learning

The notion of damaged school culture, as well as marginalised leadership alluded to earlier in this discussion, inevitably flow through to the teacher-learning agenda aimed at developing the professional and intellectual capacity of staff. It is difficult to consider this learning agenda as it applies to post-conflict schools without drawing attention to the efficacy of professionalism at both the macro-level of the education system and the micro-level of the school.

For various reasons, education in many of the settings described in this book has been blighted by teacher shortages. Furthermore, there is often a tendency for the relatively small number of qualified teachers available to become disillusioned because of the conditions they encounter in their occupation. For example, the paltry salaries and a dearth of incentives to pursue a teaching career are usually compounded by the numerous challenges teachers face in their day-to-day work. As Tanaka has emphasized (2012) specifically in relation to 'untrained' teachers in Ghana, it is very difficult for teachers without drive to perform effectively in the long term. He goes on to suggest that the kind of professional and social environment that is most likely to harness the motivation of teachers is in need of further research, a suggestion that seems pertinent to post-new war school environments in general.

This observation appears even more important when the professionalism of teachers at the micro-level of the school is also taken into consideration, an area that has received a good deal of attention throughout the commentary in the preceding chapters. Indeed, Davies suggests in her chapter, that enhancing the professionalism as well as the motivation of teachers is a key leadership challenge in Angola. In this context, such teacher behaviours as absenteeism, sexual harassment, drunkenness and corruption are commonplace. A similar portrayal of teacher professionalism has been provided by Beck and Araujo in their work on Timor-Leste, where they comment on the tendency for teachers not to turn up to work on time or not to turn up at all. They also draw attention to pedestrian approaches towards teaching and learning in the classroom, exemplified by preparing lessons that are completely teacher-centred, and following the same format day after day. It is clear, therefore, that in most post-new war settings the professional and social environment is hardly conducive to utilising the potential of teachers to create and promote change within their classrooms, schools and communities. As Shepler (2011) points out in what almost amounts to a statement of the obvious, teachers can only be enabled as agents of positive change when they are provided with sufficient information, support and resources.

If teachers' agency is to be enhanced in harnessing positive change amidst the challenging circumstances of post-new war societies, there are significant implications for the role of school principals. In particular, there is a need to consider their selection, preparation and on-going professional development. Not surprisingly perhaps, these considerations feature regularly in the discussion contained in several of the chapters presented here. For example, Earnest mentions that in Rwanda, school principals are thrust into leadership positions without preparation, mentoring or support. Furthermore, although they are often keen to enhance their knowledge and skills of school leadership and management, they are unlikely to be aware of relevant opportunities for professional development that might be available. Similar observations are made about the readiness of principals to deal with the complexity of their work in Timor-Leste, Ghana and Angola.

In sum, it would seem that the efficacy of the teacher learning agenda in its quest to promote professional and intellectual capacity in post-new war societies is inclined to be debilitated by weakened professionalism occurring at both the macro-level of the education system and the micro-level of the school. The situation is compounded because principals often lack the wherewithal to establish an environment where teachers can develop their agency in order to create a suitable learning environment for students. This observation brings us to a consideration of the students' learning agenda.

Student learning

As with the organisational and teacher learning agendas, the challenges that exist in pursuit of enhancing the academic and social capacity of students in many post-new war circumstances are daunting. Most notably, it is apparent that many students who have experienced the trauma of war have to contend with severe adjustment problems as they re-engage with the daily routine of the classroom. This difficulty in adjusting can be manifested in misbehaviour, aggressiveness, violence and lack of motivation (Al-Jaber, 1996). Maebutu, for example, in his chapter, reported that some students in Solomon Islands suffered such psychological trauma during the conflict there that they refused to attend school. Earnest, in her chapter on Sri Lanka, where the impact of conflict was compounded by the destruction wrought by the tsunami in 2004, describes how children were often displaced, orphaned and subjected to physical harm, exploitation and violence. She also refers to the plight of child soldiers who have been recruited into combat and can present enormous challenges for schools in seeking to reintegrate them back into the classroom. In this connection, Njeru (2010) has commented elsewhere that the discipline of school life can be unappealing because of children's independent lives as combatants and not many of them, particularly those who have lost their parents or guardians, will be willing to part with the few monetary resources they may have acquired.

Ideally, it would be hoped that schools are able to provide psychological support and healing for children who have been brutalised by the impact of conflict (Save the Children, 2006), but in reality this is not necessarily the case. Datoo and Johnson, for example, in their chapter, comment that a lack of awareness on the part of some Kenyan school principals about the psychosocial effects of conflict on children and staff, coupled with the scarcity of resources and support from relevant authorities, mean that associated issues continue to go undetected or are overlooked. In these circumstances, it is unlikely that the school environment will be able to alleviate patterns of anti-social and violent behaviour that might already exist. Indeed, it could well be that the school environment actually promotes the normalisation of violence through its sanctioning of corporal punishment. For example, with reference to Angolan schools, Davies, in her chapter, observed that discipline is likely to be maintained by a regime of fear and violence that has come to be accepted. In similar vein, MacBeath and Swaffield (2010) refer to 'a whip in every classroom' as a prominent feature of Ghanaian schools. This situation is echoed by Sharkey's observations (2008) about girls' schools in Sierra Leone where she frequently encountered an atmosphere in which an ethos of violence, humiliation and berating of students was customary, thereby sanctioning and permitting violence to occur.

It is also likely that this punitive attitude to discipline is accompanied by approaches to learning that are teacher dominated and uninspiring. MacBeath and Swaffield, in their chapter, contend that one reason why learning by rote is often preferred is because it facilitates conformity and order in the classroom. There are other reasons, however, why such pedestrian pedagogical practices tend to be embraced by school principals and teachers. Davies, for example, in her work on Angola, argues that the lack of creativity in the classroom is at least partly attributable to impoverished teacher professionalism. This situation is mirrored in other contexts such as Timor-Leste and Solomon Islands. In these settings it seems almost unrealistic to expect teachers who are often inexperienced, as well as being faced with intractable problems in their work, to be successful change agents. In addition, as MacBeath and Swaffield suggest, the preference for traditional, teacher-centred strategies is because children have to commit much to memory in order to pass examinations. Indeed, it would appear that many of the post-conflict contexts featured in the preceding chapters assign a heavier priority to students passing examinations than to promoting more enterprising curricula designed to foster unity and reconciliation within highly brittle communities.

Curriculum reform in post-new war settings, however, tends to be fraught with political agendas and can, as Davies has emphasised elsewhere, contribute to conflict by 'reproducing or hardening inequality, exclusion, social polarisation, ethnic/religious identities, aggressive masculinity, fear and militarism' (2006: 13). Of relevance here is Maadad's observation in her chapter relating to the different versions of the history curriculum being taught in Lebanese schools, indicating that the civil war there has been interpreted along sectarian lines. Earnest, in her work on Rwanda, also draws attention to the complexities associated with the teaching of history in the wake of the genocide, where a fear of polarisation has deterred the formulation of an official curriculum, a concern also highlighted by Bijlsma (2009).

Furthermore, the preceding chapters suggest that the inculcation of destructive beliefs is more likely to occur if the learning conveyed through the formal, overt curriculum is complemented by messages communicated through the school's day-to-day operations. Indeed, it could be argued that it is this medium, or the 'hidden curriculum', that is most influential in shaping students' (and others') attitudes, values, beliefs and behaviour. Sharkey (2008: 577), with reference to Sierre Leone, alludes to the same point, when she draws attention to the contradiction that is often apparent between teachers' rhetoric of empowerment, caring and concern, and the school context of subjugation, humiliation and demeaning treatment of girls.

It may also be that centrally imposed and highly prescriptive curricula have little relevance to students' day-to-day realities of living in a post-new war environment. This is an observation made forcibly in relation to curriculum content in the chapters on Rwanda and Solomon Islands. MacBeath and Swaffield in their comments on circumstances applying to Ghanaian schools (2010), also depict ways in which curriculum is understood and implemented which seem to be mirrored throughout a range of post-new war settings. In particular, they draw attention to the lack of alignment between what and how children learn in school and the informal learning that takes place in the home, peer group and community. This dissonance, they have suggested, tends to be manifested in children's prior knowledge remaining largely hidden and devalued in a system where it is only what takes place in the classroom and through the formal curriculum that is valued. From this perspective, Hart's criticism (2006) that understanding the impact of educational initiatives in post-conflict settings takes precedence over understanding the lives of the children who are the intended beneficiaries, appears valid.

Moreover, in some post-new war situations, the efficacy of the curriculum is affected by complications of language. The example of Timor-Leste immediately springs to mind where, as Beck and Arajou have described in their chapter, substantial difficulties arose for students and teachers when the official language of the country was changed from Indonesian to Portuguese. Similarly in Rwanda, an additional challenge for the education system has been introduced by the adoption of English as the official medium of instruction. The potentially positive impact of this development, as Earnest reports in her chapter, has been undermined by low levels of English language proficiency among teachers and a shortage of educational resources produced in English. Consequently, school principals are often in the unenviable position of needing to improve their own proficiency in the language while also being responsible for the linguistic advancement of their staff.

Glimmers of innovation and reform

A toxic combination, then, of marginalised leadership, damaged school culture, weakened teacher professionalism and compromised students can often debilitate schools' capacity to instigate innovation and reform in post-new war societies. The intractable problems besetting education in such settings represent what Fullan (2005: 53) portrays as 'adaptive problems'. These are the kinds of problems for which we do not have ready answers and which take time to deal with. Fullan describes them as 'politically charged, because solutions are difficult to discern and learn and some disequilibrium on the way to addressing the problem is inevitable' (Fullan, 2005 p. 54). In making these comments he is referring to relatively stable and predictable education environments. It seems reasonable to suggest, however, that the solutions to challenges typifying post-new war circumstances are likely to be even more difficult for school leaders to discern and learn.

Notwithstanding the enormous severity of the problems, some glimpses of ways forward have been projected by the spectrum of the post-conflict contexts presented in this volume. We are not suggesting that these glimpses of creative approaches to change are new. Neither are we suggesting that they represent a panacea for resolving challenges in post-conflict settings, either individually or collectively. We do argue, however, that it is valuable to highlight opportunities for innovation and reform with the aim of reiterating the instrumental role that school leadership plays in enabling them.

Enhancing the curriculum

The first area to which we draw attention is of enhancing the curriculum for mitigating potential conflict and building peace. As Barakat and his colleagues suggest (Barakat *et al.*, 2012: 15), this endeavour requires a commitment to creating an effective environment for all children, the provision of secure and adequate facilities, and a relevant curriculum with clearly defined outcomes. In this connection, there are numerous examples of innovative practices alluded to in previous chapters that can enhance children's experience of education in post-conflict conditions. For example, Davies mentions the creation of UNICEF-inspired child-friendly schools across Angola. Likewise, Earnest, with reference to the Sri Lankan context, describes the positive impact that a child-friendly approach can have in providing a school environment that enables children to play, be protected from harm, express their views and actively participate in the learning process. Although it could be argued that the drive behind the establishment of child-friendly schools has occurred at the macro-level, Earnest suggests that the effectiveness of the approach will ultimately be determined at the micro-level of the school by the principal's ability to mobilise the community around education and the needs of the children.

It is also likely that the efficacy of accelerated learning programmes will be influenced by similar factors at the micro-level of the school. Given their wide use in post-conflict situations, it is not surprising that these programmes receive some attention in the chapters reported here. In the chapter on Angola, for example, Davies suggests that the programmes offer a degree of hope for enabling out-of-school youth to catch up with their learning and are proving particularly successful for girls. Earnest reports that in Sri Lanka too, the programmes have been effective for students living in Internally Displaced Person camps who have missed school, and for those who have been child soldiers and returned to their families.

It might be argued, however, that just as important as the introduction of specific programmes, such as the examples mentioned above, is the content of the curriculum being communicated in schools. In this connection, Smith contends (2005: 380) that if curriculum is conceived of simply as the transmission of knowledge from one generation to another, it can become a powerful means of socialisation into particular political ideologies, religious practices or cultural values and traditions. For this reason, he goes on to suggest that a contemporary trend in many post-conflict countries is to 'modernise' the curriculum, with the intention of making it more conflict sensitive.

Here again, at least on the face of it, there are some encouraging signs of progress featured in this volume. For example, Maebutu mentions the introduction of a student-centred outcomes-based approach to the curriculum, which has been adopted in Solomon Islands. Within this approach there is a consideration of skills, values and attitudes that goes beyond the traditional focus on factual knowledge. Particular attention is paid to those skills, values and attitudes that are deemed useful for students in later life. Similarly, Goddard and Buleshkaj comment that in Kosovo there has been a major shift from a content-based to a competency-based curriculum, aiming to mobilise the potential of Kosovan youth to compete successfully in the labour market, handle the challenges of the digital age effectively and develop the knowledge, skills and attributes required for the twenty-first century world. In the same vein, Datoo and Johnson, in their chapter, refer to the implementation of a life-skills programme that has been implemented in Kenya, aiming to equip students with skills to help them perform well academically, as well as in their personal life outside of school. For this purpose, the programme incorporates specific dimensions of personal and social development requiring a learner-centred, practical approach to the classroom. According to Davies, the Angolan curriculum has also evolved along comparable lines with inter-related 'cross-cutting' topics being implemented, intending to enhance students' personal, social and moral education. Finally, in Rwanda schooling has been assigned a key role in promoting unity and reconciliation (King, 2011, p, 148). On this, in her chapter, Earnest highlights encouraging developments in the curriculum that incorporate learning for peace, human rights and life skills.

Once again, we argue that although these promising developments in the content of curriculum as well as pedagogical processes tend to be initiated at the macro-level of the education system, their efficacy will be determined by factors existing at the micro-level of the school. In this connection, it is useful to acknowledge that any curriculum operates in different dimensions, and that these need to be aligned as closely as possible if reforms are to stand any chance of being successful. This is not the place for a detailed exposition of curriculum theory. Put in simple terms, however, it is possible to distinguish between the intended curriculum as it is prescribed by education authorities, the taught curriculum as it is promoted by teachers in the classroom and, perhaps most importantly of all, the learned curriculum as it is experienced by the students themselves. We would argue that it is this third learned dimension of the curriculum that constitutes the real curriculum (Ornstein and Hunkins, 2004). As the ways in which it is experienced will be heavily dependent on the professional capacity of teachers working in the school environment, we now consider the opportunities for innovation and reform associated with the energising of teaching capacity.

Energising teaching capacity

Closely intertwined with the deliberations above is the need to reflect on the significance of energising teaching capacity. Indeed, in their chapter, Goddard and Buleshkaj suggest that in Kosovo it is necessary to assist teachers in overcoming a twenty-year deficit in their professional knowledge base. Energising teaching capacity is an especially important requirement because, in common with other contexts, the quality of the education provided for students in post-new war settings will be heavily dependent on pedagogical processes in the classroom and the knowledge, skills, dispositions and commitment of the teachers (Barakat *et al.*, 2012). As we have already mooted, and as Smith (2005) also points out, it is unrealistic to expect inexperienced teachers to embrace complex curriculum reforms in areas such as human rights education and to promote effective student learning without having developed the necessary skills themselves

Notwithstanding the inadequacy of teacher pre-service programmes that is widely reported in the chapters featured here, there are some brief glimpses of professional practices that appear to have considerable potential for developing teachers' agency in adopting new approaches to the classroom. In particular, the use of networks and learning groups for providing supportive development opportunities for teachers appear to have much potential. An arrangement of this kind, as it operates in Angola, is described by Davies. The *Zonas de Influência Pedagógica* (ZIPs) are groups of schools based on the local needs of teachers that bring them together so that information and insights are shared, common issues debated and innovative ideas tested. The indications are that engagement in these processes is likely to enhance teachers' confidence and agency, both individually and collectively, in responding critically to change.

Datoo and Johnson, in their chapter, also report that in Kenya an increased commitment to 'peace' and 'conflict resolution' in schools has been accompanied by collaborative workshops organised by churches. These are aimed at preparing teachers to deal with the psychosocial effects of conflict. The workshops encourage the use of a learner-centred approach to teaching and alternative methods of learning through the use of poems, stories, music, and voluntary activities in educating students about peace, conflict resolution and unity.

These kinds of collaboration are clearly premised on the assumption that if teachers are offered continuous opportunities for learning, leadership and participation, they are more likely to experience a sense of instrumentality and commitment. The availability of such opportunities for energising teachers will be dependent, to some extent, on the disposition of school principals in supporting teachers' professional learning and development. Nevertheless, in his observations on the principalship in developing countries, Oplatka (2004: 435) has suggested that principals are unlikely to engage with curriculum development, encourage the professional learning of staff or promote the quality of teaching and learning. For this reason, it is instructive now to examine some insights offered in the preceding chapters as to how leadership effectiveness in schools can be optimised.

Optimising leadership effectiveness

Datoo and Johnson make the point that in post-new war contexts characterised by extraordinary levels of complexity and uncertainty, it is essential that principals should be able to work effectively with the challenges they face. These authors devote considerable attention in their chapter on Kenya, to a recurrent theme emerging from the commentaries presented throughout the book; that is the importance of principals having the capacity to operate in flexible ways with the broader community. They argue that by the strengthening of ties with neighbouring schools, churches and NGOs, and enabling the exchange of knowledge and skills, it is possible for principals to alleviate the void created by a lack of resources and a lack of support from education authorities. Likewise, Davies suggests that the key to leadership effectiveness in Angola lies in principals working with energy and compassion alongside their school communities to solve real problems, and participating in networks of schools that can join forces in this process of problem-solving and assisting the development of teachers. Earnest makes a similar point in her suggestion that school leadership in conflict-affected areas of Sri Lanka needs to be developed in such a way that principals should not only be expected to be responsible for school-based tasks, but should also be supported in fostering the collaboration and commitment of teachers, students and the community in achieving innovative school change.

MacBeath and Swaffield, in their chapter, adopt a somewhat broader view in their observations about optimising leadership effectiveness. They argue that while the tensions typifying Ghana and similar contexts are unlikely to be resolved by reforming schools alone, schooling can continue to play a significant role in social and economic life providing there is a quality of leadership that has a focus on learning at the individual student level, the teacher professional level, the senior management level, and the inter-school level. They go on to report that the 'Leadership for Learning' programme they have assisted in implementing throughout Ghana, appears to be gaining some traction in shifting principals and 'significant others' understanding of school leadership to one where the starting point in their thinking is a focus on learning, the nurturing of an environment that supports the learning of a whole community, the promotion of a continuing dialogue around learning, the sharing of leadership, and a commitment to shared accountability.

This example of powerful professional learning serves to reiterate, perhaps, that the task of optimising leadership effectiveness is well-nigh impossible without providing appropriate preparation, continuous development and support for school leaders. By 'appropriate' we are referring to the capacity of these processes to be grounded in the day-to-day realities of schools as complex organisations. Given the distinctive complexities brought to bear on education in post-new war environments, this is an especially critical requirement for enhancing the quality of school leadership in these contexts. It is also a requirement that has significant implications for the research agenda in the emerging academic field of 'education and conflict'.

Implications for research

In common with a number of other commentators (see for example Tomlinson and Benefield, 2005), Karpinska and her colleagues (2007) have suggested that existing research in the field of education and conflict has failed to fill the theory practice gap. They further argue that this gap must be resolved in order to generate an adequate knowledge base of effective approaches to rebuilding education systems emerging from conflict. More recently, Baraket *et al.* (2012: 4) have suggested that these approaches should be sensitive to, and capable of being applied across, a range of country contexts.

Karpinska and her colleagues also examine ways in which scholarly research can best complement educational practice in what they describe as 'unstable contexts' in general. One area of research they recommend for its potential contribution to the field and which is especially pertinent to this volume is focused on improving good governance, including that of schools. Research adopting this focus, it is argued, should entail working with affected communities that might provide evidence for improvements in institutional systems. We agree with this line of thinking and believe it can be used to open up a rich vein of research activity that could serve to tighten the connection between conceptualising leadership development and the everyday reality of schools located in the extraordinarily challenging circumstances typifying post-new war contexts.

It seems very clear from the commentary running through the chapters in this volume that schools in many post-new war societies are characterised by disorderliness, complexity and unpredictability, determining that the work of school leaders, and above all, principals, engenders almost insurmountable challenges and pressures. It stands to reason, therefore, that principals need to be prepared as effectively as possible for the rigour of their roles. As we have already suggested in our analysis, echoing Clarke and Wildy (2010), for this preparation to be effective it is desirable that it should be grounded in the day-to-day realities of schools, rather than being driven by normative models of leadership that often have little application to those realities and make it more likely that principals will find dissonance between how they were prepared and what they experience in their roles.

The extent to which preparation processes will align with school leaders' professional needs will, in turn, hinge on the availability of a comprehensive, professional knowledge base embedded in the realities of workplaces found in schools and in the environments in which they are located. It follows, therefore, that interpretative approaches to research are potentially fruitful insofar as they can help to depict the 'lived' experience of practitioners and describe accurately the realities of their work in given contexts. It is this portrayal of lived experience that can be used to inform the content and pedagogy of principal preparation programmes, as well as processes of leadership development more generally. Indeed, Harber and Dadey made the same point nearly twenty years ago in their advocacy that in African countries 'wherever and however headteacher training takes place, it must be grounded in the reality of the nature of their work and that some form of research will be necessary to establish what the needs stemming from that work are' (1993: 159).

We would suggest that Harber and Dadey's recommendation is just as pressing now as it was then in its application to enhancing school leadership in post-new war contexts. We also hope that the work reported here represents an attempt to open up for future researchers a number of directions they could take in advancing through this relatively uncharted territory. As such, it may serve as a precursor to engaging in empirical case-study research to generate robust examples of school leadership exercised in post-conflict environments. To pursue such research would be to take a first step towards developing theoretical models for informing innovation and reform. This would be in line with Karpinska and colleagues' (2007) concern to bridge the policy-practice divide. In doing so, it could make a small, but valuable, contribution to the field of education and conflict by providing a solid body of professional knowledge on which to base advocacy to the international community and to inform the planning and implementation of effective policies and programmes that can enhance the efficacy of school leadership.

References

Al-Jaber, Z. (1996) School management in Kuwait after the Iraqi aggression: Problems for principals. *Educational Management and Administration*, 24(4), 411–24.

Barakat, S., Connolly, D., Hardman, F. and Sundram, V. (2012) The role of basic education in post-conflict recovery. *Comparative Education*, iFirst Article, 1–19.

Bijlsma, S. (2009) Teaching history: Looking for unity in Rwanda's classrooms. In S. Nicolai (ed.) *Opportunities for Change: Education innovation and reform during and after conflict*. Paris: International Institute for Educational Planning (IIEP), pp. 218–29.

Clarke, S. and Wildy, H. (2010) Preparing for principalship from the crucible of experience: Reflecting on theory, practice and research. *Journal of Educational Administration and History*, 41(1), 1–16.

Davies, L. (2005) Schools and war: urgent agendas for comparative and international education. *Compare: A journal of comparative and international education*, 35(4), 357–71.

Davies, L. (2006) Understanding the education-war interface. *Forced Immigration Review*, July, 13.

Fullan, M. (2005) *Leadership & Sustainability: System thinkers in action*. Thousand Oaks: Corwin Press.

Harber, C. and Dadey, A. (1993) The job of Headteacher in Africa: Research and reality. *International Journal of Educational Development*, 13(2), 147–60.

Hart, J. (2006) Putting children in the picture. *Forced Immigration Review*, July, 9–10.

Karpinska, Z. E., Yarrow, R. and Gough, L. M. A. (2007) Education and instability: avoiding the policy-practice gap in an emerging field. *Research in Comparative and International Education*, 2(3), 242–51.

King, E. (2011) The multiple relationships between education and conflict: Reflections of Rwandan teachers and students. In K. Mundy, and S. Dryden-Peterson, (eds) *Educating Children in Conflict Zones: Research, policy and practice for systemic change*. New York: Teachers College Press, pp. 137–51.

Knapp, M. S., Copland, M. and Talbert, J. (2003) *Leading for Learning: Reflective tools for school and district leaders*. Seattle, WA: Centre for the Study of Teaching and Policy, University of Washington.

MacBeath, J. (2012) *The Future of the Teaching Profession*. Education International Research Institute. http://www.educ.cam.ac.uk/centres/lfl/current/research/futureteachingprofession.html (accesed 1 September 2012).

MacBeath, J. and Swaffield, S. (2010) Developing leadership for learning in Ghana: Opportunities and challenges. Paper presented at 23rd International Congress for School Effectiveness and Improvement, 5–8 January. Kuala Lumpur, Malaysia.

Milligan, J. A. (2010) The prophet and the engineer meet under the mango tree: Leadership, education, and conflict in the Southern Philippines. *Educational Policy*, 24(1), 28–51.

Mundy, K. and Dryden-Peterson, S. (2011) Educating children in zones of conflict: An overview and introduction. In K. Mundy, and S. Dryden-Peterson (eds) *Educating Children in Conflict Zones: Research, policy and practice for systemic change*. New York: Teachers College Press, pp. 1–12.

Njeru, S. (2010) Dealing with the past: the youth and post-war recovery in southern Sudan. *African Journal of Conflict Resolution*, 10(3), 29–50.

Oplatka, I. (2004) The principalship in developing countries: context, characteristics and reality. *Comparative Education*, 40(3), 427–48.

Ornstein, A. C. and Hunkins, F. P. (2004) *Curriculum: Foundations, principles and issues*, 4th edn. Boston, MA: Pearson Education.

Save the Children (2006) *Rewrite the Future: Education for children in conflict-affected countries*. Cambridge: International Save the Children Alliance.

Sharkey, D. (2008) Contradictions in girls' education in a post-conflict setting. *Compare: A journal of comparative and international education*, 38(5), 569–79.

Shepler, S. (2011) Helping our children will help in the reconstruction of our country. Repatriated refugee teachers in post-conflict Sierra Leone and Liberia. In K. Mundy and S. Dryden-Peterson (eds) *Educating Children in Conflict Zones: Research, policy and practice for systemic change*. New York: Teachers College Press, pp. 199–217.

Smith, A. (2005) Education in the twenty-first century: Conflict, reconstruction and reconciliation. *Compare: A journal of comparative and international education*, 35(4), 373–91.

Tanaka, C. (2012) Profile and status of untrained teachers: experience in basic schools in rural Ghana. *Compare: A journal of comparative and international education*, 42(3), 415–38.

Tomlinson, K., and Benefield, P. (2005) *Education and conflict: Research and research possibilities*. Slough: National Foundation for Educational Research.

Wright, N. (2011) Between 'bastard' leadership and 'wicked' leadership? School leadership and the emerging policies of the UK coalition government. *Journal of Educational Administration and History*, 43(4), 345–62.

Index